What
is campaigning?

NCVO's definition of campaigning

You might call it influencing, voice, advocacy or campaigning, but all these activities are about creating change. At NCVO we use the word campaigning and define this as the mobilising of forces by organisations or individuals to influence others in order to effect an identified and desired social, economic, environmental or political change.

Whatever you call it and whether you are trying to save a local community centre from closing or lobbying government, campaigning is about creating a change. The impact is the real change created by a campaign – the difference it makes to people's lives.

How to
use this guide

'The challenge is to make things as simple as possible and not one bit simpler.' Albert Einstein

This guide brings together the last five years' work of NCVO's Campaigning Effectiveness programme, which champions best practice and innovation in campaigning and influencing work.

Taking you from the beginning of a campaign to its completion this guide follows the structure of the campaigns cycle from analysing and selecting the issue, developing strategy, planning the campaign, delivering it and monitoring progress to evaluating impact and drawing out learning.

Building on the concepts of previous Good Campaigns Guides it places campaigning and influencing into the wider context that you might be working in and explores the latest thinking about campaigning and influencing; new areas include developing an evidence base and policy proposals, developing a theory of change and embedding evaluation into it, securing funding for your campaign, communicating campaign concepts and framing the debate as well as coping with success and becoming a partner in delivering change.

We recognise that the world is a messy place and that many of you will turn to this guide when you are responding to a problem, have come to a dead end or just need reassurance that all you should be doing has been done – you may find the Quick finds section useful here.

Nevertheless, it is worth becoming familiar with the core methodologies developed in the guide's earlier sections on theory of change, campaign strategy and framing as these ideas form the foundations of any campaign and are referred to throughout.

Organisations of all sizes can apply nearly everything in the guide; much of it can also be applied by individual campaigners. One of the guide's key messages is that the insight and passion of campaigners is as crucial as the processes and resources at their command; with modern communication methods the smallest David can slay the largest Goliath.

Introduction: why campaign?

Through a combination of passion allied with theory, know-how, persistence and sometimes sheer bloody-mindedness, small groups that have grown into large social movements and organisations have taken on the powerful to change the landscape of public debate and achieve massive social change.

In the last 10 years, campaigning by the voluntary and community sector has caught the public's imagination, enthusiasm and commitment in a way that has outstripped traditional interest in political parties. Campaigning by the sector has set the agenda on everything from climate change, world poverty and human rights to a living wage, access to the countryside and dealing with the bullying of children. The sector has often brought to the fore issues that would have remained hidden or unaddressed. Injustice and need do not become social or political issues until they are given definition and crystallised in people's minds, brought to the attention of decision-makers, and solutions are presented and debated.

What campaigning can achieve

There are many reasons why voluntary and community organisations (VCOs) are increasingly taking up campaigning as a means of delivering their mission:

- Campaigning can address the causes of social problems not just their effects, releasing resources into other areas of need not so amenable to advocacy.

- Campaigning can shine a spotlight on emerging issues not yet susceptible to service interventions or reveal unmet need. It can help give a voice to those without one and promote civic responsibility and participation in areas where it is lacking.

- Campaigning can lead to social change and the provision by the state of resources, services and entitlements that are many times greater than the resources that were used to win them.

- Campaigning is sometimes the only action possible, especially when the scale of the problem is large or cannot be dealt with without state intervention.

- Campaigning can bring people together in their communities and foster greater civic responsibility and active participation in decision-making.

Crucially, only government – national and local – has the capacity to make a profound and consistent difference to people's lives through legislation and changing the context and terms of engagement in which voluntary and community organisations operate. Organisations therefore need to be aware of the overall context in which they work and need to play a part in shaping the framework for the benefit of those they serve.

[1] NFP Synergy poll (2007) quoted in: Parvin P. (2007) Friend or Foe? Lobbying in British Democracy. London: Hansard Society.

[2] Rosenblatt G. (2006) A Year in the Life: From member of public to member of parliament. London: Hansard Society. p40.

[3] Parvin P. (2007) Friend or Foe? Lobbying in British Democracy. London: Hansard Society. p24.

[4] UK Workforce Hub (2009) National Occupational Standards for Campaigning, developed by Pye Tait Consulting. Available online: www.skills-thirdsector.org.uk/national_occupational_standards/campaigning_standards/ (accessed November 2010)

[5] NCVO's Certificate in Campaigning – accredited by Roehampton University.

'Never doubt that a small group of thoughtful committed citizens can change the world. Indeed, it is the only thing that ever has.'
Margaret Mead, US Anthropologist (1901–1978)

A changing context for campaigning

Over recent years significant public support has been routinely expressed for VCO campaigning – people not only accept it, they expect it. For example, over half of those polled in one survey thought that charities should directly lobby government, and ranked lobbying as the 'most economical' and cost-effective activity for charities to engage in.[1] MPs have also expressed a willingness to meet more with charities than business interests[2] and also find their arguments more credible.[3]

This growing public acceptance has mirrored a growing professionalism over the last decade as campaigners[4] and organisations supporting them have moved to codify the best of campaigning practice including the first national standards for campaigners and a university accredited course in campaigning.[5] This growing professionalism was a necessary response for the sector to show it could effectively campaign to a high standard, deliver value for money and show it could manage the more complex public relationships with government and the commercial sectors as a result of a raised public profile.

The ever-growing focus within the sector on measuring impact has also rightly challenged campaigners to do more to demonstrate the change they achieve and illustrate how campaigning is improving outcomes for beneficiaries. Demonstrating effectiveness helped to persuade regulators to give charities more latitude, with the redrafting of the Charity Commissions Guidelines on Campaigning (CC9). Confidence also increased amongst supporters that charities could deliver social change while managing the controversy this sometimes brought. VCOs measuring the impact of their campaigns also chimed with government's drive to encourage the sector to give voice to those who use its services as well as expanding the volume and range of services.

There has, however, been a growing concern that, with more professionally honed methods of campaigning, we could lose the vital spark of anger that motivated people to take action in the first place. We need to retain the vibrant dissatisfaction of campaigners, increase the involvement of beneficiaries and communities and meld this with the best thinking about how to run effective campaigns. With growing expertise and effectiveness, we are much better placed to say what the core of good campaigning consists of and to develop a language, approach and methodology common to all.

Introduction:
why campaign? (continued)

A compelling narrative
Campaigns have to operate with many more channels of communication, with ever-increasing competition for public space in which to press for change. In this environment campaigners need a more sophisticated understanding of how to gain attention, frame their issues for maximum impact and motivate supporters into action to bring about change.

The latest developments in communication theory and practice show that people respond as much to the emotional content of an argument as its rational content. Motivations to become involved with an issue go beyond narrow calculation of self-interest to deeper held values and beliefs.

The implication of this thinking for campaigners is the need to appeal to a vision of a better world that chimes with people's existing values and beliefs as well as providing evidence and rational argument to motivate people to support their cause. How to frame arguments and tap into deeper sets of values that people to use to assess their support for issues becomes fundamental to ensuring that campaigns reach out beyond core supporters and gain momentum. Without understanding how to develop compelling narratives, campaigners can have the best of evidence and still not make headway in their campaigning.

Conversational activism
More and more people involved with an organisation, supporters, members, beneficiaries, expect to be part of the construction and execution of campaigns, not just passive recipients. This means that we need to support campaigners to co–produce campaigns, which will need new concepts of effective campaigning and fresh ideas about how we can facilitate conversations with our supporters and beneficiaries.

The continued erosion of traditional lifelong allegiance to political parties and decreasing participation in politics may lead as some predict to the end of mass membership organisations in favour of much looser alliances of individuals and groups that respond to particular events and challenges, such as the environmental and women's movements.[6]

---

[6] Fox R, Gibbons V. and Korris M. (2010) Audit of Political Engagement 7: The 2010 report with a focus on MPs and Parliament. London: Hansard Society, who note a 'five point rise in donating/paying a membership fee to a charity or campaigning organisation' and a rise in those who had signed a petition. See also: McHugh D. and Parvin, P. (2005) Neglecting Democracy. London: Hansard Society, who noted the decline in formal political activity but also that: 'People are now more likely to have signed a petition, boycotted a product, or contacted an elected representative than ever before.' See also: (2006) Power to the People. The report of power, an independent inquiry into Britain's democracy. (2006) York: Joseph Rowntree Foundation.

[7] The most obvious 'template' for this has been Obama's presidential campaign, which had been much studied for its lessons. See: D. Raymond (2009) How to Campaign Like Obama. Fairsay website: http://fairsay.com/obama-howto (accessed December 2010).

[8] Machiavelli N. The Prince. Translated by Bull G. (1975) London: Penguin Books.

These developments have led some commentators to speculate on how far this heralds new forms of organising campaigns, or indeed new types of organisations. Seeing the era of large, strong political parties and organisations with hierarchical structures coming to an end, giving way to diversified and networked groupings based around particular places, interests and causes. With the internet providing infinite ways for campaigners to collaborate, mobilise and achieve change without an organisation to co-ordinate activity.

Many people are attracted to this kind of 'networked' activism and this approach offers exciting possibilities for campaigning organisations, large and small. It also poses challenges for campaigners: can they capture these shifting alliances and interests and focus them to achieve sustainable change?

Crucial to this approach is to create and maintain conversations with key groups of people relevant to your issue(s) instead of following the more traditional 'command and control' communication mechanisms. Online and social media are becoming characteristic features of many campaigns, enabling campaigners to conduct conversations with people who become engaged with issues, join in and take action. The biggest opportunity of these developments is the ability to link disparate communities together and facilitate face-to-face meetings. To tap into this 'conversational activism', effective campaigners need to operate in an often dispersed, but also networked, world.[7]

Yet crowds, even if they are digital crowds, still need 'conductors' to co-ordinate activity. All campaigns need to develop networks whether they are online, offline or both. Organisations that have thought through the opportunities of this new way of organising will be better placed to tap into shifting patterns of involvement and activism but also be aware of its restrictions and barriers to involvement.

Sustaining change

Machiavelli once observed that: 'There is nothing more difficult to plan, more doubtful of success, nor more dangerous to manage than the creation of a new order of things... Whenever his enemies have occasion to attack the innovator they do so with the passion of partisans, while the others defend him sluggishly so that the innovator and his party alike are vulnerable.'[8]

He well understood what many campaigners can forget – the price of success is constant vigilance. Successful campaigns are not those that win short-term battles but those that build an enduring consensus around an issue or deliver long-term change for beneficiaries. For this we need an understanding of impact and how sustainable change can be achieved, this involves having a good theory of how change happens and then align this with the know-how to evaluate your campaign as you progress, promoting the learning – both good and bad. You need to know about what do when your campaign succeeds, how to make a successful exit, make the most of achievements so far, and ensure that the change you have campaigned for remains.

Introduction:
why campaign? (continued)

The changing face of policy-making

We need to recognise that the policy development landscape within government has radically changed. The old distinctions of 'insider' and 'outsider' campaigning have rapidly broken down. Organisations have to apply a sophisticated mix of strategies – engaging the public to exert pressure while also deploying influencing skills through less public channels.[9] Ideas germinate and take hold much more quickly and need a much nimbler response from the voluntary and community sector.

Government has adopted many of the tactics and methods of campaigners to source ideas and engage with the public while the Voluntary and Community sector has, at times, become more caught up in government, bringing more leverage but, some would say, a more muted voice.

Campaigners need to understand the far more complex way in which conversations now happen between policy-makers, government, campaigners and their targets, and be able to deploy a range of campaign strategies and tactics. Crucially, campaigners need a clear theory of how change comes about for the issue they are tackling and to be able to apply the right approaches to the circumstances they find themselves in.

A harsher climate for campaigning

The volume of campaigning by the Voluntary and Community sector has grown because of affluence not adversity. With the current period of economic austerity and squeeze on funds, formal organised campaigning could decline if campaigners cannot continue to demonstrate to their organisations the effectiveness of investing in campaigning, over other areas such as service provision.

Of course, campaigning and social protest have been with us throughout history, both as organised protest and passive resistance. But campaigning as an organised institutional phenomenon, attracting increasing resources and a focus on professional development, may be in jeopardy. In a world where budgets are squeezed, when many might expect that hard times and social upheaval make the need for campaigning more acute it may be less able to fulfil its promise.

---

[9] For the classic distinction between insider and outsider approaches see: Grant W. (1995) Pressure Groups and British Politics, Politics and Democracy In Britain (2nd edition,). Palgrave Macmillan.

[10] McHugh D, Parvin, P. (2005) Neglecting Democracy. Hansard Society

[11] For example see: Lloyd J. (2001) The Protest Ethic. London: Demos. While written for a different moment, it still raises some very pertinent questions about the way large global movements for social change have the potential to undermine a focus on getting things done through the democratic process.

This context will challenge campaigners to think harder about the impact they want to achieve, possibly with reduced resources. The emphasis of this guide is on ensuring that campaigners think clearly about how to bring about change and analyse the means to do that, rather thinking that they will magically change the world.

The challenge is how to continue to grow and develop in vastly different circumstances to those in which campaigning has flourished over the last 15 years. Campaigners seeking to extend obligations on the public purse, get companies to change practice and encourage public support face a harsher climate so the need for good campaign practice has never been more urgent. The pressures of austerity may also produce an upsurge of more spontaneous outbreaks of protest and more fluid social protest movements. The challenge will be how to harness this upsurge without resorting to the command and control models of the past.

A case to answer?

The fact that there are campaign organisations, such as the RSPB, have memberships that exceed political parties has drawn some to argue that campaign groups have a claim to be regarded as representative organisations on particular issues in a way that political parties cannot.[10] On the other hand, some politicians and other commentators have voiced concerns that local activism and community groups, not to mention large social movements, have subverted the relevance of democratic processes[11] and distorted decision-making and resource allocation.

This perspective on campaigning views its growth not as the expression of expanding democratic and civic renewal, but as a distortion of democracy, undermining conventional mechanisms of accountability. The remedy, from such a viewpoint, is to ensure that formal government functions better, rather than encouraging the growth of campaigning organisations.

There have also been criticisms that the rise of issue-driven engagement gives vent to the worst of democratic accountability – how easy it is for campaigners to drill away at single issues while taking no account of the compromises decision-makers are faced with on a daily basis. Party politics, runs the argument, is the only legitimate channel for those with a mandate from the public to make democratically legitimate decisions between all these competing priorities.

Such criticisms seem strangely out of kilter with the public and political mood for more devolution of power and a broader desire for engagement in communities. They also rest on a misunderstanding – most organisations do not seek to put themselves above the political process but work within it to ensure that people's views are better represented and their needs addressed. Campaigning, within the law, by Voluntary and Community organisations supports the belief that effective democracy is only achieved through the competition of ideas and by holding elected representatives to account for their actions. Taking part in this process is the fulfilment of the democratic ideal, not its subversion.

Introduction:
why campaign? (continued)

The more that different Voluntary and Community organisations contribute to debates – from climate change to abortion, assisted suicide to poverty – the more the arguments can be put before the public and politicians to decide. The success of a campaign depends on the extent that it strikes a chord with the public and decision makers. To ensure that no vested interest predominate, we need more campaigning and discussion with communities and individuals supported to voice their views.

Campaigning and campaigners in the future

This guide is founded on the belief that being more effective at campaigning adds to the capacity of individuals, communities and organisations that want to participate in society and challenge the way in which things are done.

The quickly changing context for campaigning is going to ask more of individual campaigners and campaigning organisations than ever before. The range of skills is going to be wider and the need to think more broadly about change and how to bring it about greater. Campaigners need to be more attuned to how to understand and create policy proposals, turn these into compelling messages and understand the scope and possibilities of a fast-changing environment.

Campaigners need to look both inwards and outwards, ensuring their organisations have the capacity to campaign effectively. That they can correctly interpret the shifting tides of public opinion and political will and can provide leadership across their sectors. Organisations that have the best campaigning capacities are those who have visionary leadership, actively engage their boards and beneficiaries, and continue to build both their own and others' capacity to campaign through investment in staff skills, robust planning and the nurturing of networks and co-operative working.[12]

---

[12] For a fuller account of research on this issue see: TCC for California Endowment (2009) What Makes an Effective Advocacy Organisation? California Endowment. Los Angeles. See also: Alliance for Justice (2005) Build Your Advocacy Grantmaking: Advocacy evaluation and advocacy capacity assessment tools. Alliance for Justice. Washington.

Introducing
The campaigns cycle

It is helpful to think of campaigning as a cycle from beginning through to completion of the campaign:
- Analysing the issue
- Developing a strategy for change
- Developing a plan of action
- Delivery of the campaign and monitoring progress
- Evaluate – building on success, managing failure

The campaigns cycle is a model to help simplify what happens through the course of a campaign, not a literal representation to follow whatever circumstances you find yourself in.

It is, nevertheless, a tried and tested way of thinking through the stages of a typical campaign and understanding that the general principle of campaigning is based on making choices to achieve impact.

Diagram: The campaigns cycle

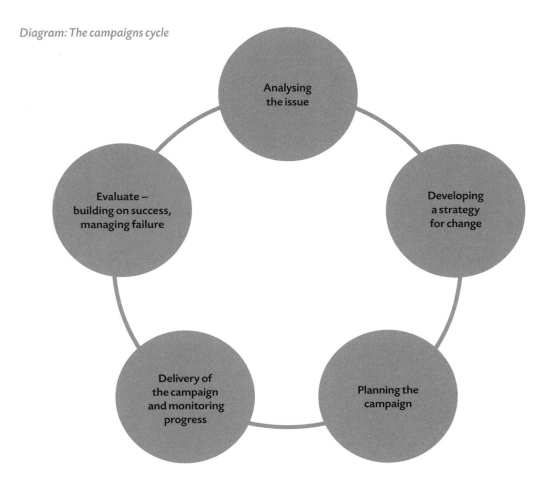

Analysing the issue

Developing a strategy for change

Evaluate – building on success, managing failure

Planning the campaign

Delivery of the campaign and monitoring progress

Introducing
The campaigns cycle (continued)

The campaigns cycle can be broken down in more detail to understand what needs doing at each stage. The guide reflects this structure and explores the essentials of campaigning, as well as placing this in a wider context of how to bring about change.

Analysing the issue
- Exploring the issue and developing a strong evidence base.
- Turning evidence into a solution for change.
- Analysing the context – both external and internal environment – to ensure you select the most suitable issue to campaign on.
- Participation is key to any campaign – think through about whom to involve in the campaign and how.

Developing a strategy for change
- Developing a clearly defined aim – overtly spelling out the change you want to see and the impact you want to make.
- Developing a theory of change of how you will achieve the campaign aim and building in an evaluation framework to ensure you stay on track.
- Ensuring that any funding strategy is fully integrated into the campaign.

Planning the campaign
- Developing an overarching campaign concept to frame the issue, bring it to life and appeal to your identified target audiences.
- Developing a plan of action and setting clear measurable objectives acting as milestones to guide you along the path to achieving the campaign aim.
- Testing plans, contingency planning and risk assessment to mitigate risk.
- This may also involve planning how to work with others – such as your beneficiaries, supporters or potential allies.

Delivering your campaign – making it happen
- Understanding your target audiences, pitching the messages right and developing tailored campaign actions.
- Communicating with target audiences through appropriate channels.
- Ongoing monitoring to check you are on track.

Evaluate
- Evaluating your impact and learning from it.
- Knowing when you have succeeded, how to manage failure and considering compromise.
- Building on success by embedding change and telling people about it.
- Building an organisational learning culture.
- Anticipating future trends.

Analysing
the issue

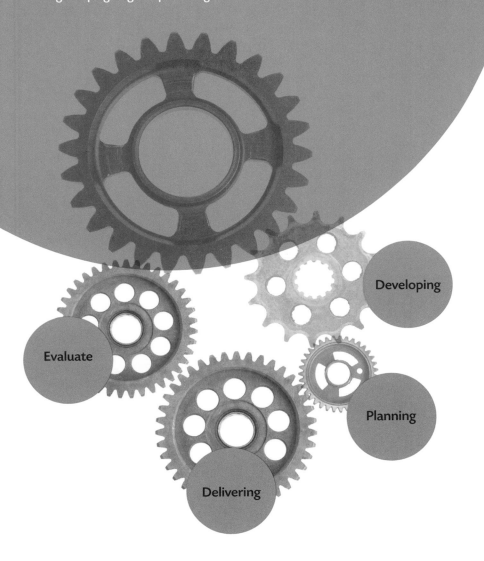

Evaluate

Developing

Planning

Delivering

Contents

This section is about identifying what you want to change, understanding the issue and ensuring that you have a strong evidence base to support your cause. It also explores how to assess both the internal and external environments in which you are working to ensure that you select the most suitable issue to campaign on.

You may not always need to embark on a full-scale campaign to achieve the change you are seeking; taking all your analysis into account you will need to consider what route to influence will be most effective.

Decisions should be based on the best possible evidence and analysis of the problem. Strong evidence backing your campaign gives clarity and a reasonable expectation that proposed solutions are well-founded. Decision-makers want evidence to underpin new policies and programmes and will need to be convinced that your proposed alterative is something that will work and not backfire on them once implemented.

Of course, once you have good evidence base you need to deploy your case skilfully to build support for the change you are seeking within whatever institution you are targeting. You also need to be aware of what improves your legitimacy and capacity to make proposals and be listened to. This section explores various routes you could take to influence, including policy work and involvement in consultations.

[1] Stone D. (2002) Policy Paradox: The art of political decision making. New York: W. W. Norton & Co. Quoted in Bales (2002) p8 Bales, S. N., & Gilliam, F. D. (2004). Communications for Social Good. The Foundation Center. New York.

[2] A Select Committee review of the overall performance of the Department for Communities and Local Government concluded that 'the weakness identified by successive reviews in the Department's willingness and ability to base its policies consistently on the evidence, rather than preconceptions' House of Commons Communities and Local Government Committee (2008) Communities and Local Government's Departmental Annual Report 2008. London: The Stationery Office p27.

'Ideas are a medium of exchange and a mode of influence even more powerful than money, votes and guns.' Stone D., Policy Paradox: The art of political decision making[1]

Developing an evidence base

Strong and compelling evidence should be the bedrock of your campaign. Before commissioning or undertaking in-depth research into your issue, look around to see what evidence is already out there that you could to tap into from sources such as the Office of National Statistics (ONS), government departments, think tanks and academic research. If you do not have the resources or capacity to conduct or commission your own research there is often evidence available that could be used to support your issue.

You can use evidence for your campaign in different ways: to provide the foundation for your own thinking about new proposals for change, and to change how decision-makers perceive an issue, enabling them to justify solutions that help your campaign's priorities. You may need evidence that assesses the possible impact of different proposals being made by government or by other organisations.

Your issue will not exist in a vacuum and you will also need to think about the competing frameworks of ideas and vested interests that you are trying to support or disrupt.[2] Take time to research if there are other groups that can also be influenced to take up your view of the issue and create a better climate for your ideas?

Decision-makers recognise that the voluntary and community sector(VCS), with strong links to communities and their beneficiaries, can often produce evidence and develop solutions based on that evidence in a way that centralised bodies cannot.[3] Government departments may bring voluntary and community organisations (VCOs) into debates about policy and consultations on law and good practice. You need to be prepared with evidence of a standard that government and other bodies expect. To do this well you need to know what else has been published that affects your area and who else is working on the same topics as you. Making contact with relevant think tanks and professional associations can save you time and resources.

Once you have built an evidence base for your campaign you should have a key proposition or set of claims about the issue, information to support your issue and proposals for solving the problem. This can be used to:
- **Inspire** – generate support for an issue or action; raise new ideas or question old ones; create new ways of framing an issue.
- **Inform** – represent the views of others; share expertise and experience; put forward new approaches.
- **Improve** – add, correct or change policy issues; hold decision-makers to account; evaluate and improve your own activities; learn from each other.[4]

You can glean evidence from your day-to-day activities or ask the people for whom your organisation exists. You can trawl existing research or your organisation may have its own research staff or money to commission research. However you gather it, strong and compelling evidence should be the bedrock of your campaign.

---

[3] 'In any policy area there is a great deal of critical evidence held in the minds of both front-line staff... and those to whom the policy is directed. Very often they will have a clearer idea than the policy-makers about why a situation is as it is and why previous initiatives have failed' Strategic Policy Making Team (1999) The Cabinet Office. Professional Policy Making For the Twenty First Century.

[4] Pollard A. and Court J. (2005) How Civil Society Organisations Use Evidence to Influence Policy Processes: A literature review. London: Overseas Development Institute. Available online at www.odi.org.uk (accessed October 2010) and NCVO In Focus guide Building your evidence base.

Developing an evidence base
(continued)

Example
Woodland Trust: online mapping

Woodland Trust is the UK's leading woodland conservation organisation. For several years the Trust kept a record of woods under threat as no other organisation, not even the government, was doing this. Its initial idea was to build up a resource of publicly available information to reveal the extent of the threat to this irreplaceable resource. It realised, however, that without help from the public it would be impossible to keep track.

In 2008 Woodland Trust developed a prototype website with digital mapping tools that highlight areas under threat; this is the clearest way of conveying the situation visually. The digital mapping included the government's ancient woodland inventory – the record of known ancient woods across the UK, which was the first time this resource had been made available digitally.

The next step was to get the public more involved as Woodland Trust's eyes and ears. Previously people had reported threats to precious woodlands via letters, phone calls, and occasionally emails. The first five years of the Woods Under Threat website helped the Trust build its information base. It started with around 100 cases and has grown to over 800. The map provides a template to capture the threat and prompt people to offer more information to increase the evidence base. The website has proved a cost-effective and efficient way of gathering information that can be dealt with in a more managed way.

The site allows the public to communicate quickly and easily, locating the woods under threat and specifying what is threatening them. Having this evidence has led to real policy change, helping to persuade government to protect ancient woodland better through the planning system. Such a commitment does not necessarily lead to practical action to protect ancient woods on the ground, so Woodland Trust also encourages and supports individuals and communities to campaign. The people engagement programme works to create a UK-wide network of volunteer Threat Detectors. Phase two for the project involves adding a tool to the website that calculates the loss and damage to help visualise the impacts of development on woodland.

Source: with thanks to Ed Pomfret, then Head of Campaigns at Woodland Trust (2006–2009) writing for Fairsay Campaigning Insights[5] and additional material supplied by Alice Farr, WoodWatch Campaigner, Woodland Trust.

[5] Gathering campaign information online: Woods under Threat: http://fairsay.com/tools/campaigning-insights/gathering-campaign-information-online-woods-under-threat.

[6] Mulgan G. (2003) Government, Knowledge and the Business of Policy-making. Prime Minister's Strategy Unit, Conference paper for Facing the Future conference, Canberra. Available online at: www.odi.org.uk (accessed November 2010).

Tapping into government research and knowledge

Government departments are among the largest funders of research in the country and produce a large volume of analysis and reports; many also have their own foresight and research programmes, much of which is publicly available. In all, there is a rich source of evidence available for campaigners to tap into including:

- Statistics, for example, of population size and migration.
- Policy knowledge, for example, suggestions about what reduces reoffending.
- Scientific knowledge, for example, data about climate change.
- Opinion poll data and qualitative data.
- Practitioner views and insights, for example, how teachers view exams.
- Political knowledge, for example, the balance of opinion in the ruling party.
- Economic information and trends, for example, which sectors are growing or contracting, national and local job markets.
- Information on other countries' actions, for example, development and anti-terrorism policies.[6]

It is always worth checking what relevant research government has undertaken or commissioned. However, you will need to ask how that research was framed: the questions government asks may differ from how you would frame them.

How are you going to deploy the government's research findings? You can of course use much of the government's own research 'against it' and show up any weaknesses of its policies, if that supports your campaign. For example anti-poverty campaigners have for many years effectively used the government's statistics to take them to task on their lack of progress towards a stated aim of reducing poverty.

The parliamentary process is another way of finding information. Asking parliamentary questions (PQs) via MPs who support your campaign to obtain evidence not only gets you that information (free of charge), it also puts that information straight into the public realm in a way that is likely to be picked up and used. PQs alert government departments that there is interest in an issue. The libraries of the House of Commons and the House of Lords contain a wealth of research on legislation and government policy which is available online at no cost.

Developing an evidence base
(continued)

Freedom of Information

Freedom of Information (FOI) legislation gives access to any non-personal recorded information held by or on behalf of central government, local authorities and other public bodies, unless a specific exemption allows the authority to refuse to give the information. The FOI Act (FOIA) is supplemented by the Environmental Information Regulations (EIRs), which give people a right to know about environmental matters.

Both of these can be used as powerful campaigning tools to help build up the evidence base of a campaign or to gain crucial information on how decisions were arrived at. The onus in the legislation is quite clearly in favour of disclosure; if requests are rejected appeals can be made – first for an internal review by the public authority, then to the Information Commissioner's Office (ICO) and, if need be, litigation can be pursued to the Information Tribunal, and potentially to the High Court.

All public authorities are now also required to produce a Publication Scheme detailing specified types of information they hold and how to access it. It is important to check these first to see if the information you are seeking is already disclosed. To get the most out of FOI, much depends on how you frame the language of the request; key to this is asking for specific information within certain time periods if possible. This can be done through developing a series of requests or through building up a dialogue with those you are requesting information from.[7]

Example
Using Freedom of Information requests

The charity Rarer Cancers Forum surveyed primary care trusts (PCTs) in England about decision-making processes on patients with rare cancers. This showed that PCTs used inconsistent and often secretive processes for determining whether they would fund life-extending treatment. Using the FOIA, Rarer Cancers

Forum collected more detailed information and demonstrated the variations in PCTs' processes. The Forum was able to estimate how many patients were missing out on life-extending treatments, publishing its findings in two reports: Taking Exception and Exceptional England.[8] The evidence provoked a policy change that unlocked significant extra resources for cancer treatment.

---

[7] For further guidance, insight and research, see Hadley P. (2010) Voicing Your Right to Know: A guide to using Freedom of Information in campaigning. London: NCVO. Available online at: www.ncvo-vol.org.uk/yourrighttoknow.

[8] Rarer Cancers Forum (2008) Exceptional England: An investigation of the role of Primary Care Trusts in making cancer medicines available through exceptional cases processes. Canterbury: Rarer Cancers Forum. Available at: www.rarercancers.org.uk/news/archive/winter_2008_12_03/exceptional_england_new_report_from_rarer_cancers_forum (accessed December 2010).

Other sources of evidence

Professional bodies, such as the British Medical Association, or umbrella organisations, such as the CBI (Confederation of British Industry), or individual trade organisations and trade unions will also conduct research. Networks and research associations linked to universities, such as the Third Sector Research Centre and the Voluntary Sector Studies Network can also be extremely useful; some of this information will be easy to access but much may also be in specialist journals and research publications, which may take time to source or need to be paid for.

Conducting research

All research should be based on a clear need and should seek to create new knowledge, giving you further insight into your issue. You can do research 'in house' if you have the expertise and capacity. Otherwise you may need to commission it. Either way, research can eat up budgets so be clear about what you are expecting to discover.

Commissioning external researchers can both bring independence and provide greater credibility with your target audience(s). It can sometimes enhance the credibility of your research with your target audience by using a research organisation that the target uses or by using an organisation, such as a think tank, that has a significant profile and important connections to your target.

Developing an evidence base
(continued)

Developing a research proposal[9]
Stage one: Scoping

Establish the aims and purpose of the research and draft your research questions. These will form the 'route map' for the rest of the project. Consider:

- Can research realistically answer your questions?
- What evidence or information will be generated by the research?
- Can your questions be answered in the time you have available and with the resources you have (money, staff, staff time)?
- How are the questions relevant to your existing campaigning and influencing work and how do they drive forward your understanding and insight?

Stage two: Developing the brief

If the stage one answers are positive you can work up a research brief. Typically this includes:

- Research aims and objectives – what you want to find out and how this will contribute to your policy and campaigning work.
- Research outputs – what you will produce: for example, a report, a film, a toolkit.
- Intended outcomes – what changes you hope will result from the research.
- Research methods – how you will gather the information and what principles guide your methods.
- Research participants – who will take part in the research, how many participants are required and how they will be selected.
- Timescales – duration and timing of activities, including key milestones.
- Budget – total budget, including breakdown of costs by activity.
- Research ethics – what ethical issues are raised by the research and how you involve research participants.

Methods of research

Undertaking secondary research helps to establish what gaps there are in the evidence you may need and also to ensure that you are not 'reinventing the wheel' by doing unnecessary work.

Secondary research **is also known as desk research, it involves collating and summarising existing research:**

- **Literature reviews** are an objective overview and analysis of existing research on a given issue.
- **Analysis of existing data** may include internal case study or service information or data from sources such as the census, the British Crime Survey, Labour Force Survey, etc. It can include your own previous policy evaluations, research appraisals and literature reviews.

Primary research involves collecting data that doesn't already exist. There are two basic approaches:

- **Quantitative** – often referred to as 'hard' evidence seeking information that can be readily measured, such as prevalence, cost or frequency.
- **Qualitative** – often referred to as 'soft' evidence seeking descriptive information, such as behaviours, attitudes or beliefs.

---

[9] Based on: NCVO (2010) In Focus Guide: Commissioning Research. London: NCVO.

This can be collected in various ways including:

- **Focus groups** – facilitated small group discussions.
- **Internet polls** – organisations are using the internet as a quick and easy means of testing opinion or gaining information. You need to think carefully, however, about how convincing this will be to your target audience, especially if you do not have a random sample of respondents. Specialist companies that carry out polls via the internet also exist.
- **Surveys and questionnaires** – a series of set questions, which you conduct online, by post or face to face.
- **Randomised control trials** – the 'gold standard' in the health and education fields for assessing the effectiveness of different interventions. One group of people is given a treatment or intervention and a 'control group' is not; the results are measured between the two groups to judge the effectiveness of the intervention. This method is insisted on in many government-commissioned projects.

- **Interviews** – may be structured, with set questions, and analysed for content or statistical significance or semi-structured, with a looser set of subject areas for discussion, which are normally analysed for predominant themes or clusters of issues. These can be done face to face or by phone.
- **Service or project evaluations** – may involve evaluating an organisation's own services or evaluating an external publicly funded service or initiatives. This method can assess and compare the effectiveness of different approaches to the same issue.
- **Informal 'evidence'** – this can be dipstick testing of opinion, embedded knowledge from running your services or users' views and general organisational learning. While not traditionally part of research and evidence-gathering, it is important to acknowledge how much this informal 'knowledge' shapes decision-makers' opinions and needs to be taken into account. This can also include informal feedback from the direct services to beneficiaries that your organisation undertakes.

Research ethics

The ethics of your research are important – are people under pressure to give you information? Will their identities be protected? Voluntary and community sector research needs to address such ethical questions scrupulously. Without ethical principles, respecting the people participating in your investigations, your research will not have a sound basis.

Developing an evidence base
(continued)

Table: Research ethics

Questions	Evidenced by
Is the research necessary?	Can you show that the research will generate knowledge that is not available elsewhere?
Have those involved given informed consent?	Do those involved know how the research might affect them – can they withdraw if they are not happy?
How will you deal with privacy issues?	Are you confident that the privacy of participants will be respected at all times?
Can you ensure that all participation is voluntary?	You need to ensure that no explicit or implicit coercion was applied – this can be complex if you are interviewing recipients of your services and they may feel obliged to take part.
Have you addressed issues of the potential harm that could be caused by the results of the research?	Do you have a process in place to assist participants who have been distressed as part of the process?
Have you catered for the specific needs of the people you are interviewing?	You need to ensure that you are using age- and culture-appropriate research methods and that you are being sensitive to the needs of those you are working with. You also need to ensure that premises and methods are accessible to all participants.
Does the research use appropriate methods of research practice and are these applied correctly?	Do the researchers have the expertise and qualifications to administer and contact the research?
Are there conflicts of interest?	What is the source of your funding and background of those doing the research?

Source: Adapted from NCVO, In Focus Guide: Commissioning Research.[10] Based on NSPCC 2009 CPSU Research ethics guide.

[10] NCVO (2010) In Focus Guide: Commissioning Research. London: NCVO.

[11] Oz A (2010) 'Against ideas, Israel's force is impotent'. Guardian, 2 June 2010.

'To defeat an idea you have to offer a better idea. A more attractive and acceptable one.' Amos Oz, author and activist[11]

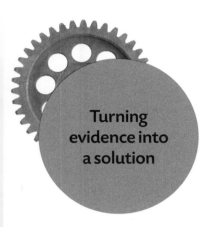

Turning evidence into a solution

Of course not all issues are resolvable simply by reference to the evidence, which can often be disputed. Evidence is the first step to framing an issue and providing a solution. Saying that a particular community suffers more from ill health such as heart disease or early death is only the start of a debate – you then need to think about what response you want local health providers to have, what responsibility local communities have and what the causes of that ill health are. What your research and analysis gives you is the possibility to structure the options on the basis of evidence. Often, decisions about what you campaign on will then come down to choices based on resources, completing explanations of what the best solution will be and value judgements about what is most important between completing demands for resources and time.

Example
When the End Child Poverty Coalition was campaigning in 2007-8 for increased resources for anti-poverty measures, it needed to demonstrate what the positive impact of this would be as a means for the then Labour government to reach its policy aim of reducing child poverty in the UK by half in 2010 and eradicating it by 2020. The Coalition also needed to continue to demonstrate the level of need to ensure that related benefits were increased.

Using independent research produced by the Joseph Rowntree Foundation on the costs of eradicating child poverty provided a powerful platform for the Coalition to coordinate its lobbying. This resulted in the Coalition securing an additional £1 billion in welfare and other measures to end child poverty in the 2008 budget.

Source: Hilary Fisher, Director of End Child Poverty Campaign 2006–2009.

Working out what change needs to happen and how is a process usually known as policy development – whether this involves proposed changes to policies, legislation, behaviour of individuals or a company, or the development of services. It involves formulating the changes you think are necessary into a clear narrative that you can convey to those whom you want to influence.

Policy development can sound complex confined to organisations with vast resources and policy functions. Yet anyone who has ever said 'why do they not think of doing this differently?' or 'I have an idea about how this could be done better' is taking the first step in developing policy proposals and framing an issue. All campaigns should be underpinned by a clear argument of why things should be different (or need to stay the same) and how this can be achieved.

You may not always need to run a public-focused campaign to achieve the change you are seeking. Some issues may comprise part of your organisation's wider policy and influencing work. To launch a campaign or not is a decision that often depends on the issue and the context you are trying to influence, as well as your organisation's capacity or priorities.

Turning evidence into a solution (continued)

Tools for policy development

Whether you are a policy specialist or not, there are tools that can help you break down a problem into causally related areas to help you think it through and analysis both the issue and solutions: 'problem trees' and 'fishbones' are two examples. These tools are best done in groups, part of the benefit is the discussion that the exercise provokes and you have a better chance of getting all the relevant information into the analysis and then testing out if it stands up. Try to involve a range of your stakeholders to account for multiple viewpoints.

Problem trees

In the middle of the tree define the main problem or question you want to answer. Above (the branches) identify the effects or consequences of the problem you wish to address. Then ask yourself why these occur. Below the main problem (the roots) break down the problem into causes; keep asking why to get to the real roots of the issue.

Diagram: Problem tree example

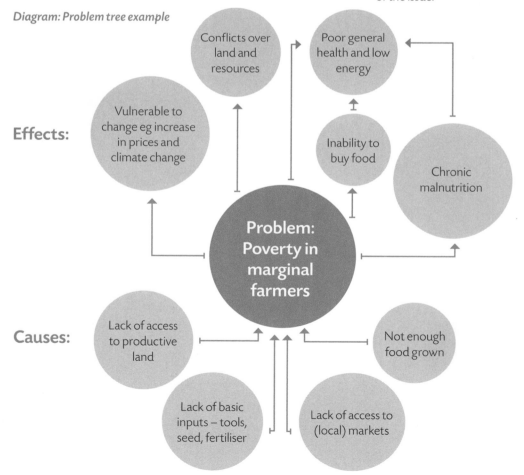

Effects:
- Conflicts over land and resources
- Poor general health and low energy
- Vulnerable to change eg increase in prices and climate change
- Inability to buy food
- Chronic malnutrition

Problem: Poverty in marginal farmers

Causes:
- Lack of access to productive land
- Lack of basic inputs – tools, seed, fertiliser
- Lack of access to (local) markets
- Not enough food grown

Solution trees

Put your ideal situation, the change you wish to see or impact you want to make, into the middle of a solutions tree. Discuss solutions to the problem in a group. What policies or practises need to change and who can bring about the change? Be as specific as possible. Write your solutions under the change you wish to make on the solutions tree (roots). Above the middle box write what difference this would make, the effects you hope to see if your vision is achieved (branches).

Think through which solution brings benefit to the greatest number of people?

Which solution is most achievable within your means and the current political, economic, social etc... climate?

Come back to this thinking after you have completed analyses of the external and internal context.

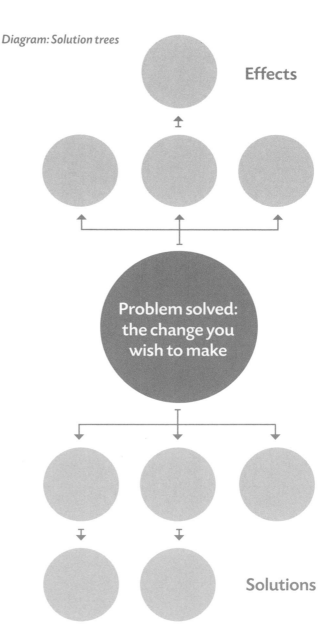

Diagram: Solution trees

Effects

Problem solved: the change you wish to make

Solutions

Turning evidence into a solution (continued)

Fishboning

The fishboning technique was first developed by Professor Ishikawa of the University of Tokyo as a technique for solving problems that have many different dimensions.

This exercise is best done as part of group to ensure that you get the widest possible perspectives on the issue. It can also help you to select policy options, especially when there is a wide range of potential ways of solving your problem. To use it in this way, write your desired impact, change you wish to see on the head of a fish. Draw a spine and then a series of diagonal bones. Each of these bones will be a generic group, for specific options such as limited resources, policy issues, environmental factors and so on, that might affect achievement of your ultimate objective. You will need to vary the titles and number of bones as you start to stick the options to them.

Once you have a number of options attached to your fishbones, you can sift out any duplicates. Pay attention to options that appear on several different bones – they may be worth closer consideration. You then need to group your options and discuss which ones you need keep or to exclude. At the end the fish should be displaying several broad groups of options. You can then either weigh options within a group against each other, or you can weigh groups of options against each other.[12]

Whether or not you have used any of these tools to analysing your issue this is a good point at which to consider:

- Is your analysis consistent with the overall vision of your organisation?
- Does your analysis contribute something new?
- In what aspects of the issue does your organisation have particular expertise?
- Are there still gaps in your knowledge?
- Have you spotted areas where evidence is unreliable or contested?
- Are other organisations also working on these areas and could you work together?

Diagram: Fishbone example

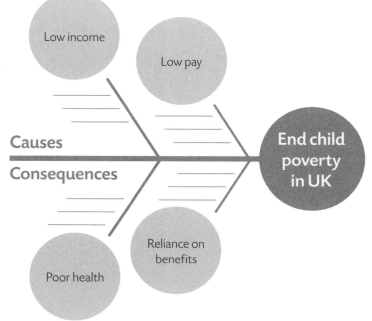

[12] Adapted from: National Government Office (2005) Making Policy that Happens National Government Office (2005) Making Policy that Happens. National School of Government .

[13] For more on the often complicated progress of discussions about policy see Brock K., Cornwall A. and Gaventa J. (2001) Power, Knowledge and Political Spaces in the Framing of Poverty Policy. Institute of Development Studies Working Paper 143. Brighton: Institute of Development Studies.

Which route to take?

By this stage you have identified the issue you want to change, have developed a strong evidence base and good solution to the issue. Next, you have to think how to deploy your innovative idea. The following section explores possible routes to take either directly progressing the issue through a policy agenda (covered here) or as part of a broader campaign for change, which is explored throughout the whole guide.

The policy cycle
Timing is everything. More often than not you will have to fit in with the decision-maker's timetable for change. You need to think about whether your evidence shows the links between possible interventions and the outcomes you are aiming to achieve. Is it presented in a way that is convincing for the research and policy community?

If possible, tell a clear story and have a narrative that either fits with what the target is trying to do, or that disrupts the target's thinking in a way that brings them to a fresh view of what is needed. It is up to you to define how the policy discussion takes place, its concepts, values and criteria.[13]

It may help you to think of the typical cycle through which policy develops and its different uses at different points.

Policy-making in government tends to follow a fairly set route – from consultation papers through to legislation, after which guidance is issued and good practice recommended. You have significant opportunities along the way to influence where and how government chooses to intervene, how the questions are framed and speed of change – the latter often depends on how contentious the proposals are. But don't get too fixed on this overly rational model of making logically sound decisions based on weighing up the facts alone – debates about policy are always contested and open to reinterpretation.

Diagram: Typical stages of policy development

Policy Stages

- Identifying the problem
- Raising the problem's profile
- Developing a solution and getting it adopted
- Implementing the policy
- Assessing the impact

[14] Young, E. and L. Quinn (2002) Writing Effective Public Policy Papers: A Guide To Policy Advisers in Central and Eastern Europe. Budapest: LGI p12 (redrawn and adapted). For a more sophisticated version of the policy cycle see the following briefing paper, which outlines ODI's RAPID outcome mapping approach: Young, J. and Mendizabal, E. (2009) Helping Researcher Become Policy Entrepreneurs. How to develop engagement strategies for evidence-based policy-making. ODI Briefing Paper 53. London: ODI.

Source: Young, E. and L. Quinn (2002) Writing Effective Public Policy Papers: A Guide To Policy Advisers in Central and Eastern Europe (redrawn and adapted).[14]

Which route to take?
(continued)

Policy formation and implementation will involve a range of pragmatic considerations and imperfect approaches. Those developing policy may have an incomplete knowledge of the alternatives and their likely consequences, vested interests may also influence which issues make it onto the agenda, something we will look at further in *understanding power and power relations* page 46.

Setting the agenda through policy
Your evidence can be used to establish your own frame of reference or help set an agenda to support your issue. Key is identifying workable solutions – potential wins; leaving the solution open can leave you vulnerable to your target imposing a solution, that could be unpalatable. Timing is also crucial for the policy process: it is little use having the perfect research or policy once the opportunity has passed.

Evidence needs to be able to go beyond the very specific circumstance or unique situation; decision-makers need to see its wider relevance or applicability to immediate problems. You therefore need to demonstrate relevance, how your solution fits with the question they are trying to answer. If it doesn't, how could it be made to do so?

There are a number of ways you can deploy your evidence or policy proposals; which route you take may well depend on how the issue or organisation is positioned, how receptive your targets are and what resources you have to draw upon.

Information approach – the quantity of knowledge counts; influence rests on getting your evidence in front of the decision-maker in as many places as possible. If you rely on this approach you need to be adding to your information base as you go providing new insights and ensuring your messages are consistent.

Evidence-based approach – the quality of knowledge counts; influence depends on you having high-quality, contextually relevant policy proposals that win the respect of the people who matter.

Value-based approach – whose knowledge is what counts; make your evidence as credible as you can or build your 'brand' by developing networks with the communities that you represent.

Relational approach – it's not the knowledge that counts but the dialogue; facilitating a shared approach by developing relationships with communities affected by the issue and coming to shared solutions and policy proposals. This approach relies on your capacity to facilitate conversations.[15]

Making the most of public consultations
Central and local government mechanisms aiming to give the public more of a voice in decision-making have been proliferating. Commercial organisations are also trying to reach out to customers, especially around their corporate social responsibility measures. These attempts at dialogue offer campaigners an opportunity to influence. Some general questions to answer for deciding whether to take part are:
- How crucial is the issue to furthering your campaign aim?
- How many organisations are being consulted and what is your standing among them?
- What is your particular positioning in the decision-making process?

Consultation can be used to slow down an issue when organisations are pushing for quick decisions or where they have leverage in a situation. Public consultations can sometimes allow divisions to emerge in a campaign, which can then be exploited by those in power. Organisations can waste valuable time trying to challenge the way questions in the consultation, or the whole agenda, have been reframed. It can also be used to legitimise decisions that have effectivly been made.

15 These types of influence are developed from Sumner A., Ishmael-Perkins N. and Lindstrom J. (2009) Making Science of Influencing: Assessing the impact of development research. IDS Working Paper 335 Brighton: Institute of Development Studies p14.

Co-option?

Governments sometimes try to enlist critical groups into backing a policy agenda by setting up working groups and reviews. This can be a high-risk tactic for both parties; if the campaign later withdraws it may seriously damage any prospects of further dialogue. If, however, the campaign keeps quiet, it can be publicly perceived as approving the policy. For the government, the risk is having its policy exposed in a high-profile public row.

Consultation process can be a means of pushing a controversial topic 'into the long grass' when problems seem intractable or seem costly to implement or not be politically popular.

Decision-makers have powerful weapons at their disposal: they can affect who gets selected to be consulted, especially who ends up being in the room. While most public procedures now encourage everyone who wishes to respond, that openness means that any impact you have depends less on the formal process and more on who is going to be represented in other places, such as working parties, who sees the officials – off the record – and who is invited to give further submissions.

If a campaign is trying to achieve a change within a specific time, say before the end of a parliament, all these deliberations can spin things out until it is too late to change anything.

These methods can all have a boomerang effect on those who try them. Sooner or later the consultation or inquiry ends and frustrated or excluded organisations can regroup, forming powerful alliances that can loudly undermine the validity of the consultation if they feel it is flawed.

Think tanks

A senior civil servant observed that 'It is useful when think tanks agree with our stance as it makes the announcement [of a new policy] easier. Colleagues in the civil service know it gives them some kind of legitimacy they wouldn't normally have on their own'.[16]

Think tanks play a powerful role in the development of policy. Originally conceived as a means of developing innovation in policy-making, many have taken on a wider remit of developing mainstream policies and have been used to justifying pre-existing policies. In the UK think tanks can be seen as the point at which research and ideas get turned into policy and transmitted into the political mainstream with ministers, MPs, journalists and opinion-formers all key consumers of their work.

You can make use of think tanks to help you in several ways:
- Commission research or think pieces – this can be done from a think tank that you know is close to a particular minister, adviser or the general inclinations of the government.
- Influence work – by acting as an expert resource for the completion of think tank work commissioned by others you can exert influence on how that work frames policies; generalist think tank researchers often seek the advice of specialists in the sector.
- Testing ideas out – you may get a chance to test ideas that are ahead of either your target audience or own members and supporters enabling you to push a debate or develop your thinking without having to be totally aligned with a position.
- Away from the spotlight – by attending think tank seminars or conferences you can discuss key issues often in the presence of ministers or opposition spokespeople.

Because think tanks are often aligned with particular political perspectives, before you commission work from one, think carefully about its position and ensure that your own independence is not going to be compromised.

[16] Com Res for Hill and Knowlton, (2007) Think Tanks, their role, influence and future, London.

Analysing the environment

When deciding whether to embark on a campaign you need to assess both the environment and decision-making process that you want to influence and the wider work of your organisation, including the views and needs of the people you represent and support.

The world around you

Many campaigns underestimate the time it can take to achieve change. Some changes can happen quickly in the face of major threats or when there is massive public demand for action. However, most shifts in policy and practice are the result of years of careful nurturing of evidence, like the slow drip of water on stone, until a particular view achieves the status of common sense without anyone having been aware of the change.

Remember the law of unintended consequences – legislation and policy interact with other social forces to produce consequences that no one has foreseen, which can be both positive and negative. You need to recognise this and ensure that your issue and campaign strategy open to revision and development.

Undertaking a risk assessment and addressing how risks can be mitigated will minimise this. See more on risk assessment and mitigation, page 32. However, there may still be some consequences that you had not predicted and you need to be able to respond to those as they happen.

Tools for analysing your environment

There are several well-established and simple tools to help you analyse the environment to decide if you have found the right issue to embark on and launch a campaign.

SWOT

SWOT stands for strengths, weaknesses, opportunities and threats. A SWOT summary categorises information that you have gathered while investigating the campaigning climate and your organisation's priorities and capacity – your internal and external analyses.

In a group brainstorm what are the strengths, weaknesses, opportunities and threats to the campaign?

Things to think about could include:
- Resources, expertise, skills, capacity, funding
- The current environment and future trends
- How the issue is positioned
- Your stakeholders such as beneficiaries, supporters and funders

SWOTs are usually laid out on a grid. By placing the answers to these questions in a SWOT summary, you will identify problems at an early stage. SWOT analysis is a simple way to analyse both your external and internal environment.

PEST

PEST stands for political, economic, social, and technological. PEST is a tool for assessing the political, economic, social and technological factors likely to influence your ability to effect policy change. Variants of PEST analysis also look at the environmental, legal and ethical factors (PESTEL and STEEPLE).

PEST is a manageable way of arranging a large amount of information into categories that might affect your chances of success. Try to stick to your specific issue rather than general issues that will not really make much difference to your campaign.

How to do it

Step one – under each heading consider the key trends or forces that may affect policy-making generally. These trends are often referred to as 'drivers'. Decide on a timeframe to guide your thinking, for example, in the next year, next five years, next 10 years. Decide whether you want to focus on the policy environment as a whole or a specific area that concerns you directly.

Step two – think about what each driver means for your organisation's campaigning and influencing work.

Step three – list the opportunities and threats that these drivers present for your work. You should highlight those that are likely to have the greatest impact on your work and those that are most unpredictable or uncertain.

Step four – now you may be able to specify what you need to do next. You might decide to monitor a specific political development more closely, establish contact with potential allies or to clarify how decisions are going to be made about an issue. PEST analysis is good for flagging up gaps in knowledge and areas needing more research.

Questions to ask could include:
- What is the political climate?
- What are the decision-making structures?
- Who is most powerful within these in relation to your issue?
- Who is going to be most sympathetic and who is going to oppose what you want to do?
- How well are you positioned in relation to those decision-makers?
- How do the public, members, and others with an interest in the issue see your organisation?
- Is your issue regarded as important in the general political environment the decision-makers work in?
- What developments are already likely to happen related to the area you are campaigning in?
- What economic factors will affect your campaign?
- What is the economic climate and how will this affect your campaign proposals?
- What is the general state of the economy or the sector in which you are hoping to campaign and how will this affect it?
- What social factors influence your work?
- What do you know about public opinion on your campaign issues?
- What is the media's general attitude to those issues?
- Are other organisations likely to support or oppose your campaign?
- What are other opinion formers' views?
- What other social trends might have an impact on your issue?
- What scientific or technological issues might make a difference?
- Does the science support your position?
- If scientific views are divided what can you do?
- What developments are on the horizon that might give support to or undermine your cause?
- How might changes in communication technology change the way you conceive your campaign?

Working through these questions will improve your analysis and show you how your campaign might progress.

Analyising the environment
(continued)

Forcefield analysis
Once you have completed SWOT and PEST analysis it can be helpful to analyse the forces for and against any change that you are contemplating to see how realistic your idea is and what key issues you would need to address to help bring about change.

Start by describing the change you wish to make in the middle of a page and then list all the forces 'for' it on one side and the forces 'against' it on the other side. Next assign a score to each of the factors you have listed from 1 (weak) to five (strong). Add up the totals for each column and this will

give an indication of the overall positives and negatives. You then need to see how you could address or neutralise any of the negatives and enhance the positives to redress the balance in your favour or further increase the strength of your position.

Diagram: Force field analysis example
Example: a campaign against airport expansion

Forces for policy change ▶	Desired policy change:	Forces against policy change ◀
Will help curb growth in CO2 emissions in the UK (2)	A government commitment to prevent UK airport expansion	Significant and sustained growth in demand for air travel, both in UK and internationally (3)
Key heritage and wildlife sites will be irrevocably lost (2)		Job creation: within aviation, service and construction industries; strong union support (3)
Financial and political costs for re-housing and compensating local residents; protracted legal battles (3)		Support economic growth: positive impact on UK service sector, particularly tourism (3)
Increased noise pollution from increased number of flights (1)		Will increase UK's competitiveness in the global economy (3)
Expansion costs, particularly in face of pressure to curb public spending commitments (3)		
Total: 11		**Total: 12**

Source: NCVO, In Focus Guide: Making Sense of the External Environment.[17]

[17] NCVO (2009) In Focus Guide: Making Sense of the External Environment. London: NCVO.

Other voices speaking on your issue

You are probably not alone in presenting your case to decision-makers. You may be in the company of the private sector lobbies with their own research and policy sections, or professional bodies and groupings such as the Local Government Association, all with extensive policy and lobbying experience and resources. Other VCOs may also be raising their voices.

They can either be allies in your work or conduits to be influenced and hopefully carry your message, or opponents to your issue. You need to see that as far as possible they understand and support your agenda and work with them as another means of influencing your ultimate target. Often, even when the overall aims of other institutions do not match yours, it is possible to find some common interests where their research or policy can be used to support your case. For example, during the passage of the Equalities Act in 2010 the disability lobby secured the support of major employers' organisations for stronger requirements of employers not to screen for pre-existing disabilities as this could be used to discriminate in employment. The support of a lobby that might have been thought to oppose such measures was very powerful and based on evidence that both parties agreed on.

Organisations may exist and be campaigning in opposition to your campaign. You need to think about what actions they may take, how they will counter your campaign arguments and whether they have access to decision-makers you are trying to reach. It can be really useful to systematically go through all the arguments in your campaign with a colleague playing devil's advocate and suggesting what the counter arguments – 'the other side' – may take.

Analyising the environment
(continued)

Stakeholder analysis
Stakeholders are people or organisations who are affected by the issue or can influence the issue. Stakeholder analysis is used to identify allies and opponents and prioritise whom to target. It helps you determine your influencing strategy and priority audience(s) to focus your resources. To be effective you need to be clear on the issue that you intend to campaign on. If you need further resources to support your campaign or technical expertise, include a section on pro bono support in your stakeholder analysis.

How to do it
Step one – brainstorm
Sit down, ideally with a group, and list all the possible stakeholders that are either affected by your issue or can influence it. Aim for a long and comprehensive list, be as creative as you can and try not self-censor as you go along. Then divide the results into groups with broadly the same position and interest.

Step two – analyse the results
You need to analyse the stakeholders to identify the most important players in the campaign to focus attention and resources where they will have most effect. Consider the following questions for each stakeholder and record the answers in a table.

How much influence do they have over the issue (compared with the other stakeholders)?
• High Influence
• Medium Influence
• Low Influence

How much do they agree or disagree with us?
• Strongly in favour
• In favour
• Neutral
• Against
• Strongly against

How important do they think the issue is, (compared with the other issues that they face)?
• high importance
• medium importance
• low importance

You may also have a can't agree/don't know group, so
• Sub-divide the category and/or
• Investigate further and/or
• Make an educated guess

Diagram: Stakeholder analysis

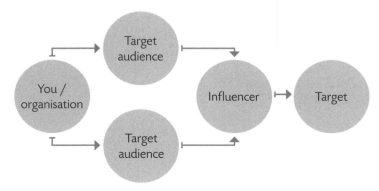

Step three – sort the results

You will be left with a large amount of detailed intelligence so to make the results stand out you can transfer the results onto a matrix. This can be drawn onto large sheets of paper.

Step four – interpret the results and select your target audiences

The matrix will enable you to interpret the results and determine your influencing strategy; the answers to the following questions should be clear:

- Who are the priority stakeholders?
- Who are your most important allies and opponents and who is neutral?
- What options do you have for shifting the balance of power and ideas?
- Who can help increase your influence?
- How can you reduce the influence of opponents?

See diagram: Allies and opponents matrix.

Source: This version of a stakeholder analysis has been developed by Ian Chandler, of the Pressure Group, for use in advocacy and campaign planning to help us to make these choices of target audiences on a rational and systematic basis.

Diagram: Allies and opponents matrix

Influence of the stakeholder over the decision maker

HIGH
- Here will be your main opponents
- Here will be the main battle ground, you might need to persuade these groups to agree with your issue
- Here will be your main allies

MEDIUM
- Here you may need to increase your influence

LOW
- Here you may need to increase your influence

VERY ANTI — VERY PRO

Attitude of the stakeholder to your position

Analyising the environment
(continued)

Influencing options

For the audiences you select to target, you have five influencing options:

- Persuade them to agree with your position – with influential neutrals and soft opponents.
- Persuade them that the issue is important – with disinterested allies.
- Build alliances with them – with influential and interested allies.
- Increase their influence – with allies of low influence.
- Decrease their influence – with opponents of high influence.

You can also map out your list of stakeholders onto a power interest matrix to help you determine your strategies for engaging with each of your stakeholders and resources needed. By doing this you will be able to focus your efforts on those who have the most power and interest to make a difference to your campaign. Review it from time to time to ensure that stakeholders have not moved their position since you started your plan.

Stakeholder analysis will help you identify who are the most important allies to your campaign and alert you to the size of potential opposition to your issue. These are important factors to consider when deciding whether this the right issue for you to be campaigning on, whether you need to work in alliance with others, or whether you need to reassess your issue.

Diagram: Power interest matrix

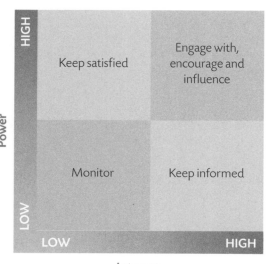

Power

HIGH — Keep satisfied | Engage with, encourage and influence

LOW — Monitor | Keep informed

LOW ——————— HIGH

Interest

---

[18] For a fuller analysis of the sources of power and credibility for research in the policy process see for example: Court J., Hovland I. and Young J. (2004) Bridging Research and Policy in International Development: Evidence and the change process. Rugby: ITDG.

How to decide if a campaign is right for you

Once you have analysed the external environment you will now need to decide whether you and your organisation have the capacity to undertake running the campaign. Does it fit with your organisation's capacity and its priorities and mission? If you are a charity the campaign will need to be demonstrably linked to the achievement of your charitable objectives. Answering the following questions may help you to decide.

- Are you well placed to campaign on the issue?
- Does this campaign fit with the vision, mission and aims of your organisation?
- Do you have any authority – expertise and the backing of your members – to conduct a campaign?
- Have your members, beneficiaries and other stakeholders been involved in the process?
- Does the issue fit in with the priorities of the people that your organisation supports or represents?
- Do you have enough resources and capacity – in terms of staff time, money and expertise – to campaign on this issue?

- If the campaign takes off, how long can you sustain it?
- Do you need to raise more money before you embark on a campaign?
- What are your weaknesses?
- What are the implications of the campaign for your reputation and operations?
- How far the issue is amenable to campaigning? Are there different approaches?
- Are there different solutions?

Your authority to campaign

What business is it of yours? Who do you represent? What do you know about this, anyway? Questions such as these challenge the legitimacy of your campaign; you need to be able to speak from a position of strength and authority. There are a number of ways in which you can establish the legitimacy of your campaign and enhance your claim to be listened to by key targets.

Moral legitimacy – you may be able claim persuasive moral authority, deriving from your established role as champion of human or animal rights, or being the acknowledged representative of a section of the community because you provide services to them.

Technical competence or providing services – authority can stem from having expertise; you may provide services and have specialist knowledge as a result of that. Local community groups can have as much credibility here as large national organisations due to the uniqueness or innovative nature of the work they are engaged in.

Political clout – if you have a large membership, network or community and are clearly accountable to them, this gives you political strength. If you provide services and the services users have a voice in shaping services this can be a powerful additional source of political credibility.

Legal – another base for legitimacy is in knowledge or expertise in the law or professional practice around legislation or policy. This is often again backed by direct service provision through helpline advice or legal services and advocacy to clients, which means the organisation is well placed to comment on the consequences of policy.[18]

Using a number of these sources of legitimacy together can make your claim to be heard even stronger.

**Involving
people**

Participation is key in any campaign, giving people – citizens, service users, specific communities, consumers.... a voice to influence the decisions that affect their lives. Enabling your organisation's members, beneficiaries, users, supporters or other stakeholders to engage with your work could happen in many different ways but involving people in your campaign is essentially about giving them a voice, supporting them to be heard and acting on what they say, in order to bring about positive changes to the world they live in.

At this stage of the campaigns cycle active participation of your wider stakeholders could help to determine the issue you campaign on, ensure that your evidence base is relevant and grounded in the experiences of those you are representing, or help propose alternative workable solutions for change.

Diagram: Levels of participation

Inform	To provide members/service users/ other stakeholders with balanced and objective information.
Consult	To obtain feedback on an issue.
Involve	To ensure that the problems, needs and aspirations of your members/ service users/other beneficiaries are identified, understood and considered.
Collaborate	To develop solutions or an agreed course of action in collaboration with members/service users/other beneficiaries.
Empower	To place final decision-making powers in hands of members/service users/ other stakeholders: to enable them to directly engage in policy process or campaigning efforts[19]

[19] Based on International Association for Public Participation template quoted in: Involve (2005) People and Participation, How to put citizens at the heart of decision-making. London: Involve. See also: NCVO (2010) In Focus Guide: Involving People That Matter. London: NCVO.

[20] For more on the different methodologies of involvement see: Involve (2005) People and Participation, How to put citizens at the heart of decision-making. London: Involve and: Cabinet Office (2008) Better Together: Improving consultation with the third sector. London: Cabinet Office, designed essentially as a guide for public officials but includes many of the key methodologies and principles for good consultation.

Deciding whom to involve

Ensuring that you are involving a range of stakeholders can make a crucial difference to the relevance and appropriateness of your campaign. There are two main approaches to deciding whom to involve, depending on your aims and the wider context:

- Open – allowing anyone who is interested to participate.
- Selective – those involved are identified as part of the process.

How will you recruit your would-be participants? How will you support people to participate? What barriers might stop people participating and how can you address these?

Be careful that you do not engage with the same people in every campaign you run. Choosing the 'usual suspects' over and over again undermines your campaign's authority and could also give these people a dose of 'consultation fatigue'.

When involving a range of stakeholders it is important to have processes in place to ensure that different voices and priorities are heard as appropriate. There may be a distinction between your beneficiaries and your audience and/or campaigns or fundraising supporter network. So think through the terminology that you use and whose voice is prioritised.

Some methods for getting views and involving people

Involvement could range from informal consultation to involvement of a governing body of the organisation where beneficiaries have a meaningful stake in the oversight and scrutiny of a campaign. These might include:

- **Written consultations** – good for getting views on more complex issues but give little opportunity to question the premise of the issue being consulted on.
- **Questionnaires** – good for finding out views on specific issues and measuring opinion at one moment in time but poor as a means of engaging people in shaping issues – at best a snapshot of what people are thinking.
- **Public meetings** – the usefulness depends on the skill with which they are handled: if the agenda is open and people have good opportunity to participate they can be very effective. It can be difficult to decide the outcome of a meeting or what it has changed; it may require follow-up with other methods.
- **Focus groups** – good for getting to people's more deeply held views and to be able to theme responses.
- **Open space** – meetings where all participants have the opportunity to set the agenda based on open questions or themes in an informal atmosphere, which seeks to give everyone the same chance to contribute.
- **Citizen panels** – large groups of people (hundreds), useful for tracking issues and changing views over time.
- **Citizen juries** – smaller than panels so allow more in-depth consideration of the issues through calling of witness and evidence. They normally last a number of days. It is then possible to measure how views change during the process. You need to be aware that they are expensive and time consuming to run and it is difficult to replicate the process on a larger scale so insights are not always transferable.
- **User advisory groups** – typically around 10–30 service users or beneficiaries who meet to inform and advise organisations about internal or external policy issues. You need to ensure clarity of expectations about what they can and cannot change.
- **User-led management committees** – users or beneficiaries in the majority or all of the management committee and can sign off campaign plans.[20]

Beneficiary involvement

Beneficiaries

By beneficiaries we mean people whose lives will be improved by your campaign's success. People may object to the term because they feel it implies that beneficiaries are passive subjects, rather than potentially active agents of change. Alternative terms – users, stakeholders, partner, rights holder – all have limitations, and few are applicable in all contexts. While recognising the difficulties, the terms 'beneficiary' or 'beneficiaries' are used here because they are short and simple.

You may want a range of stakeholders' inputs into a campaign but it is important to separate and prioritise the views of wider stakeholders from those groups who will be affected directly affected by the change you wish to make – the beneficiaries of the campaign.

Different campaigns may have different groups of intended beneficiaries. It may already be clear who your beneficiaries are or it could involve a complex process, drawing out audiences from stakeholder analysis. Many organisations may have different beneficiary groups and it is useful to map these out to identify who should participate in which campaigns and when.

For example, what happens if your organisation has different sets of beneficiaries with different experiences and needs – whose voice is prioritised? Or if you are an international organisation whose beneficiaries are abroad, you may need to convince them that the campaign is relevant to them. How do you manage a diverse range of views when involving hard-to-reach groups? You need to have a clear plan for how you will handle these potential conflicts.

An organisation campaigning for changes to enhance the lives of people with a specific health condition may, for example, have the following beneficiaries:

- People living with a specific condition.
- People affected by a condition, for example, family, friends
- People caring for someone who is living with a condition.

Then there may be a wider group of stakeholders, who may have an interest in a specific campaign. These could include:

- Other experts such as researchers, trustees, staff and volunteers, people who work with people with a condition such as specialist nurses or doctors, campaign supporters, donors or funders and partner organisations.

Stakeholder analysis tools will help you identify and priories those you should work with see page 36.

See more on beneficiary involvement, pages 42 and 134.

[21] www.ncvo-vol.org.uk/countmein

[22] See Charity Commission, Speaking out guidance on Campaigning and Political Activity by Charities (CC9) http://www.charity-commission.gov.uk/Publications/cc9.aspx

[23] Crutchfield L. and McLeod-Grant H. (2008) Forces for Good: Six practices of high impact non profits. Chichester: John Wiley and Son.

[24] Public Administration Select Committee (2007–08) Public Services and the Third Sector: Rhetoric and Reality Eleventh Report of Session. London: House of Commons.

Ramblers is Britain's largest walking association, with nearly 140,000 members. Its highly participative membership runs Ramblers' campaigns. The membership elects the board and approves its policies, including prioritising campaigns and scrutinising their progress.

The highest decision-making body of the organisation is its General Council. Each year around 300 delegates, selected by their area, attend General Council and vote on the programme for the year ahead. General Council is the culmination of a lengthy and highly participative process. In the run up to it all local Ramblers' groups from 53 regions will have their annual general meeting, in which any member can propose motions to be sent to General Council.

The motions that are passed at General Council become policy or the campaign aim and are carried out by staff who report to General Council the following year. The democratic nature of campaign selection creates a large workload for the staff but the association strongly believe its benefits outweigh the costs.

Source: Adapted from Campaigning Effectiveness, NCVO Count Me In web resource.[21]

Combining campaigning and providing services

Campaigning often grows out of and remains embedded in the service experience of the communities they work with. If you are a registered charity, campaigning activities must routinely be a subsidiary activity except in exceptional circumstances according to charity law.[22] Therefore, campaigning and service provision have never been mutually exclusive. A recent study found those organisations that do both are more effective at achieving change than those who only undertake one of these activities.[23] As a select committee observed:

'It is clear that pursuing and delivering public service contracts is not necessarily a barrier to independent campaigning and advocacy. In particular, there may be positive effects of entering into a contracting relationship, as it can deliver stability of income; organisations which rely on grants for core funding are arguably more at risk than large service delivery organisations' Public Administration Select Committee (2007–08) Public Services and the Third Sector: Rhetoric and Reality Eleventh Report of Session.[24]

But this dual role is not without its strains. Recent government policy has encouraged the voluntary and community sector to provide more and more services and to be a voice for local communities and the individuals that they serve and represent. The continuing drive for organisations to operate increasingly commercially, taking on contracts on behalf of the public sector, may sit uneasily with the public bodies that issue the contracts when the VCOs then advocate for their service users with those same bodies.

Combining campaigning and providing services (continued)

If the organisation's main source of income is from contracts that they are under pressure to retain then this can be perceived as a potential brake on their role as vigorous advocates, with smaller organisations feeling particularly vulnerable. Many VCOs have reined in their campaigning, thinking that 'you can't bite the hand that feeds you'. However the evidence does not really bear out these concerns.[25] Campaigning and providing services can sit well together but need careful and active management.

Feedback from your service users can strengthen your campaigning work. You can ask users not only about the service that you are providing but whether the wider context of current laws, policies and practice is making life harder or better for them? Think about your relationships with contractors before you launch into campaigns that they might see as damaging to them; if you are indeed going to 'bite the hand that feeds you' must have a clear idea about the possible consequences of your actions and how you are going to manage the relationship.

Resisting pressure

Organisations can find themselves vulnerable to undue pressure from public bodies that may restrict their ability to campaign, especially if they are dependent on grant aid or similar contracting arrangements. The renewed Compact states that Government will: *'Respect and uphold the independence of CSOs (civil society organisations) to deliver their mission, including their right to campaign, regardless of any relationship, financial or otherwise, which may exist.'* [26]

Any public body exerting formal or informal pressure on your organisation not to campaign should be reminded of this undertaking. The acceptance of the key role of campaigning is even reflected in examples of local contracts specifying that organisations not only provide services but also give local communities a voice.[27]

Undertaking a risk analysis will help you to explore the consequences of your campaign activity and will highlight any potential risks you may encounter, enabling you to explore ways to mitigate those risks before you run into them. Embarking on a public campaign should follow on from other routes to influence that you have explored; if you can demonstrate that other forms of dialogue have already been pursued and met with dead ends it may well strengthen your campaign. As will having a clear aim including alterative solution(s) to the issue you wish to tackle.

You should also ensure that that people in your organisation, especially those who provide services, and your trustees are aware of the content of your campaign before it is launched, and ideally that they are involved in it all the way – from the selection of the issue, developing the evidence base or backing the campaign and helping with the delivery.

---

[25] National Consumer Councils evidence to the Select Committee's inquiry into the voluntary sector concluded on campaigning that 'A lot of third sector organisations worry about the potential that there will be some negative knock-on effects, but we do not have any evidence that that is necessarily a problem.' Public Administration Select Committee (2007–08) Public Services and the Third Sector: Rhetoric and Reality Eleventh Report of Session. London: House of Commons.

[26] The Renewed Compact is an agreement between the Coalition Government, and their associated Non-Departmental Public Bodies, Arms Length Bodies and Executive Agencies, and civil society organisations (CSOs) in England. The agreement aims to ensure that the Government and CSOs work effectively in partnership to achieve common goals and outcomes for the benefit of communities and citizens in England. http://www.compactvoice.org.uk/about-compact (Accessed December 2010).

[27] See the Local Government Association's evidence to Public Administration Select Committee's investigation Public Administration Select Committee (2007–08) Public Services and the Third Sector: Rhetoric and Reality Eleventh Report of Session. London: House of Commons. Par 224. A recent study found that local organisations where skilled at managing the potential tensions caused by local campaigning: see Cairns B., Hutchison R. and Aiken M. (2010) 'It is not what we do, it is how we do it' managing the tension between service delivery and advocacy. Voluntary Sector Review 1 (2).

Developing

a strategy for change

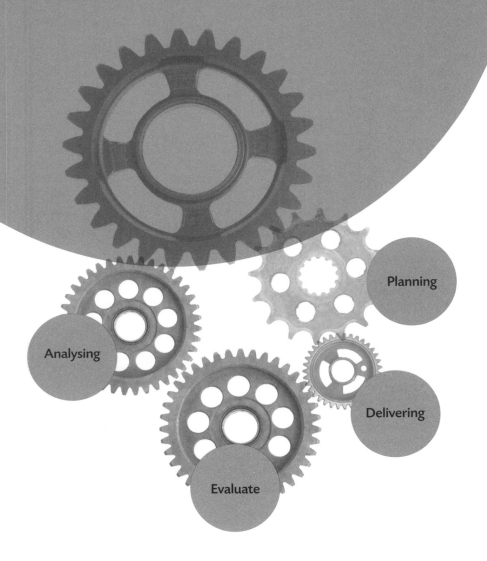

Analysing

Planning

Evaluate

Delivering

Contents

Understanding power and power relations
- Power and why it matters
- Types of power
- Increasing your sources of power
- Becoming more powerful
- Power in practice

Strategy
- Setting the campaign aim
- Developing a theory of change for your campaign
- Theory of change – how to plan for impact
- Theory of change model
- Understanding how change comes about
- Anticipating the consequences of change

Evaluation
- What you can evaluate
- Measures
- Some monitoring and evaluation models
- Avoiding the pitfalls
- Plan how you will communicate your results

Funding your campaign
- Co-ordinating campaigning and fundraising
- Working together
- Campaigning integrity
- Online campaigning and fundraising
- Corporate fundraising link-ups
- Trusts and foundations
- Pro bono: a different way of giving

Campaigners are often fired by the passionate need to make change happen. Sometimes sheer enthusiasm and intuition can get you a long way. There are, however, far more campaigns that fail because they lack a clearly defined aim, a campaign strategy and ways of checking that they are on track. This section sets out these essential elements of your campaign, but first it explores power and power relationships, as these are fundamental to bringing about any change.

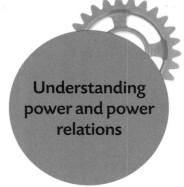

Understanding power and power relations

Power and why it matters
If you already had the power to change something there would be no reason to campaign. Campaigning is nearly always about attempting to alter the balance of power within a situation. This change can stem from a range of tactics from gentle persuasion through to open public confrontation. The main route to bringing about a change in power relationships is being able to focus pressure directly on those with power to solve the problem that you are addressing or on those who can influence the targets of your campaign.

Understanding how power is deployed positively and negatively in different situations is crucial for campaigners in thinking about how change comes about. It is crucial that you understand how power is applied and understand your own sources of power and those of the communities you work with and support. There are many approaches to power, set out below are some of the most relevant.

---

[1] Lukes S. (2005) Power: A radical view (second edition). London: Palgrave Macmillan.

[2] See for example Gaventa J. (2006) Finding the spaces for change: a power analysis. IDS Bulletin 37 (6)., which summarises the idea of a power cube – a three-dimensional analysis of power based on the idea of a Rubik's cube with different levels of power exercised at local, national and international levels all of which can have the different types of spaces in which power is exercised and the different dimensions of power outlined by Lukes. See also www.powercube.net and Gaventa J. 'Levels, spaces and forms of power: analysing opportunities for change'. In: Berenskoetter F. and Williams M. (Eds) (2007) Power in World Politics London: Routledge. and VeneKlasen L. and Miller V. (2002) A New Weave of People, Power and Politics: The action guide for advocacy and citizen participation. Oklahoma: World Neighbours.

Types of power

Steven Lukes' classic book, Power: A radical view, distinguishes three different dimensions or 'faces' of power – visible, hidden and invisible.[1]

Visible power is contestable in the public realm and open to challenge – through legislatures and other formal processes of consultation and engagement. Campaigning activity here means participating in existing structures or trying to challenge them through accepted procedures. Decision-makers may also prefer to operate through building up consensus and support for their decisions, investing time and resources in formal process and consultations. Campaigners' effort and focus is therefore often aimed at influencing this formal exercise of power through persuasion tactics. It can mean that campaigns with little formal power can nevertheless deliver big changes.

Hidden power is when powerful groups try to control access to decision-making by controlling what is put on or left off the formal agenda, and how the rules of engagement are framed. This directly or indirectly results in certain issues being excluded from the agenda and others promoted. The more power an organisation has the more easily it can influence the agenda.

Campaigners faced with the challenge of disrupting hidden power may try to redress the balance by working with communities to alter embedded assumptions about a particular issue or group and seek to frame issues differently to counteract an inherent bias. Reframing an issue is a way in which campaigners can challenge the conventional 'political wisdom' that marginalises or keeps issues off the agenda. Also measures such as the Freedom of Information Act offer scope to challenge hidden power by increasing the transparency of public authorities.

Invisible power is the shaping of the public domain through the beliefs, values and wants that are considered normal or acceptable. This is manifested in everyday assumptions and bias towards certain states of affairs and against others. Often assumptions about what is 'natural' or 'unchangeable' reinforce particular groups' advantages. Depicting poverty as an issue of personal responsibility, for example, makes it much more difficult to campaign for measures that would reduce poverty and its causes. Campaigns facing this kind of power have to take on not only the way in which a problem is perceived but may also want to work with disempowered groups to help challenge accepted assumptions.

To achieve change you need to be aware of all these dimensions of power, how they may affect your campaign aim and what options you have to disrupt and challenge the exercise of power.

A useful addition to this explanation of power has been developed by academics such as Dr John Gaventa at the Institute of Development Studies, University of Sussex, which focuses on the 'spaces for participation' – invited, claimed or created and closed. This explanation points to how groups and organisations can lay claim to the spaces in which power is exercised or support others to do so.[2]

Invited space is a useful concept for examining how campaigning groups can directly influence the policy and public agenda by being part of formal or informal but relatively open processes, such as consultations, public discussion forums, user panels, meetings and so on. All these provide direct routes through which you can engage with powerful structures of national and local government, where there has been a major attempt to develop more meaningful engagement. Geoff Mulgan, Chief Executive of the Young Foundation, summed up the aspiration for this type of engagement:

Understanding power and power relations (continued)

'Public participation could radically improve our quality of life. It can contribute to creating more active citizens, help manage complex problems in public service design and delivery, help build the new relationships and shifts of power required for 21st century governance, and develop individuals' skills, confidence, ambition and vision.' Mulgan G., People and Participation: How to put citizens at the heart of decision-making[3]

Remember that it is government or public body, however, that often sets the agenda for these discussions and decides who is at the table.

Closed spaces occur when those with power do not want consultation or advice at any price; they want to pursue their own agenda. This type mirrors Lukes' concept of hidden power. It is a means of restricting access to decision-making. Campaigners can challenge this through questioning the legitimacy of those who have closed down the space through public exposure of the issue, research and bringing the issue to light or the legitimacy of the decision-making process itself.

Claimed or created spaces are self-created spaces that excluded groups make for themselves. These could range from mass social movement to small community associations, to small groups of like-minded people meeting to discuss and debate.[4] Sometimes these can be planned or sometimes can result from a spontaneous outbreak of personal or group anger that captures interest and attention. Claimed spaces occur where excluded groups claim an invitation to take part in an existing issue or area, or seek to reframe the issue. Created spaces occur if groups put an issue on the agenda when there is no existing debate or interest.

All these types of 'spaces' can cut across national boundaries with clusters of supra-national policy forums and spaces where power is also contested. So campaigns will also need to think about the space boundaries or levels at which that power is exercised, which could be at of community, national, European or global level. Depending on the campaign and or organisation different levels of politics will be important.[5]

Increasing your sources of power

It is important to remember that groups can have latent or unrealised power. Which relatively powerless groups might become active depending on the issue? Campaigners need to assess how potentially powerful groups could be brought together or mobilised to influence the agenda. London Citizens is a good example of where, by working at community level, groups who previously did not have a voice have been able to campaign on a living wage for Londoners. Conversely, governments will often not act for fear of disturbing a particular interest that is seen to be powerful or where public opinion is presumed to be strongly against or for a particular issue, for example this was seen by the last Labour government's concern about how far an alliance of National Trust members and environment groups would go when brought together to protest against the expansion of Stansted Airport.[6]

---

[3] Mulgan, G. (2005) People and Participation: How to put citizens at the heart of decision-making. London: Involve. Online at www.involve.org.uk (accessed October 2010)

[4] Adapted from www.powercube.net/analyse-power/spaces-of-power/claimed-spaces (accessed December 2010).

[5] John Gaventa, the power cube http://www.powercube.net/

[6] Beetham, D. BLick, A. Margetts, H. and Weir, S. (2008) Power and Participation in Modern Britain. A Literature Review by Democratic Audit.

Becoming more powerful

In order to address different forms of power campaigners can utilise and build on a range of sources of potential power including their own organisation's positioning:

- **Persuasion** – public opinion and anger, once mobilised, put targets under pressure; public exposure and criticism can be a very powerful sanction.
- **Expertise** – investing in or using expertise to lay claim to an area of debate – the quality of your evidence, its presentation and type of work you are engaged in will improve perception of your expertise.
- **Legitimacy** – mobilising sections of the public or your members and ensuring that they are seen as the 'legitimate' voice.
- **Reputation** – is connected to legitimacy – the higher your reputation with public or decision-makers, the less likely that your views will be contested or can be ignored.
- **Position** – VCOs that are linked to communities that they represent or work with have credibility to do so and are respected.
- **Authority** – community representatives who are regarded as authoritative, perhaps through a combination of their experiences or their personal charisma, can boost a campaign; there is a danger that if such individuals withdraw from a campaign it is weakened.

- **Capacity to react quickly** – VCOs can often respond more rapidly than government bodies or large corporations to changing circumstances and shifting public interests.
- **Independence** – is a core part of the voluntary and community sector. It is fundamental to most people's understanding of the sector and highlights the importance of organisations managing their own affairs and being accountable to their mission and their beneficiaries.
- **Longevity** – VCOs can take a long-term view that often goes beyond the horizon off a particular minister, government, official, CEO or corporate policy, ensuring that expertise and knowledge can be deployed more consistently and over time.
- **Legal challenge** – formal processes, such as the Human Rights Act 1988 (and under the European Convention on Human Rights) freedom of expression, assembly, and freedom of information can be used by campaigners to challenge power. More specific laws, including the Equality Act 2010, provide a growing body of individual redress, and can set powerful precedents for groups. More generally they can also be used for more collective forms of action through judicial review and similar mechanisms.

Power in practice

Power relationships are not always a zero sum game in which everything you gain becomes an equal loss of power for others. Targets may, in fact, benefit from the participation of campaign groups and may seek their co-operation, with both gaining from building consensuses and working towards a shared aim, even where the means of getting there can be in dispute. The implication of this view is that there doesn't have to be only winners and losers – a view that may be more appetising to your target as well.

Campaigners constantly have to evaluate how power is used against them and what kinds of power they can exercise. Much campaigning involves mobilising supporters and beneficiaries to challenge decision-makers in order to lay claim to the spaces in which public debate takes place and institutions take decisions. This is how organisations with no formal power can challenge governments and vast corporations, with little more than their ideas, the legitimacy garnered from their work and a supporter base.

Understanding power and power relations (continued)

Key features of political power

Power is the ability to achieve a purpose. Achieving that purpose will depend on what it is and a combination of your position and the opportunity to influence.

Power is structured and exercised in relations between people. People's capacity to achieve their purposes can be realised:

- **Through** others by influence or persuasion.
- **Over** others by the power to grant or withhold some resource or service that they need.
- By virtue of a position of authority, **with** others, through co-operation and organisation in a common enterprise or activity.

The ability to form groups is crucial to acquiring power; bringing together groups to work collaboratively to achieve an aim is key to the exercise of power. The relatively powerless may need to co-operate with others to achieve their purposes. This is one of the main reasons why campaigning in coalitions has become so prominent although the obstacles in forming a coalition and maintaining it over time can make them vulnerable to failing. See more on working with others page 125.

Power is structured and concentrated in institutions such as government and corporate bodies. Two features are common to all institutions and corporate bodies in a democracy.

First, they have to meet publicly validated criteria of legitimacy, both for the way they are organised (accountability, etc) and for what they do (satisfying needs, not causing harm, etc). These criteria for legitimacy both reinforce and set limits to institutional power, public challenges to them can form some of the most serious challenges to that power.

Second, in a democracy these institutions – public or private – also have to provide space for the voices of different groups of stakeholders – whether as citizens, consumers, shareholders etc.– including opportunities for individual complaint or redress. This is the realm of visible power.

A further aspect of power is the 'law of anticipated reactions', which suggests that people adjust their behaviour in the context of the 'powerful' because of the anticipate reactions, including the consequences of what might happen if they do not adjust their behaviour towards more powerful people. This happens without power having to be exercised or even made explicit. This logic is what explains the 'invisible face' of power.

In contrast, the 'power' of the relatively powerless has to be visibly exercised, sometimes in apparently confrontational or disruptive ways, if it is to achieve any effect; precisely as the group in question only has the power of public embarrassment or the threat of it – the threat of such action could be considered their 'latent' power.

Power is fluid and has differing effects and impact in different circumstances and between people, depending often on whether people are in agreement or opposition. A powerful authority may accept a proposal or demand from others if it is judged to be in the authority's interests, or reject it when it is not. Sometimes one part of government or a corporation might also actively encourage representations or protest in the service of increasing their power or leverage with another part of the system, such as government departments encouraging lobby groups as a means of strengthening their own hand with the treasury. UK governments may encourage public protest over global poverty to increase their power within international bodies for example.

Power is affected by the prevailing ideas and beliefs – the power to shape or influence ideas is one of the most significant powers there is.

Source: Adapted from Beetham D., Blick, A., Margetts H. and Weir S, Power and Participation in Modern Britain.[7]

Understanding concepts of power and power relations will help you identify who has the power to make change happen, how they might behave when challenged and how much power you have and how to increase your sources of power. This checklist can help you think this through:

- What type of power relationship are you up against? Is it visible, hidden or invisible? Which institutions are you targeting?
- What type of change are you trying to bring to those power relationships? Does this depend more on changing the visible exercise of power or unearthing the hidden assumptions or entrenched values of invisible power?
- Do you have the ability to mobilise resources, supporters or evidence or have organisational reputation to claim or dispute open and closed spaces at local or national level, and if so how?

- Can you start a debate that claims space for your campaign and drives the debate in new directions?
- Do you have a power analysis to map out who the most important players are and how you can target them? See page 85.

Answering these questions will help you develop you theory of change and in turn build your campaign strategy.[8]

[7] Beetham D., Blick, A., Margetts H. and Weir S. (2008) Power and Participation in Modern Britain. A Literature Review by Democratic Audit,. London: Carnegie Trust UK.

[8] For more on Power and how it effects decisions around campaigning see Mayne, R, Coe, J. Power and Social Change, NCVO, 2010.

• Analysing • **Developing** • Plannning • Delivering • Evaluate
a strategy
for change

Strategy

Once you have pinpointed the solution you wish to achieve (see analysing the issue section) and looked closer at power and power relations a clear campaign aim will act as a beacon towards which everyone involved in the campaign should head.

Setting the campaign aim
In one sentence you need to set out a clear campaign aim, encapsulating the ultimate purpose of the campaign, the change you want to see and the impact you want to make. It should be easily communicable – that is:
• Compelling and inspiring.
• Targeted – identifying who or what needs to change.
• Focusing on impact – articulating what change will result.
• Succinct.

An aim is not the same as objectives, which are the changes you will need to see to contribute to achieving your overall aim. You may have several objectives, each of them stepping stones on the path towards your aim, but you will only have one campaign aim.[9] For more on objectives see page 87.

To have a realistic aim you need to understand the context and environment you are working in so you can develop the capacity to make change happen. Understanding power and power relations are fundamental to this.

Developing a theory of change for your campaign
To build a theory of change you need to start with your ultimate aim, the change that you wish to make. Everything that you do must contribute towards achieving your campaign's ultimate aim. By now you should have already worked out what is achievable given the resources of your organisation and the environment you are working in (see section analysing the issue from page 15).

There are a variety of models of how change happens, some of which are addressed as we work through the campaigns cycle in this guide. A 'theory of change model' is a powerful tool for focusing your campaign strategy and planning. It brings a focused view of how to make change happen and explores the assumptions behind each of the stages on the way, identifying the conditions needed for change to happen and what campaign activities might produce that change. The steps and actions identified will represent your thinking derived from research work and other knowledge as well as your analysis of potential influencers, power relationships and the appropriateness of different campaign approaches.

This process forces campaigners to list in sequence their planned activities and to draw logical connections between these and their expected outcomes and impact. Any particular campaign theory will not necessarily be fixed but will change as you take on board new evidence or as the theory is tested by the impact of your campaign actions.

---

[9] Adapted from: Tess Kingham and Jim Coe (2005) the Good Campaigns Guide, NCVO.

[10] See for example Theory of Change: A Practical Tool For Action, Results and Learning. (2004) Organisational Research Services. (ORS).

[11] For a fuller outline of the basic logic model see: W. K. Kellogg Foundation (2004) Logic Model Development Guide. Michigan: W. K. Kellogg (adjusted here to take account of campaign context).

Theory of change – how to plan for impact

Theory of change (TOC) is an extension of a basic planning tool usually referred to as the logic model.[10]

A logic model looks at the process from identifying resources through to activities, outputs, outcomes and impact as a logical chain of events to form a project plan. Often they are more useful for describing the progress of an existing plan or monitoring delivery.

- **Resources** are everything drawn upon to carry out the activities. These include people, equipment, money and services you need. They might also include more intangible elements such as time, morale and knowledge. Resources are sometimes referred to as **inputs**.

- **Activities** are what the campaign does with the resources. The tasks you do to make sure your campaign outputs happen such as planning, recruiting supporters, campaign actions etc.
- **Outputs** are things generated by your activities – the amount of media coverage secured, production of new research, marches, meetings with minsters etc.
- **Outcomes** are the effects the campaign actually has – the benefits of changes that it has brought about or helped bring about, for example, new legislation, new guidelines, a change in policy. The results can be short term – one to three years or long-term – four to six years.
- **Impact** is the difference your campaign makes. The impact is the real change created by a campaign – the difference it makes to people's lives or environment.[11]

Some people use the terms 'outcomes' and 'impact' interchangeably; others don't. Here we separate the two as distinct terms – this helps to distinguish what you wish to achieve. The passing of legislation is an outcome, whether or not the legislation has the desired effect set out in your campaign aim. The real impact will be the changes on the ground, the difference it makes to people's lives or environment. It's also useful to distinguish between 'outputs' and 'outcomes'. Outputs are the things you do – meetings, marches, media coverage – to reach your outcomes, such as new legislation and change in policy or practice.

The logic model rests on the idea that you should make clear what the logical links are between your activities, outcomes and impacts. This process is essentially the building block for any type of strategic planning.

Diagram: Logic model

Resources / Inputs ↦ Activities ↦ Outputs ↦ Outcomes ↦ Impact

Strategy (continued)

Theory of change model
'A theory of change lays out **what** specific changes the group wants to see in the world, and **how** and **why** a group expects its actions to lead to those changes.'[12]

TOC process is more sophisticated than the logic model in recognising that campaigns need to cope with complex social processes and theories about what actually brings about change. By introducing more focus on the rationale for change it can illuminate strategic choices and how to implement these.

How does the theory of change model work?
The main elements of the TOC model are as follows:
- Stating a clear aim or ultimate impact you want to achieve.
- Mapping the activities that campaigners should undertake to achieve that campaign aim.
- Using 'so that' chains.
- Building an outcomes map.
- Understanding different ways of achieving social change.
- Identifying how to build the capacity of the organisation to achieve change.
- Building evaluation into the model.[13]

The basis of the TOC model is to state a final aim or impact and then describe what would need to happen to arrive at that point. TOC involves having both a theory, or theories, about different ways in which change can be brought about and what methods and interventions will work best. TOC looks across the whole campaigning cycle to achieve its ends and then provides a framework for evaluating progress, which is built into the planning assumptions and methods.

TOC models suggest that you start with the desired end result and work backwards through what would be needed at each stage of the process to achieve the intended result. This is often done through mapping each stage of the process onto a framework, listing the barriers, assumptions and steps that need to be taken to achieve your campaign aim. Therefore most theory of change models follow a similar set of processes outlined next. Working through TOC planning is best undertaken in a group or team or with a range of your stakeholders, such as your beneficiaries, to ensure multiple views and options are explored.

[12] Guthrie, K., Louie, J., David, T., & Foster, C. C. (2005). The Challenge of Assessing Policy and advocacy activities: Strategies for a Prospective Evaluation Approach my emphasis.

[13] For a fuller explanation and evaluation of this approach see NCVO Lamb B. (2010) Campaigning for Change: learning from the US.

Theory of change

Stating a clear aim

The first stage of the process is to start with the ultimate campaign aim. The aim should be a visionary statement that encapsulates the ultimate purpose of the campaign. List the ultimate impact at the bottom of a page and work backwards from this aim.

Examples of campaign aims could be:
- Carbon Emissions will be decreased by 30% in England and Wales.
- Child Poverty in the UK will be abolished by 2020.

Mapping activities to achieve your campaign aim

This stage examines the specific activities that would be needed to bring about the campaign aim. These activities may include campaigns to change policy or practice, bring about changes in law, behaviour change or public opinion, capacity-building efforts, community activity and so on.

Some examples could be:
- Development of alliances.
- Recruiting supporters.

These activities need to have a causal or logical relationship to the end aim that you are trying to achieve and you need to be aware of the appropriate type of strategy to achieve these. This assumes an overall understanding of what types of actions lead to different types of changes. See more on different approaches to campaigning page 93.

Outcomes and how to get there – using 'so that' chains

This process checks the logical links between your different activities by drawing all the logical links between a number of stages in a campaign. Start with the impact or aim and work backwards to the outcomes and outputs that would be necessary to get to that point.

This takes the first activity and associated strategy listed and creates a 'so that' chain based on the following statement:

'We do X or Y activity/strategy so that it results in (blank) for individuals, families, organizations or communities' X or Y should be the direct outcome or result of the strategy. Repeat this exercise until you have linked each strategy to your aim.

A typical example of a worked up 'so that' chain from a campaign to establish short breaks for parents of disabled children:

Strategy:

More rights to support for families to care for their disabled children.[14]

To do this we need to work together across the sector as one organisation will not be able to deliver change and
(Activity)
so that...
we can campaign to establish new rights through legislation establishing a right to short breaks and funding streams to be able to pilot new approaches from local authorities,
(Activity)
so that...
legislation is passed we need a campaign with MPs to pressure government,
(Activity)
and...
a review of funding is undertaken with new resources for local authorities
(Activity)
so that...
new legislation gives rights to parents to have more support
(Outcome)

Strategy (continued)

so that...
funding streams are established as
a result of the legislation and local
authorities provide more
resources
(Outcome)

and...
parents have a right to expect
more support as of right and feel
more secure about the future
so that...
parents will have more resilience
and a better quality of life and be
better able to parent their children
through having the additional
support.
(Impact)

'So that' chains can be very simple
or complex depending on the
issue, size of the project or level of
analysis. If you are dealing with
multifaceted issues there may be a
number of chains looking at
different aspects of achieving one
aim or a number of aims that may
be interrelated. This approach can
also be applied to much smaller or
micro processes at the community
level, but the crucial point is always
to align the different activities
undertaken with the expected
effects or outcomes in working
towards the desired result.

A key part of this process is also to
be aware of the factors that might
help or hinder that change and
what strategies are deployed to
address these factors.

External factors can help or hinder
your ability to carry out your
planned activities and the outputs
and hoped-for outcomes. Focus
on why you think the particular
activities and outputs you are
working on will deliver the
outcomes and impact you are
seeking. Go back to your planning
to test these out. Test whether
logical linkages occur between the
strategies, outcomes and impacts.
Have you included the most
relevant outcomes and all the
relevant strategies? Complete the
analysis by making clear the
assumptions that influenced the
design of the map. If you are
assuming, for example, that
challenging public opinion in a
particular way will alter your ability
to make the change then state this,
and link it to your campaign
activities, with evidence that this is
realistic.[15]

It is useful to describe the
principles that underlie the
outcome map, the assumptions
you have made and why. Often
these statements will be part of
the discussion while you are
constructing the map and that is
one of the strengths of the
exercise. It keeps driving you to
elucidate your assumptions and
connections between actions and
outcomes. If you have identified
these factors as prerequisites for
achieving your campaign aim you
can monitor progress towards it.
See diagram Typical theory of
change outcome map.

**Putting together a theory of
change outcome map**
By putting all of these different
activities together it is possible to
arrive at a fully formed TOC model
for your campaign, which can be
mapped out relatively simply with
the arrows in this diagram
representing the 'so that' links
between the different
intervention strategies and actions
taken to achieve them.

TOC models also help you analyse
your organisation's capacity for
carrying out the campaign as they
require you to look at possible
activities and the resources that
you need for them. Planning tools
such as SWOT or PEST analysis
also help do this see page 32.

[14] Author's example; for worked examples from campaigns in the USA see: Organizational Research Services
(2004) Theory of Change: A practical tool for action, results and learning. Prepared for the Annie E. Casey
Foundation. Seattle: Organizational Research Services.

[15] Adapted from: Organizational Research Services (2004) Theory of Change: A practical tool for action,
results and learning. Prepared for the Annie E. Casey Foundation. Seattle: Organizational Research Services.

[16] Organizational Research Services (2009) Ten Considerations for Advocacy Evaluation Planning: Lessons
learned from kids count grantee programme. Seattle: Organizational Research Services.

Understanding how change comes about

Central to the thinking about how change happens is an overall understanding of what types of strategies bring about what types of change – then ensuring that the types of activities you take match the overall strategy being pursued.

Anna Stachowaik from Organizational Research Services provides a helpful typology of different strategies for change drawn from a number of academic studies and approaches, which is set out in the table on page 58.

Anticipating the consequences of change

The essence of all these methods is about scrutinising your assumptions about how change happens. Good campaigns look forward in their planning to the potential consequences of change and later evaluate the impact of what they achieve. Securing better public services might mean more people wanting to use them, thus putting up the cost of reform: has this been factored into the plan?

How will you react to unexpected things that can throw you off course? A good understanding of the external and internal environment in which you are working will help you prepare for these possibilities. See analysing environment page 32.

Diagram: theory of change example

Source: Adapted from: Organizational Research Services, Ten Considerations for Advocacy Evaluation Planning: Lessons Learned from Kids Count Grantee Programme.[16]

• Analysing • **Developing** • Plannning • Delivering • Evaluate
  a strategy
  for change

Strategy (continued)

Table: Strategies for change

Theory	Background	How change happens	Strategies for change
Major change or large leaps	Looking at big changes to government or how corporate sector undergoes major change. Look for the conditions that bring about major changes.	Normally through a complete shift in thinking, often accompanied by a change of government or a decisive event in an industry or sector.	People typically become mobilised through redefinition of the prevailing policy issue or story, a narrative that should include both facts and emotional appeals.
'Coalition' theory	Major change comes about when significant coalitions come together and either change the terms of debate around an issue or exploit a change in socio-economic conditions to promote a new solution.	Policy core beliefs are unlikely to change unless major external events such as changes in conditions or public opinion are skilfully exploited by proponents of change.	Influencing like-minded decision-makers to make policy changes. Affecting sections of public opinion via mass media. Altering decision-makers' behaviour through boycotts or demonstrations.
Policy windows	Problems: the way social conditions become defined as problems to policy-makers, whether the problem is perceived as solvable with clear alternatives. Policies: the ideas generated to address problems. Politics: political factors, including the national mood.	Policy can be changed when a window of opportunity occurs or by linking up a number of areas of the policy process by influencing the way in which there issue is perceived or by finding the perfect solution.	Changing the definition of the problem. Conducting research to demonstrate the magnitude of the issue and/or engaging beneficiaries to feedback to decision-makers.

[17] Anna Stachowaik A. (2007) Pathways to Change. Six theories about how change happens Seattle: Organizational Research Services.

Theory	Background	How change happens	Strategies for change
Strategies and tactics (part of a broader aim)			
Messaging and frameworks	People develop responses to issues based on how the issue is framed (presented to them), not simply on self-interest but how it aligns with their values and experiences.	People are presented with information in new ways that 'frame' a decision or issue in a way that gets their attention and support, where it might not have before.	Ensuring that research and policy can help to 'frame' the question and produce evidence to help move individuals to taking the action either to support a cause, or change their own individual behaviour.
Focus on who holds power and how it is exercised	Based on the assumption that there are a number of faces of power, formal, informal and hidden.	Change happens through a process of targeting those who are in power and reclaiming space in which to conduct public dialogue and/or making visible the ways in which hidden power operates.	Focus on key decision-makers at all levels within the target institution. Can be combined with more public campaigning to structure the 'internal' conversation.
Community-based or grassroots campaigning	Power really resides with community... or should do! Aim is therefore to help communities to mobilise and have a voice. By doing so they can claim power back from other more formal routes	When enough people coalesce around an issue it is possible for change to happen. This normally means mass activism at the community level to bring pressure onto the target.	Focus on building the capacity of key groups to mobilise and campaign.

Source: adapted from Stachowaik A., Pathways to Change. Six theories about how change happens.[17]

Evaluation

Without monitoring and evaluation you cannot check progress to see if you are on track, demonstrate your effectiveness, or be held accountable. Building in a clear evaluation framework will compel you to be more explicit about your theory of change.

Over the medium to long term (more than six months but fewer than five years) you need to have a way of monitoring – to test whether outcomes really do lead to the impact you had envisaged. Has the change in legislation actually been used and been effective? Have better school meals brought about healthy eating by the pupils and led to better health and social outcomes? Did the improved planning approach lead to better buildings that people are happier with? Test your strategies to see if they could have ever produced these outcomes.

What you can evaluate
When constructing an evaluation framework you need to be clear about what you are trying to achieve. You could be trying to do any or all of these things:
• Improve decision-making and impact.
• Promote learning – campaigning culture.
• Ensure accountability to stakeholders – beneficiaries, funders etc.
• Influence targets and funders.
• Motivate campaigners, supporters your members etc.

Learning and accountability, for instance, are two very different things and you may need distinct processes to capture information for each. If you follow the theory of change you will have a very good basis for evaluating a campaign. It is possible to take each stage in the process – from identifying assumptions and resources through to assessing impact – and align these with different types of evaluation methods.

Evaluation can be made overly complex and off putting; this can often stop organisations doing the simplest of things, which can make a huge difference. By attempting a basic approach as a first step, you can learn to evaluate and build in more ambitious mechanisms as you go. The tools below pick up on different aspects of evaluation, which you can apply depending on your resources, time and needs.

If you follow the TOC model you will have very good platform for evaluating campaigns. There are a number of processes that could be examined at each stage of evaluation that follow the stages of the TOC model of planning:

[18] Collins J. (2005) Why Business Thinking is not the Answer. Good to Great and the Social Sectors. Boulder.

[19] Adapted from: Coffman J. (2009) A User's Guide to Advocacy Planning and Evaluation, Cambridge, MA: Harvard Family Research Project, to show in logical sequence.

'It doesn't really matter whether you can quantify your results. What matters is that you rigorously assemble evidence – quantitative or qualitative – to track your progress. If the evidence is primarily qualitative, think like a trial lawyer assembling the combined body of evidence. If the evidence is primarily quantitative, then think of yourself as a laboratory scientist assembling and assessing the data.' Collins J., Why Business Thinking is not the Answer. Good to great and the social sectors[18]

Measures

This step involves identifying specific measures (indicators or benchmarks) that, when captured and tracked over time, will signal whether the campaigning strategy elements have been successfully implemented or achieved.

Activity/tactic measures

Commonly known as outputs these 'measures of effort' count what and how much campaigning activities or tactics produce or accomplish. Although these measures capture what was done, they do little to explain how well it was done or how well it worked with target audiences. Because they count tangible products, people, or events, activity/tactic measures are the easiest of all evaluation measures to identify and track.

Output/outcome measures

Linked to outputs and outcomes, these measures signal progress towards achieving the campaign aim. Unlike measures that are associated with activities and tactics, they are 'measures of effect' and demonstrate changes that happen – usually within target audiences – as a result of campaigning efforts.

Impact measures

These measures demonstrate what will happen after a campaign aim is achieved. They show the effects of a campaign aim for the programmes, systems, or people that it sought to improve.[19]

Some monitoring and evaluation models

There are some basic models of evaluation that you can apply to your campaign.

Evaluation (continued)

Table: Evaluation methods

Method	Process	How to measure
Social return on investment	Assigns a monetary value to the impact you are seeking and measures this against the amount of money spent to achieve it.	Normally used to evaluate service interventions but can also be used to evaluate campaigns. Can be complex to assign a monetary value to all campaign interventions and also outcomes but a powerful indicator of effectiveness and good for comparing current interventions against proposals for future change.
Distance travelled or gap analysis – best for assessing overall impact	Asks you to be clear about the original aim of campaign, state the means of achieving those and then report on the outcomes on a regular basis. The gap is the distance between the stated aim of the campaign and the current outcomes. It could also be an indication of how far the campaign has come but also indicating how far this still has to go, hence distance travelled.	Can be applied to any aspect of the campaign, such as the gap between the stated outputs and actual ones or the outcomes and impact. This can be done as a desk exercise, by assembling all the relevant evidence of progress towards the end result of each stage of the process. It could also involve surveying beneficiaries to see what their perception of change has been.
Process evaluation – best for looking at activities and outputs	Looks at any particular activity undertaken during the campaign to ensure that it has been completed to the best effect. It assumes that the methods used were the correct ones, and focuses on ensuring that they were carried out.	Essentially a comparison between what was planned and what actually took place. For example, if MPs were the target of a campaign did your briefing reach the required number, was it timely and how did they respond? If the media was involved again did you contact people at the right time, and what response did you get?

Method	Process	How to measure
Comparative evaluation	Compares your organisation's activity with others in a similar sector or activity, typically used in fundraising and benchmarking – more widely in business. Difficult to employ in campaigning. Gives you an indication of the leverage and impact your campaign is having on target audiences or the efficiency of your work compared with others.	Comparisons against similar campaigns or agencies to see how your campaign performs relative to theirs on key issues of recognition, profile and take up. Review of media commentators or contacts to see how your issue is perceived against others'.
Outcome and impact evaluation	Evaluate how far your outputs and outcomes actually changed the situation. Go back to the overall aim of your campaign and judge how far the ends were achieved.	The measures here must be the final impact on those who are supposed to benefit.
Stakeholder analysis – best used to assess how effective your activities and outputs are	Seeks to elicit the views of key stakeholders who are involved or affected by the campaign. Can improve accountability to key stakeholders as well as making your campaign more effectiveness.	Formal methods such as focus groups and surveys, or less formal ones such as asking people at a meeting how they perceive the campaign to be going.

Evaluation (continued)

In more detail
Distance travelled model
The simplest method is the 'distance travelled' model. Write down the impact you wish to achieve and what outcomes would lead towards that impact then define your expected progress – year one, year two, and so on. Assess the campaign against the plans you detailed and outcomes specified and review them regularly. This works for both for straightforward campaign aims to more complex ones. It also helps focus evaluation on measuring the outcomes and impact not just outputs.

Outcomes and impact frameworks model
Evaluation grids can be used as a means of creating a framework for the different stages of the TOC model, for example in relation to outcomes and impact.

With the grid filled in and your key outputs and impacts identified you can establish an evaluation framework. You may return to this at some later point during the campaign to monitor progress or leave it until the end. This will help you focus on impact rather than outputs; you may have had plenty of activity, but not actually to be any closer to your campaign aim.

Outcome and impact framework grid

Outcomes	Indicator	A target of what you were trying to achieve	How to gather evidence
Healthy school meals	Meals served meet new school nutritional standards.	X% of meals in schools are healthy/meet nutritional standards. X% of children in schools are eating healthier meals.	Survey of schools, inspections, self-reporting from children, examination of school menus etc.
Impact	**Indicator**	**What you were trying to achieve**	**How to gather evidence**
Children's health improved	Children are less overweight. Better attention spans and behaviour due to good nutrition. Children can make healthy choices and take school meals.	X% of children could concentrate better in class. X% of children understand why they should eat healthily.	Surveys of teachers' perceptions of classroom performance, objective evidence of improved outcomes, monitoring over time of weight and choice of meals, monitoring of meal choices and shifts in these.

Social return on investment model

A more complex method of evaluation is social return on investment (SROI), for which there are a number of different models of varying complexity. Essentially this involves allocating a financial value to a social outcome and comparing this with current practice and current or future investment. The method has much wider application than just campaigning but campaigners have also applied its methods in spend-to-save models for example in order to demonstrate that an intervention will deliver greater social benefits than continuing with a current practice such as means of delivering services. This has been used as a way of arguing that government or others should invest in spending programmes that will deliver better outcomes. Showing how investment can bring social benefits can give campaigners powerful ammunition in demonstrating the impact of their proposals or justify existing campaign expenditure in delivering social benefit.

For example, the National Committee for Responsible Philanthropy in the US undertook a number of reports using a SROI methodology and evaluated the impact of campaigning on New Mexican communities and was able to demonstrate that every dollar invested in advocacy and organising garnered $157 in benefits for New Mexico communities.[20]

Good SROI models put the benefits for the stakeholders of the campaign aim at the core of what it measures. Campaigning can offer cost/benefit analysis, showing the difference between continuing with current policies and taking a different path, for example offsetting the cost of a new health screening programme against the benefits to people's health from having early intervention and the higher costs of medical services when diagnosis is delayed. Recent examples of this have been the work around obesity and heart disease and newborn hearing screening for deafness.[21] SROI models can, however, be very complex and costly to set up and undertake depending on the model followed.[22]

Evidence

Evidence that you might need for evaluation could include the following indicators:

- Quantitative – answers questions such as what, how many, when and measures changes that can be expressed as numbers/ratios.
- Qualitative – answers questions such as why and how, assesses quality/processes/relationships, and explores perceptions – often expressed through narrative description rather than precise numbers.

Think through how (and when) you will gather information and how you will account for the activities of others. Focus on:

- The information you and your stakeholders need to know to answer your key questions.
- The things that the campaign intends to change.
- Being accessible and accountable to stakeholders especially your beneficiaries. Add in how you are going to communicate what you are measuring
- Providing evidence that, taken together, can reasonably be used to assert a connection between your activities and subsequent change.
- Evidence that can be comparable over different groups and over time.
- Using pre-defined indicators and also use open-ended questions but be adaptable as you progresses and goalposts shift.

[20] Ranghelli L. (undated) Strengthening Democracy, Increasing Opportunities Impacts of Advocacy, Organising and Civic Engagement in New Mexico. Washington: National Council for Responsible Philanthropy.

[21] For an analysis of the benefits of using this approach for evaluation and reporting see: Wood, C. and Leighton, D. (2010) Measuring Social Value. The Gap Between Policy and Practice. London: Demos.

[22] See: Cabinet Office (2009) A Guide to Social Return on Investment. London: Cabinet Office for a comprehensive guide to this approach with worked examples for service context. See also New Economics Foundation (2009) Seven Principles for Measuring What Matters. A guide to effective public policy making. London: New Economics Foundation.

Evaluation (continued)

Avoiding the pitfalls

Evaluating campaigns can be complex. The biggest challenge is working out whether it was your campaign's specific activities that made a difference. Campaigns can happen over long timeframes and assessing and assigning how far organisations have progressed towards more long-term aims can be very difficult.

Measuring impact – outcomes and impact can be difficult to measure. Cause and effect are often difficult to discern because it can be complicated to disentangle actions and motivation. However, this is precisely what makes it crucial to have your own benchmarks about impact and how you intend to achieve it.

Attribution – campaigns rarely start with an entirely blank sheet of paper and seldom make progress in isolation. Many campaigns are achieved through some kind of collaborative working. It is important to show how your actions have made a difference, worry less about trying to assign a precise weighting of your contribution compared with others. To do this you need a very clear statement of what the campaign was trying to achieve and by what measures you are evaluating against.

Timeframe – measuring impact, rather than just outcomes, will probably leave you with a long timeframe going beyond yearly planning cycles. It can be very important to set benchmarks against which to judge progress towards your final aim.

The firmer your evidence, the more clearly you can trace cause and effect in your campaign activities. Techniques for researching your impact are similar to those you would use for research generally. What is different is that you should already have your stated outcomes as criteria for your research agenda and for assessing evidence. You need to link your objectives to the best indicators to assess your progress. You also need to be realistic about the prospects of being able collect your evidence affordably and in proportion to the overall effort and cost of your campaign and the information's usefulness. [23]

Plan how you will communicate your results

Once you have developed a good evaluation framework you also need to think about how you are going to report on this to you organisation, beneficiaries and other stakeholders such as funders. You cannot be accountable if you do not communicate. Charities already have obligations to the Charity Commission to report against outcomes and you may feel that this satisfies your requirements. However, you may want to think about going further in how you promote the results of your activities.

Impact reporting can provide a powerful model that gives focus to evaluations, you know you have to report every year and you can also influence the planning process by providing a method of tracking your progress. Making information open can also help in justifying the deployment of more resources to your campaigns and motivate supporters by allowing you to promote success. See more on inspiring supporter action page 129.

Funding your campaign

Securing funds for your campaign can be a crucial factor in deciding what level of campaigning you can undertake. This section looks at possible ways to fund campaigning work and successfully combine both campaign and fundraising asks and functions.

Co-ordinating campaigning and fundraising

Campaigning and fundraising are closely linked; most organisations fund their campaigning out of voluntary income and cannot campaign unless they are also raising the funds to do so. What's more, campaigning and fundraising share a core objective to present the issue in the most powerful way possible to raise awareness and generate action and support to help resolve the issue.

Coherent presentation of the issue is essential for an organisation as a whole to demonstrate credibility and consistency of messages, speak out on an issue and galvanise action. If campaigning and fundraising messages are significantly different you may confuse or put off potential supporters, allies and the targets of your campaign.

Working together

While the benefits of co-ordinating campaigning and fundraising objectives are clear, tensions can often arise between these two areas of activity. Campaigners may fear that messages could be diluted so as not to alarm donors, in turn fundraisers may become frustrated at the lack of engaging and emotive appeals that donors can easily relate to. Internal conflict can be managed by ensuring clarity of roles and agreed expectations. Sometimes organisations merge departments to ensure co-operation, while others keep them separate; many have tried both approaches at various stages of organisational development.

What counts more than whether functions are formally joined, is clarity about the aim of the campaign or supporter journey. During the early stages of any campaign there needs to be a clear planning relationship with the fundraising function, whoever or whatever form that takes. Everyone needs to be part of the planning process ensuring a synergy or an acknowledgement of when plans differ from what is being communicated and to whom. A system to ensure that all communications are jointly signed off by everybody involved will also help.

23 For a detailed guide to evaluation with methodologies with worked examples see: NCVO (2008) Is Your Campaign Making a Difference? London: NCVO; Guthrie K., Louie J., David T. and Foster C. (2005) The Challenge of Assessing Policy and Advocacy Activities: Strategies for a prospective evaluation approach. Funded by and prepared for The California Endowment. San Francisco: Blueprint Research and Design, Inc; Guthrie K., Louie J., David T. & Foster C (2006) The Challenge of Assessing Policy and Advocacy Activities: Part 2 Moving from theory to practice. The California Endowment. San Francisco: Blueprint Research & Design, Inc.

Funding your campaign
(continued)

It is helpful to develop guidelines that clearly spell out both your organisational tone and style and how your beneficiary group(s) will be depicted. These may state, for example, that images of beneficiaries should not be used without an explanation of who the beneficiaries are, where they are from and, if possible, an explanation of their involvement with the organisation.

You should be segmenting and targeting your audiences – supporters, campaigners, memberships, users etc. Your organisation may hold this data in different ways so you need to agree with other areas who hold information on your audiences what the process is for contacting them – for example the frequency and style of communications you are going to use and who will sign them off.

Campaign integrity

Evidence may be presented in different ways but cannot be simply bent out shape to fit the needs of raising money without causing damage to the integrity of the cause. Campaign aims must be guided by working towards their identified impact and not to bolster a fundraising proposition.

Raising funds in support of a campaign that exaggerates the impact of proposed solutions is not simply unacceptable ethically, it also misrepresents your ultimate aim to the public. Doing so may also may breach charity law, which states that you have an obligation to ensure that expenditure on campaigning can be seen to have a legitimate chance of success.[24]

A joint approach to campaigning does not mean that communication messages need to be the same; appealing to different audiences may require a different approach and presentation. Having a clear campaign concept will help you keep an overall tone of your messages to keep coherence.

Online campaigning and fundraising

Donating online opens up many opportunities for raising campaign funds. Online action enables you to provide speedy and flexible responses to topical issues; combining a pressing deadline with a compelling appeal for money can be a winning formula. There is strong evidence that many donations are made on the spur of the moment, when an opportunity to give arises, rather than because of a particular allegiance or understanding of the cause. Could your campaigns spark giving opportunities even when there is not yet a clear commitment to your cause?

Example

Combining a compelling ask and a tight deadline

Open Rights Group and 38 Degrees Digital Economy Bill

The Open Rights Group and 38 Degrees joint campaign highlighting the dangers of the Digital Economy Bill being rushed through Parliament without proper scrutiny before the end of the parliament in April 2010 achieved high levels of both supporter actions and donations, from a standing start and with no dedicated resources.

Although the ultimate campaign aim failed – the bill was passed – campaigners brought the issue from relative obscurity and placed it firmly on the political agenda, persuading 23 Labour MPs to vote against the party line and Government. One MP commented at the time that the campaign was 'one of the most sustained commercial lobbying operations in recent years'.

Taking a technical issue, already being pursued by a powerful music industry lobby, the campaign reframed the issue to highlight its implications, namely, the power to disconnect millions of people from the internet. It built up an online movement: over 20,000 people emailed their MPs expressing concern and further supporters calling their MPs directly to intensify pressure. In their communication messages the campaign successfully broke down a complex message into simple calls to action combining a compelling demand with a tight deadline. An online appeal raised over £20,000 within three days to fund newspaper adverts on the day the Bill was debated.

Corporate fundraising link-ups

There has been huge growth in corporate marketing linked to good causes in recent years. From promotional campaigns on product packaging, to charity of the year sponsorships, they have obvious advantages to a company associating themselves with popular causes whilst also helping VCOs promote issues and gain added weight, credibility and visibility with audiences that they would otherwise not reach. There are, however, potential risks that need to be considered.

Any risk analysis conducted before entering into a relationship with a commercial partner should explore the issue of organisational fit: is it in the best interests of an organisation and its beneficiaries to be associated with that commercial partner? If your independence to be a critical voice can be questioned as a result of your links to a company, this may not only damage your reputation but could be a breach of charity regulations.

---

[24] See Charity Commission Speaking out: Guidance on Campaigning and Political Activity by Charities (CC9) http://www.charity-commission.gov.uk/Publications/cc9.aspx

Funding your campaign
(continued)

You need to ensure you have clear criteria in place, often at senior management or even board level, to deal with conflicts of interest. It will be important to keep a balance between short-term gains in income and the long-term effects on your supporters and their understanding of the cause. It helps to have clear criteria in place about commercial relationships and conflict of interest so these issues are decided in a consistent way.

Three types of corporate link-ups

Transactional
This is the most widespread model of consumer philanthropy. Each time someone buys a bottle of shampoo or a packet of tea, the company contributes a small amount to a social cause. When Ikea, for example, sells certain children's products it donates a proportion of sales to UNICEF.

Promotion based
Corporations promote a cause and make charitable contributions. The donations are not necessarily tied to sales and are not necessarily monetary – they could involve employee volunteering or charity of the year relationships for example – but promote both the cause and the corporation.

Licensing
A charity, such as the World Wildlife Fund, licenses the use of its name and logo to a company such as Visa. The company then donates a percentage of every transaction associated with the logo to the charity.[25]

There has been a growing uneasiness about the impact of some of these types of relationships from commentators. Concerns have included:

- Confusion about commitments, when asked to donate personally people may think they have contributed by buying the product, this can undermine people's long-term willingness to give or associate with the cause as they will already feel they have contributed.

- Products may be linked to consequences that the campaign opposes – for example clothes brands implicated in poor employment practices and promotional wristbands that contained the very environmental toxics the campaign was complaining about.

- The alignment between your cause and the company you are working with needs to be carefully monitored as business practices or general reputational issues may damage your standing or could directly contradict your cause. For example, simply wearing an armband could undermine any incentive to actually engage more fully with the issue (in a survey of wearers of the white arm band to promote Make Poverty History many did not actually know what the campaign was targeting).

- It can be hard to promote the campaign concept – and therefore be a poor way of changing awareness or promoting any understanding of the organisation's work.[26]

---

[25] Outlined in: Eikenberry A. M. (2009) The hidden costs of cause marketing. Stanford Social Innovation Review (Summer 2009).

Trusts and foundations

A survey of UK philanthropy in 2006 rated four of the greatest achievements of philanthropy in the UK as the abolition of the slave trade, suffrage for women, the banning of handguns and landmines, and civil partnerships. The survey report concluded that 'A combination of money and passionately held beliefs can create enough momentum to change the world.'[27] Trusts and foundations can be motivated by supporting campaign work and leveraging their resources to bring about real lasting social change, which you can build on.

Trusts and foundations can provide sources of funding, often over a number of years, which you can use to build your campaign capacity as well as on the campaign itself. Campaigning and political activity are sometimes regarded as more of a risk (controversial publicity, perhaps) than providing services and you may need to acknowledge this in your applications for funds. Transparency and good communications will help you work closely with your donor foundation so that everyone knows what to expect. Trusts may also want organisations that can demonstrate a good reputation for managing public relationships with decision-makers and the media.[28]

Change can often be long-term or unpredictable and your applications to trusts and foundations may need to address this. Using your theory of change and providing a framework for evaluating your effectiveness may well improve your funding chances.

---

[26] Some of these issues are usefully reviewed in Eikenberry, 2009. Angela M. Eikenberry, The Hidden Costs of Cause Marketing, Stanford Social Innovation Review Summer 2009.

[27] Breeze B. (2006) UK Philanthropy's Greatest Achievements: A research based assessment on philanthropic success. London: Institute of Philanthropy. Available online at: www.instituteforphilanthropy.org/content/Archive (accessed December 2010). See also: Rosser A. and Shimmin S. (2008) Funding for Sustainable Change: Exploring the extent to which grantmaking trusts fund campaigning, advocacy and influence. London: Directory of Social Change.

[28] For a fuller review of the issues around trust funding see: Lamb B. (2010) Supporting Campaigning a Funders Guide. London: NCVO.

Funding your campaign
(continued)

Example
Every Disabled Child Matters

Every Disabled Child Matters is a consortium founded in 2006 by four VCOs: Contact a Family, Council for Disabled Children, Mencap and Special Educational Consortium. In the same year The True Colours Trust gave it a grant to employ a full-time team to pursue its campaign aims: better rights and services for disabled children and their families.

The campaign's first step was to persuade the treasury to review provision for families with disabled children. The group also campaigned for carers to have their needs properly assessed.

The theory of change was clear: additional support to families would alleviate the need for even more statutory help later, prevent family breakdown and lead to better outcomes for children.

To win support among MPs and peers the group again lobbied the treasury, which helped them get a cross-party parliamentary inquiry set up. This interviewed many parents and young people about their needs. As a result of the inquiry the then-Department for Children, Schools and Families introduced a major £340 million initiative 'Aiming High for Disabled Children' in 2007. This enabled local authorities to provide a range of extra help to families with disabled children.

The original funding has since been matched by money from the NHS. The right for carers to have their needs assessed became law. The True Colours Trust's original investment was £200,000 over two years; the Trust has renewed its funding and campaigning activities aimed to make sure that local authorities implement the initiative. Esmée Fairbairn Foundation has provided further money for research, helping a co-ordinated approach between funders for different aspects of the campaign. The foundation has also funded the support bodies to work closely with parents to help them campaign locally for better services and to promote a charter for local authority services.[29]

---

[29] Broach S., Coleman B and Franklin L. (2009) Winning a new priority for disabled children: the every disabled child matters campaign Journal of Public Affairs 9 (3).

Pro bono: a different way of giving

Don't underestimate people's good nature. The Latin phrase 'pro bono' means 'for the public good' and is used to describe professional work done voluntarily without charge. You don't have to wait for people to make themselves known to you – your stakeholder analysis could include identifying potential support for your issues in the form of pro bono support. It could be the case that a senior person within an advertising agency or law firm may be a supporter of your cause or have experience of your issues that would help you make a connection. Media firms and law practices traditionally offer the most scope for helping campaigns but there is a wealth of expertise for you to benefit from. Film makers or web designers may be interested in your issue or looking for an opportunity to showcase their skills and social media platforms are a great way to tap into potential support for a campaign.

If you are asking for pro bono work, however, be clear about how your campaign might appeal to the motivations of those offering the support – not everyone will immediately see why cause stands out from all the others.

If your campaign is trying to break new ground, advertising agencies may welcome the opportunity this offers them to try out new approaches that they may later be able to use with paying clients and express their personal commitment to your cause.

Producing advertising or communication campaigns is one thing – placing them or getting published is another. Ad agencies sometimes have partners that help secure cheap and sometimes free advertising space for your campaign. But you need to be realistic about what the agency can do for you for free and where you may have to pay for, or at least contribute to, costs of producing adverts and promotions, as well as to the cost of buying advert space. You may get less control within a pro bono relationship than if you were a paying client. It is not that the agency will give you less quality – they often put some of their best teams onto the project – but inevitably there may be more negotiation around timescales and creative concepts.

Funding your campaign
(continued)

With pro bono ad-agency help many organisations have been able to mount public awareness and advertising campaigns that they simply would not have been able to afford. An agency's scrutiny of a campaign's aims and objectives can also compel organisations to focus more clearly on what they want for their key messages. This has played a part in improving campaign communications as a whole.

The legal profession has a longstanding tradition of providing pro bono support to VCOs or those whom they in turn support. Historically this has meant taking on cases where there is a major legal issue at stake. Law firms have also acted pro bono in more routine cases, which are of course just as important for the people directly affected by the outcome. Pursuing legal challenges can be a very powerful method for securing long-term change as well as securing individual rights.

Judicial reviews have been some of the most effective uses of pro bono legal support; these cases are important as they often establish broader principles of how the public authorities should be operating or interpreting the law. An example of effective use of judicial review was the case of R(JL) v Islington in 2009. In this case, the parents were supported by a chambers who has a specialism in this area. The High Court found that the eligibility criteria used by Islington Council to restrict access to disabled children's services were unlawful. Islington had reduced the family's short breaks entitlement from 92 to 42 nights a year following the introduction of new eligibility criteria. The Court held that the criteria were unlawful and quashed both the criteria and the resulting decision to cut JL's services. As a result of this judgement, not only was support restored to the individual family but also all local authorities have been required to review their criteria. This has resulted in more families getting a short breaks service or having access to existing ones protected.[30]

Some specialist companies have also helped VCOs draft amendments and interpret the consequences of existing legislation.

There have been moves to introduce a more structured approach to pro bono working. Pro Bono Economics is a new charity whose aim is 'to broker economists into the charitable sector to help on short- and medium-term assignments, typically addressing questions around measurement, results and impact'.[31] Given the trend towards having an economic underpinning in policy work, pointing out 'spend to save' arguments, the ability to access high-calibre economic thinking could be a very valuable resource.

---

[30] Case is reported in LBC [2009] EWHC 458 (Admin). Thanks to Steven Broach of Doughty Chambers for providing this example.

[31] www.probonoeconomics.com

Planning
your campaign

Delivering

Developing

Evaluate

Analysing

Contents

Framing the campaign

Framing the campaign
- Setting the campaign aim – recap
- A campaign concept
- Facts are not enough
- Placing the right frame on the issue
- Connecting with your audience
- Using framing
- Presenting your issue
- Discourse analysis
- Making ideas stick
- Defining an enemy?
- Passion in campaigning

Targets and influencers
- Who makes the decisions?
- Influence mapping
- Who do you want to reach and what do you want them to do

Objectives and work planning
- Setting objectives
- Work plans
- Timeframes
- Monitoring and evaluation (again)
- Planning for the unexpected

Campaign intelligence
- Managing information
- Managing and mitigating risk

Types of campaigns
- Influencing government
  - Central government
  - Developed government
- Local government
- European Union and the Council of Europe
- Influencing private sector targets
- Changing people's behaviour
- Legal advocacy
  - Judicial review
  - Human rights
  - Human rights-based approaches

Campaign activities
- Right tactic, right time, right audience
- How radical do you need to be?
- Direct action

Working with others
- Working collaboratively with other organisations
- Inspiring supporter action
- Beneficiary involvement
- Tips on how to involve people
- Going off message
- Recognising the limits to involvement

Charity law– some key points
- Charities and political parties
- Elections
- Party political activity
- Balance of activities
- Complaints and the Charity Commission

Setting the campaign aim – recap

In one sentence you need to set out a clear campaign aim, encapsulating the ultimate purpose of the campaign, the change you want to see and the impact you want to make. It should be easily communicable – that is:
- Compelling and inspiring.
- Targeted – identifying who or what needs to change.
- Focusing on impact – articulating what change will result.
- Succinct.

An aim is not the same as objectives, which are the changes you will need to see to contribute to achieving your overall aim. You may have several objectives, each of them stepping stones on the path towards your aim, but you will only have one campaign aim.

To have a realistic aim you need to understand the context you are working in and what shapes the environment in which you can develop the capacity to make change happen.

[1] www.msf.org.uk/hands_off_Video_msf_president_20101019.news (accessed December 2010).
[2] www.bartleby.com/268/9/23.html (accessed November 2010).

'Public sentiment is everything. With public sentiment nothing can fail; without it, nothing can succeed. Consequently he who molds public sentiment goes deeper than he who enacts statutes or pronounces decisions. He makes statutes or decisions possible or impossible to be executed.' Abraham Lincoln, 1858, In the First Debate with Douglas.[2]

A campaign concept

The campaign concept is the big picture vision that you want to communicate throughout your campaign, it should be developed out of your overall campaign aim to ensure your campaign stays focused on achieving its aim. Campaigning is about translating your key insights into clear and compelling messages about the change you are seeking. A campaign concept will help you exemplify and bring your issue to life, and develop conversations with your audiences, motivating them to take action – without it, your campaign and how you communicate it can be incoherent.

Example
Médecins Sans Frontières' Europe Hands off our Medicine campaign is trying to challenge the EU's attempt to stop the production of some generic medicines in India to treat HIV. The 'hands off our medicine' concept frames the whole debate in a simple way, allows themes to development around cost and pricing and points responsibility at the target of the campaign.[1]

The messages derived from your campaign concept may be deployed differently for different audiences but there should be a core idea uniting your positioning and communications that reflects how your issue is framed.

Facts are not enough
One of the biggest mistakes in campaigning can be assuming that the facts and figures alone will move people to give their support. Campaigns need a mixture of analysis and an appeal to our underlying values and how we feel.

How campaigners think about persuading people to support an issue has largely rested on the rational choice theory, which holds that if people are presented with all the information they need i.e. 'the facts' they will base their decisions about the issues they care about on a rational calculation about what is best for them. But are 'the facts' all they are cracked up to be?

As Drew Westen observes in The Political Brain, people's reaction to political issues engages the part of our brain that governs emotional responses: 'In politics, as in everyday life, two sets of often competing constraints shape our judgements: cognitive constraints, imposed by the information we have available, and emotional constraints, imposed by the feelings associated with one conclusion or another.'[3] He goes

onto argue: 'when reason and emotion collide, emotion invariably wins. Although the marketplace of ideas is a great place to shop for policies, the marketplace that matters most... is the marketplace of emotions.'[4]

Western sees our responses to political issues located in our own framework of values and beliefs into which we select what 'facts' we find convincing and reject those we don't. It is with this empathic side of the brain that we react to messages about values; we quickly assess messages and fit them into a pre-existing framework. What motivates us is therefore often not based on a rational cost-benefit analysis.

The assumption that if we give people enough facts often enough they will come around to our point of view is mistaken. While facts are important, they will be trumped in many situations by people's empathic response to them. Our emotions and values are tied up with our personal identity, and we are more likely to resist facts that contradict or challenge our identity if they challenge our sense of self. Thus, perversely, the more people are confronted with 'the facts' about an issue that challenges their identity and values, the more they are likely to resist its conclusions.[5]

[3] Western D. (2007) The Political Brain. New York: PublicAffairs. p99. Also Westen notes that voter's preferences for parties do not align with their material self-interest. p120. Lakoff also comes to similar conclusions: Lakoff G. (2009) The Political Mind: A cognitive scientist's guide to your brain and its politics, London: Penguin.

[4] Western D. (2007) The Political Brain. New York: PublicAffairs. p35. Campaigners have been slow on picking up on the implications of this work on this side of the channel – see: Lamb B. (2008) Winning hearts as well as minds. Third Sector (13 February).

Analysing • Developing • **Plannning** • Delivering • Evaluate your campaign

Framing the campaign
(continued)

We have seen this dramatically enacted in the debate around climate change where, despite massive amounts of scientific data evidencing climate change, the public's propensity to believe what is happening is limited by how that information is fitted into a pre-existing framework of thinking and feeling. Dan Kahan, working at the Cultural Cognition Project at Yale Law School has made this point when he noted that: 'a growing body of work has suggested that ordinary citizens react to scientific evidence on societal risks in much the same way. People endorse whichever position reinforces their connection to others with whom they share important commitments.'[6]

Providing a level of what Kahan terms 'protective cognition' screening out what does not fit with their, and their close friends' pre-existing views or frames of reference.[7]

The implication of this means that campaigners need to think about the value frameworks in which people understand and make decisions about issues. Gathering support often means working with the way people think and believe, not against. Proclaiming the 'truth' could be a wasted effort unless your message gets through to your target audience(s) and you achieve the change in their opinions and generate the action that you need.

People will work with both types of thinking, but tend to revert to their default frame of reference, especially when challenged and attempts to persuade them otherwise will make them only dig deeper into their pre-existing views.

Lakoff, a cognitive linguist and academic, argues that facts are important but they need to be used in the right way: 'Facts are all-important. They are crucial. But they must be framed appropriately if they are to be an effective part of **public discourse**. We have to know what a fact has to do with moral principles and political principles. We have to frame those facts as effectively and honestly as we can.'[8]

Many values are shared across wide groups of people but also become associated with different policy solutions. Part of framing an issue is to show people how a particular value can be aligned with policy solutions that accommodate their views. If you can it's best to start a campaign from where people are and frame the issue in a way that will appeal to them.

For example the campaign by Plane Stupid to stop the proposed third runway at London's Heathrow Airport started from residents' concern about noise pollution, health and the effect on the local community (likely to generate empathic responses) before going on to challenge aviation policy and air travel's effects on global warming (more rational concerns).

[5] See for example: Western D. (2007) The Political Brain. New York: PublicAffairs. p112 describes a number of experiments where people's reactions to key political events was determined by their pre-existing views and the evidence did not alter their thinking.

[6] Kahan D. M. (2010) Fixing the communications failure. Nature 463 296–297.

[7] Kahan D. M. (2010) Fixing the communications failure. Nature 463 296–297.

[8] Lakoff G. (2004) Don't Think of an Elephant! Know your values and frame the debate. White River Junction, VT: Chelsea Green Publishing. pp109–110 – my emphasis.

[9] Lippmann W. (1922) Political Opinion.

'The real environment is altogether too big, too [...] too fleeting for direct acquaintance... And althoug[...] act in that environment, we have to reconstruct it on a [...] model before we can manage with it. To traverse the wor[...] (and women) must have maps of the world.'[9]

Placing the right frame on the issue

Why is framing so important to the campaigner? The basis of any communication – the frame – triggers what Walter Lippmann famously called 'the pictures in our heads'[10] – the models or maps we have made over time to make sense of our world and then use in understanding issues and ideas.[11]

Importantly, as Susan Bales, a leading proponent of framing analysis says: 'A frame isn't simply a slogan repeated over and over; rather, it is a conceptual construct capable of helping us organise our world. When frames fail to do so, they are discarded in favour of other frames. But more often, when new facts are submitted that do not resonate with the frames we hold in our heads, it is the facts that are rejected, not the frames.'[12]

Framing analysis therefore focuses on how people process information, and distinguishes what kinds of narratives support different views of the world. So, for example, it looks at whether you are more likely to attribute public or private explanations of responsibility for action, whether poverty is a social condition reflecting society's problems or individuals' unwillingness to strive to better themselves.

If something is viewed as a private problem then it is unlikely that you will be seen to have the power to campaign on it.

The principles of framing apply whether you are trying to get your point across in a small group discussion or if you are running a large-scale campaign. When people argue over each other and there is no true dialogue it is often because they are using different ways to frame and present an argument. If you are trying to frame an issue in a completely different way you need to be aware how this differs from the way the issue is currently framed and whether you are trying to disrupt that frame or build on it.

Frames can activate and develop one set of values over another and trigger one set of associations and views over another. The extent to which these resonate with your audience or not will depend, to some extent, on what they already think and feel.

By appealing to general values we can provoke people to think about social issues and encourage them to consider particular solutions and not others. Justice, responsibility, community, fairness and freedom are all examples of frames you could use initially, and then look more deeply at the role of specific communications and communities in addressing climate change, legal entitlements to a minimum wage and other issues.

Discussions about framing relate strongly to theories on power (see page 46) through more subtle and insidious ways in which invisible power can shape the agenda through society's ingrained values and unchallenged assumptions about how things are organised. Campaigners will need to frame issues in ways that aim to shift those underlying assumptions. Framing analysis and behavioural economics (see page 105) can help by using the most sophisticated techniques of developing ways of addressing issues, bringing to the surface hidden assumptions and values behind the debates and ensuring that campaigns are presented in a way that is relevant to the way the target audience(s) think about the issue.

[10] Lippmann W. (1922) Political Opinion.

[11] For more on how this impacts within a policy and communications environment see: Bales S. (2002) Framing Public Issues. Washington: Frameworks Institute.

[12] Bales S. (2002) Framing Public Issues. Washington: Frameworks Institute. p3.

complex, and
we have to
simpler
d men

problem, a...
with enough power in the society,
agree that there is. Social problems
are produced by public opinion,
not by particular social conditions,
undesirable or otherwise.'[13]

Connecting with your audience

Framing can trigger the values and
emotive content of people's
reactions to what they are hearing
and seeing. In planning your
campaign you need to think about
your overall vision of a better
world, think about how to get
people to commit to that vision
and then think about how you can
get them to commit to action to
deliver that change. The
communications and language
that you use need to strike an
emotional chord – think about
winning hearts first and then
minds.

Table: Using framing

How to frame	Why?
State what the 'story' or 'narrative' is.	Use the story or reference point to link to a familiar way of looking at a problem or issue for your target audience(s).
Explain the problem.	Without a problem you cannot demonstrate and move onto the solution. Focus on the institution that needs to change or law or policy that needs to be made, rather than focusing on an individual figurehead.
Describe how big the issue is.	Don't make it overwhelming – you may want to abolish world poverty but peopleople need to see where they fit in. If the problem seems too big people become disheartened about how they could make a difference. [14] You may need to build in milestones along the way or run a series of campaigns.
Present the solution.	Present the solution your or your beneficiaries would like to see. Not presenting a solution leaves you open to your opponents doing so.
Keep the message simple.	People can get overwhelmed with too much information and become less certain, not more convinced. Unless you are presenting to an expert audience, keep it simple and concise.
Appeal to people's values.	Demonstrate how what you want to do fits with your audience's values and frame of reference.
Establish responsibility.	People need to understand how they can take action and can make decision-makers accountable. They therefore need to know who should be doing something about the issue.

Source: Adapted from Frameworks Institute research[15]

[13] Mauss A. and Julie Wolfe J. (Eds) (1977) This Land of Promises: The rise and fall of social problems. Philadelphia, PA: Lippincott. p2.

[14] It is also the case that if you overload people with too many negative 'facts' you simply destroy their capacity to respond as the issue becomes too large for them to have any individual impact. See, for example: Ereaut G. and Segnit N. (2006) Warm Words: How are we telling the climate change story and can we tell it better? London: IPPR; Futerra. Sell the Sizzle. The new climate change message. Available online: www.futerra.co.uk (accessed November 2010) who argue that you need to sell a compelling vision of low-carbon heaven, not a climate hell, to motivate people to take action.

Presenting your issue

There are some key ingredients in a compelling narrative to your campaign. The best narratives fit with, and bring to life, the underlying evidence with a human story that activates emotions and values, motivating people to act. Look at the values of your audience and their views in relation to your issue.

Westen,[16] outlines some key criteria for a compelling narrative:

- It should have the structure of narrative so it can actually be told as a story that your audience can understand and can repeat.
- It needs to be coherent and obvious and not require too many leaps of logic or faith to be credible.
- It needs to personify the issue and have protagonists and antagonists – either real people that stand for an issue or categories that represent and define the issues, helping to define what you stand for and against.
- It should express clearly the values that your issue is promoting.
- It should be vivid, memorable and capable of moving people to action.

- Ideally it should be able to incorporate a wide appeal to existing or underlying values.
- It should help you frame the issues how you want people to perceive them– not from your target's viewpoint.

Campaigns to cut cigarette smoking made better progress when campaigners started to frame tobacco as a dangerous product, rather than focusing on smoking as a pleasurable but dangerous individual behaviour. Once the public perceived it as a dangerous product it became much easier to put the responsibility on manufacturers for making and selling it, as well as to depict dependency on tobacco as an addiction rather than a personal vice. It was then easier to focus on the manufacturers and their sales policies as the targets of the campaign and on the solution being a tax on tobacco. This success was a result of shifting the way (frame) in which people think about cigarettes.

[15] http://fp.continuousprogress.org/toolkit/item/39

[16] Adapted from: Western D. (2007) The Political Brain. New York: PublicAffairs. He is referring to a political narrative but the underlying principles are the same.

Framing the campaign
(continued)

Discourse analysis
Example

In preparation for the 2009 General Election and potential change in government the National Housing Federation's (NHF) commissioned a discourse analysis study from a from research and communications agency just as the main parties began to release policy proposals. The study analysed the language and ideas favoured by the Conservative Party and compared it to the way the Federation and housing associations express themselves.

"The result was not a list of 'good' and 'bad' words, just food for thought. The Labour Government had shaped much of the discussion around housing, welfare, support and neighbourhood issues for 13 years. NHF was keen to challenge its own assumptions about how best to continue those discussions with the next government.

The vocabulary used by the Conservative Party in relation to social housing gave us a strong clue to their approach. Positive words were 'aspiration', 'right to move' and 'exit opportunity'. Negative phrases included 'calcifying', 'dependency' and 'inflexibility'. There was little evidence that the Conservative Party intended to adopt the idea of people making a positive choice to remain in social housing.

Comparing the Conservative discourse with that of the NHF and other housing associations more broadly, it noted four key areas that NHF needed to be aware of:

- **The Federation used different terms for the same apparent meaning**
  For example, 'vulnerable' and 'marginalised'. Conservatives perceive an element of victimhood in 'marginalised', whereas housing campaigners often see it simply as a statement of fact.

- **The Federation used the same term with different meaning**
  For example, 'aspiration', which housing campaigners tend to mean prospering, even if remaining in the same tenure, while Conservatives tend to mean getting out of social housing, ideally into home ownership.

- **The Federation use different terms and mean very different things**
  For example, Conservatives use the word 'family' a great deal and with much warmth, while the social housing sector uses it rarely and tends to mean all kinds of families, not just nuclear. Housing campaigners often use 'household' to avoid this confusion.

- **The Federation have grown accustomed to terms with difficult associations**
  For example, 'stakeholder' is a very convenient word. It encompasses subtle definitions but is very New Labour."

The NHF used these observations to shape its communications and challenge its own thinking during the following months.

---

[17] Heath C. and Heath D. (2007) Made to Stick: Why some ideas take hold and others come unstuck. Random House (2007).

In practice

Discourse analysis like this can form part of your campaign to help develop a deeper understand the language you and your target audience is using.

Simply collect relevant materials of the target you are wishing to influence – policy documents, think pieces, speeches, manifestos etc and with some colleagues set time aside to sift through them and identify where there are:

Words or terms that are different but have the same apparent meaning;

Words or terms with that are the same but have different meaning;

and where there are different words and terms that hold different values.

After analysing positions you do not necessarily have to adjust the language and emphasis you use adopting words that resonate with your targets automatically but you will have a more detailed idea of their thinking and frames of reference.

Source: with thanks to Chloe Hardy, Head of Campaigns at the National Housing Federation.

Making ideas stick

What makes us remember ideas? Analysis of urban legends, rumours, proverbs, conspiracy theories and jokes has thrown up some common themes about what makes something memorable. The best ideas are those that are:

- **Simple** – complex ideas do not stay in our memories.
- **Unexpected** – they grab our attention.
- **Concrete** – the more dimensions to the detail of a story, the more hooks our minds create to store that memory and we are then able to recall it later.
- **Credible** – it must fit with someone's frame of reference or they will not credit it.
- **Emotional** – we remember emotional experiences more than anything else, we care more about individuals than groups and we think more about things that affect our identities and values.
- **Tell stories** – information is more memorable and meaningful when it tells a story.[17]

Defining an enemy?

While it is better to start with a positive idea – Martin Luther King had a dream not a nightmare – you may also need to motivate people by defining an enemy and how to defeat them, or providing an alternative. Campaigns are often against something as well as for something. Focusing on a clear wrong that needs to be put right can be a core part of a campaign's narrative. A representative event or consequence of a policy can define and crystallise an issue. In 1942 William Beveridge launched his national social insurance scheme as a positive crusade against the five evils of the age – a short and memorable list that people could recall and is still referred to today.[18]

Passion in campaigning

Passion is a key part of campaigners' armoury – it's what inspires people to do something and you need to tap into it in others to succeed in your campaign. Passion is not the same as emotion; caring about an issue is not necessarily enough. Campaigns should link vibrant dissatisfaction to the firm underlying rational arguments for change. The emotive appeal, properly argued and harnessed to the argument, will stir others to action.

---

[18] Beveridge is still worth quoting for, as Timmins notes, in one short passage he 'encapsulated much of post war aspiration'. Beveridge wrote his plan was 'an attack upon the five great evils; upon the physical Want with which it is directly concerned, upon Disease which often causes the Want and brings many other troubles in its train, upon Ignorance which no democracy can afford amongst its citizens, upon Squalor... and upon Idleness which destroys wealth' quoted in: Timmins N. (2001) The Five Giants. A biography of the welfare state (2nd edition). London: Harper Collins. p24.

• Analysing • Developing • **Plannning** • Delivering • Evaluate your campaign

Targets and influencers

In setting your campaign aim (see page 52) you should have identified the campaign target(s). Who do you have in your sights? Influence mapping will help you identify and prioritise your routes to influence your targets.

Who makes the decisions?
Be clear who the targets are. Find out exactly who makes the decisions and at what levels – often there may be more than one decision-maker or chains of decision-makers. How can you get to your target? Often you will have to go through others to exercise any influence (for example via local authority committees, civil servants, special advisers, MPs).

Think creatively about potential influencers, such as any personal contacts you or your stakeholders may have. Use your organisation's trustees, other organisations, shared interest groups, etc. Having multiple entry points is useful if officials are blocking you and you need to get to your target from other angles.

Diagram: Influence mapping example

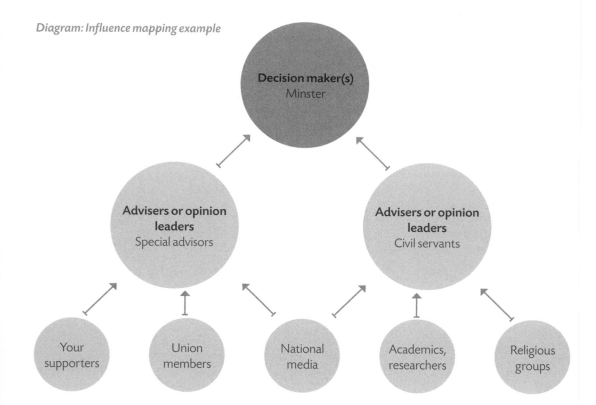

Influence mapping

You can draw up an 'influence map' to help capture this information. Influence mapping takes stakeholder analysis one step further by indentifying the specific individuals and groups with power to affect a decision. It looks at their motives, position and channels through which to influence them.

Brainstorm a list of your targets and influencers. Are they potential allies? If so how can you involve or co-opt them? Are they opponents? Do you need to be wary when you are in contact with any opponents about giving away too much about your campaign strategy? Are there some floaters or undecideds who need persuading? How can you bring allies together and how can you minimise your opponents' influence?

Who do you want to reach and what do you want them to do

To influence someone you need to understand what makes them 'tick'. For example, the way you persuade an MP who has no particular interest in your issue will not be the way you engage local health unions or GPs who already have detailed knowledge on the subject. Try to understand what people think about your issue, test out your assumptions and explore the best ways to reach them. The tactics you develop will depend on:

- The target's current views – ideally the person or group will be receptive, vulnerable to pressure in some way and have the power to actually get things done.
- The issue's resonance with target audiences – it must stand out and it helps if a connection can easily be made between the problem and the solution you are advocating. If the audience is sceptical, a different type of approach is needed.

- Your organisation's credibility– do the targets consider your organisation is entitled to comment on behalf of your beneficiaries and what evidence do you have?
- What type of change are you trying to achieve? For example, are you attempting to achieve a one-off change in behaviour, a health check or commitment to a different way of living? This may change what methods you use.
- Does the organisation have the resources to make a difference and if not who could you work with?

Targets and influencers
(continued)

The mnemonic **AIDA** is a useful way to check that your communications are on track. (think of Verdi's opera, Aida).

Attract attention
Reason: People are inundated with information. Your communication needs to attract attention to get noticed. Start with your campaign concept and build up a narrative around your issue.

Generate interest
Reason: Your audience has to be able to relate to and be interested in your message or the issue. Tailor the message to the audience. Don't be afraid of passion, if it's called for.

Encourage a desire to respond
Reason: Create a narrative. Facts or statistics alone may not command the moral and emotional force that motivates people to act. Your communication has to persuade people to want to do something by resonating with their values and motivations and setting any facts within these, not the other way around.

Prompt action
Reason: You need to be crystal clear about what action you want people to take. Make it as simple as possible and ensure the audience feels it is within their power, or that they are supported by your campaign.

Objectives and work planning

Setting objectives

An aim identifies what the campaign is designed to achieve. A strategy gives you an idea of the most effective routes to get there. In most campaigns there will be several outcomes that lead to the achievement of your ultimate aim – these may be short, medium or longer term.

Setting objectives is the process of making these outcomes explicit, to act as milestones on the path to your final aim. They not only help you make the most of your resources, but also provide a yardstick against which you can assess your progress.

Objectives need to be measurable. They should:
- Identify a specific target – who or what is going to change?
- Define a specific change – what will they know or do differently?
- Stipulate when change will happen.

A useful way of thinking about objectives is to ask – are they **SMART**?
- **S**pecific
- **M**easurable
- **A**ttainable
- **R**elevant
- **T**ime bound

Objectives should be about the outcome you're seeking to achieve, rather than the activity you need to undertake in order to get there, so for example 'the government to increase spending on mental health by 20% in the next budget", would be an objective 'to lobby the government to increase spending on mental health by 20%', wouldn't be an objective.

Campaigns do not usually progress along a straight path so objectives need to be flexible; be prepared to adapt them as the campaign develops. Your objectives should primarily be about measuring your progress towards the campaign aim, not about measuring how busy you are. See more on building a monitoring and evaluation framework, page 52.

Work plans

Think about what resources the campaign will need in order to achieve the objectives. The next stage is to develop work plans to show how activity will be managed to achieve the objectives. Work planning enables you to think about and allocate resources for the campaign and helps to indentify any gaps.

Work planning involves:
- Identifying the tasks that need doing to deliver the objectives.
- Ensuring that resources are available for the assigned tasks.
- A timetable for the tasks.

Work plans help everyone understand and agree what the campaign will be doing, enable people to be clear about what is expected of them and provide a way of monitoring progress. You need to ensure that the overall campaign is discussed and 'owned' throughout the organisation so it is a good idea to share plans with teams across the wider organisation.

Objectives and
work planning (continued)

Work plans should be developed with the team that is going to do the work. If you are leading this team do a skills audit to check that people are confident that they can perform their allotted tasks. If there are skills gaps, you could get more experienced members of the team to train or mentor the less experienced ones.

If you do not have a campaign team around you for support, planning helps to identify tasks that need to be done and the resources that can be allocated to them. Where can you find additional support and help? The point of planning is that it highlights these issues early on.

Timeframes

Many campaigns for change will need to be sustained over long periods of time so you will need to be committed to a long haul. Be wary of setting arbitrary timeframes that fit into organisational planning – stopping after six months, a year or two years of activity. With your external analysis (see page 32) you will know when your key windows of opportunity arise. This should be the deciding factor for the length of your campaign, rather than an artificial date.

Planning things in a logical sequence to support the different stages of your campaign is often called 'critical path analysis'. Not all actions are necessarily sequential in a campaign, but many will be. Your theory of change looks at the steps you need to take sequentially, providing a path for your plans to follow.

Monitoring and evaluation (again)

With objectives acting as milestones you also need to allow time to monitor and evaluate the progress of the campaign, adjusting plans as required. Monitoring and evaluating as the campaign goes is simply a process to check how things are progressing and if plans need adjusting. Plan opportunities to get feedback from those involved in the campaign – supporters, members, beneficiaries, even your targets. Monitoring can be very motivating for you and your supporters if you can celebrate successes along the way and build up a picture of how on track you are to achieve the ultimate campaign aim.

Diagram: Simple planning tool

Objectives towards aim	Outputs or what is generated by your activities	Indicators and timeline
Key opinion formers put pressure on target... X number of complaints demonstrating widespread support	Meetings with decision makers Petition March Demonstration Boycott...	X meetings over X months ...

Planning for the unexpected

Work planning gives you a final opportunity to test the overall plan and the thinking behind it. Is it robust? Is it achievable? Is it coherent?

Check that your external analysis is sound by getting reactions from key audiences and testing your key messages on your target audiences. Check that you have the resources to be able to deliver the campaign. It is important to keep revising your approach and checking the assumptions behind it.

The idea is not so much to plan things, as to plan for things. How will you manage contingencies – the unexpected things that are bound to emerge and could throw any plan off course? Plans with only one tactic or approach have less room for manoeuvre so allow for some flexibility both in timescales and assumptions about how your targets will react.

A good contingency plan anticipates the possible reactions of the targets of your campaign.

- What will the target's response be – defensive, accommodating and open to dialogue or attacking?
- What opportunity and/or threat does this create?
- How are you going to respond to attacks on your position or an invitation to talk?
- How should strategy and tactics be adapted? What is your bottom line and how will you know when you cannot make further progress?

Managing and mitigating risk

A crucial part of the planning process involves assessing and analysing the kind of risks that may occur along the course of, or as a result of, the campaign to make informed decisions about how to handle and mitigate risk. Whilst this process should be done in the planning stages, it should also be reviewed and updated throughout the delivery of the campaign.

Risk analysis tools are used to help categorise, prioritise and assess the impact of any potential risk.

- Start by listing all the potential risks posed by the campaign or that the organisation faces and the assumptions made.
- You can devise categories for all the risk areas, such as financial, legal etc, and add potential risks under the relevant headings. Review the lists – can you simplify long lists by grouping any that are part of wider root causes?

Objectives and
work planning (continued)

- Assign a score to each risk on an agreed scale (1–5 or low/medium/high), by assessing the likelihood of it occurring.
- Assess the severity of impact that would ensue if the risk occurs or the assumption doesn't hold; assign it a score on an agreed scale.
- Plot the risks on a map to help inform the strategy you take to address any risk. Think about the following questions:
- What are the implications of the findings?
- What needs urgent attention?
- What can you influence?

Mitigating risk
After completing this exercise you will be in a better position to reduce possible risk factors. This could include:
- Undertaking more research to test your assumptions about the potential risk.
- Devising strategies to reduce the likelihood of the risk occurring.
- Devising strategies and contingency plans to reduce the severity of the impact if the risk occurs or the assumption doesn't hold.
- Decide if the risks are acceptable or you need to adjust the campaign.

Source: this section has been adapted from materials from NCVO's Certificate in Campaigning developed with Ian Chandler of the Pressure Group.

Diagram: Risk map

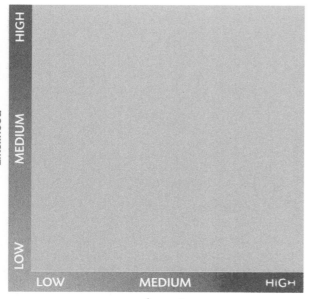

Campaign intelligence

Good intelligence is vital to any campaign. Campaigns should be based on a sound evidence base on the issue, an understanding of the context in which you operate both internally and externally and insight into your targets. To work effectively you need to ensure that you are capturing information or intelligence as the campaign progresses and storing it centrally (not just in someone's head). Building a campaign intelligence base provides a systematic approach to managing information; without it organisations will not be able to learn from their successes and mistakes and the same lessons may be re-learned again and again.

Campaigning intelligence systems help you to focus on the right information needed for the campaign – from its design, planning and delivery to evaluation. Ultimately however, it's not about gathering information but making it accessible and useful and saving you time and energy. You might need to be asking and answering the same questions throughout the course of the campaign. The trick is to indentify key questions and ensure you can answer each question to the right level of detail, with minimal effort.

Start by thinking about the following questions:
- What information is needed?
- How can you gather the information?
- How should you manage the information?

More useful questions to consider are:
- What important decisions are needed as the campaign progresses?
- What information do you need to make those decisions?
- What do you know already?
- What are the best ways to find out what you don't know?
- What resources do you have to find this out?
- What is the benefit of this information and does it outweigh the cost (time, effort, money)?

You may need to collect information gathered from your own research, from information that is already available or records of your own activities. How often you need to update this information will depend on the questions you need to answer and the nature of the campaign. For example, information on the targets and key routes of influence may need continual tracking but an internal review might only happen every other year.

Campaign intelligence
(continued)

The following questions could help you to collect intelligence:

The issue
- What are the problems?
- What are their causes?
- What are their effects?
- What are the potential solutions?
- Which solution are you focusing on?
- What personal testimonies can be used to illustrate the problem/campaign?

The campaign environment
- Who are the key players (ie. targets and primary routes of influence)?
- How much influence do they each have?
- What is their position on the issue?
- How important do they believe the issue to be?
- How susceptible are they to influence?
- How can you influence them?
- What wide trends are affecting the campaign environment?

The internal context
- Do you have clarity of purpose?
- Do you have the necessary resources, skills and expertise?
- Do you have legitimacy to speak on the issue and the credibility to do so with authority?
- Are you accountable to stakeholders?
- Is your organisation oriented in ways that enable effective campaigning?

Managing information
You need to ensure that you make any information accessible and useful to your campaign and use it to increase your campaigning effectiveness.

The minimum you should be capturing and recording is:
- Detail about campaign targets – the institution and routes of influence.
- Detail on the key targets – updated regularly to reflect any changes.
- Detail on whom you meet and responses, promises made and when.

However complex or simple your campaign intelligence system is, it needs to be backed with organisational buy-in – being championed and resources allocated – to make it work.

Source: this section is based on Kingham T. and Coe. J (2005) The Good Campaigns Guide. London: NCVO. p163-179.

Types of campaigns

There are many different theories of how change happens. Whether they are explicit or not, all campaigns operate on some kind of theory of change, a set of assumptions mapped out as to how change happens and how this particular campaign is going to influence that process.

Broadly speaking, there are campaigns that aim to influence public opinion, attitudes or change behaviour and those that seek changes in practice or policy or legislative or regulatory change by influencing decision-makers.

The latter may target government, local authorities and/or private bodies – either through direct lobbying or by mobilising support and pressure behind the issue.

You can combine the two: influencing public opinion on an issue and combining this to pressure decision-makers to change the context or to reinforce what is 'acceptable' by changing the law or policy.

Some approaches focus on building people's capacity to campaign and become more active and engaged in society while the organisation supports whatever action and campaigns they want to take.

Another route is to combine these approaches with legal advocacy. Many community development

organisations and international non-governmental organisations (NGOs) use the term 'advocacy' interchangeably with 'campaigning'. Here, 'legal advocacy' means legal or personal representation in court cases that secure rights through existing provisions or clarify or extend the way law is applied.

At various stages campaigns may use just one of these approaches or a combination of all of them. Your theory of change should have already helped you to identify the type of change you are trying to secure and who or what has the power to make that change – this will structure the type of campaign you will need to run. See more on developing a theory of change page 52.

Diagram: Types of campaigns[19]

Building capacity to campaign		
Awareness raising	Public policy and legislative change / Changing policy and practice of private sector	Legal and personal advocacy
Behaviour change/ public campaigning		Influencing
More public engagement		Less public engagement
Range of campaigning and influencing all aimed at achieving change		

[19] Adapted from Adapted from Davies, R. (2001) A Review of NGO approaches to the evaluation of advocacy work. (DIFD)

Influencing government

The focus of many campaigns is to bring about change in policy, legislation or practice of government or public authorities, or to resist a proposed change.

Tactics can range from direct influencing, which involves developing contacts with key targets, such as civil servants, ministers, councillors, to indirect influencing, which involves mobilising others to pressure your targets – this could be your supporters, peers of the target, or a high-profile figure.

Central government

Influencing central government provides the potential for achieving a great deal with relatively few resources, especially if a major public campaign is not required and you have good relationships with the key ministers or civil servants. This approach is not always possible for every issue, or always the desired route to achieve change. Even if you are embarking on a legislative or influencing route, it does not mean that your campaign should not demonstrate support and involvement of your beneficiaries or supporters: in fact they can add extra legitimacy to your issue and be powerful additional support and pressure in reinforcing your message.

The political system is a direct route for many campaigns to establish how far their proposals are acceptable: start with the most senior policy official you can interest in your issue and test out the government's reaction. Only then should you think of directly approaching a minister to flag up your issues, make proposals or seek a meeting. Otherwise you risk simply wasting time as your concerns could be dealt with further down the chain.

How close should you work?

It can be difficult to work out how closely an organisation should be focused on working with the government or the opposition. How close you can afford to get or how oppositional do you need to be? If you are challenging the principle of a government policy you will have to decide whether you have the resources to mount a long-term public campaign to shift opinion and pressure government, as in the short term you are unlikely to be successful in getting government to change. If you are contesting how policies are being put into practice you can probably talk to ministers and officials more easily, although you may still need a robust public campaign and energetic lobbying.

Be clear which strategy you are undertaking and at what stage of the campaign. For example, an oppositional stance might be sustainable at the early stage of new proposals but not once they are being implemented. At some point all successful campaigns to get changes in legislation or policy have to develop a relationship with the relevant government departments to ensure the implementation. You need to remember this in the heat of the campaign and ensure you are thinking about what happens when you get to this point.

[20] For more on how to manage parliamentary campaigns see: Zetter L. (2008) Lobbying: The art of political persuasion. Petersfield: Harriman House Publishing; and NCVO (2010) In Focus Guide: Working with Whitehall. London: NCVO.

[21] See, for example: nfpSynergy (2005) Ten Campaigning Tips for Lobbying MPs. London: nfpSynergy, which surveyed MPs on the most effective routes to influence them.

Remember government is not monolithic; a department sometimes not only welcomes pressure from interest groups, but can even seek to orchestrate or provoke it. This can be by proposing unpalatable solutions to a problem so that the lobby will react negatively, thus saving the department from having to take further action. Departments may also rely on lobbying from groups to propose solutions that are difficult for them to introduce from within government but would, in fact, welcome and strengthen their hand.

You will have to judge at what point you risk being co-opted into someone else's agenda or being manoeuvred into accepting less than you should by early concessions or promises of consultation after the legislation has been passed.

Parliamentary bills (they are bills before they are passed and become acts when passed) have long 'gestation' periods and it is crucial to be involved from the beginning. You have to be talking to officials and ministers to influence the content of any proposals even before green papers and white papers are published and formal consultations begin.

The nearer that proposed legislation is to reaching parliamentary approval, the less scope there will be for change. Occasionally, however, the legislative process moves very quickly, in response to a perceived emergency or a sudden gap in the legislative programme, so do be on the lookout for these opportunities and be prepared to move quickly to take advantage.

Success in navigating the parliamentary process often demands compromising on particular issues. Think about what is realistic – small gains may be the best you can achieve. Once a bill is introduced into the parliamentary process your chances of getting it thrown out as a whole are limited. Are government proposals vulnerable to challenge from their own supporters as well as the opposition? Can you frame changes in a way that the government can accept and that does not damage the overall principles behind the bill? The victory is not in winning the amendment; it is in getting the government to accept it and holding it to account to make sure it's implemented.[20]

There are several other ways to influence central government.

Working with MPs

MPs are a key access point to parliament, especially if your approaches directly to government departments are getting nowhere or you want to increase the pressure. MPs sympathetic to your issue will normally make representations to departments on your behalf or arrange meetings with ministers to which you could be invited. Ministers rarely refuse to meet with MPs especially if a consistency issue is involved. MPs say the single most powerful pressure on them is constituents making representations.[21]

Select committees

Select committees scrutinise the work of government departments by shadowing and interrogating ministers, their officials and the delivery of the department's work. They also examine key issues and topics relevant to the remit of the department. They can call witnesses and their reports are influential. A committee's request for evidence is a big chance for you to push your case and appearing in person before the committee gives you a major platform.

Influencing
government (continued)

A select committee chair can be a powerful ally. You may be able to prompt or influence an inquiry. Talk to the chair and committee members as well as to the clerks to the committee who can advise the chair. Make sure the committee's specialist advisers are aware of your views. Parliament's website explains the committees' work and their upcoming programme;[22] you could also offer to host a visit to one of your services if they are investigating a topic that is relevant to your work.

All-party groups

All-party groups are less formal than select committees. The membership mainly comprises backbenchers from both houses but may include ministers, shadow ministers and non-parliamentarians. Some of the larger groups exercise considerable influences and ministers will attend their meetings when invited. Groups are classified either as subject groups (for instance, forestry) or country groups (relating to a particular country or region). The chairs of such groups are influential and ministers respond when asked to meet them, sometimes accompanied by representatives of interest groups.[23]

Prime minister's questions and parliamentary questions

Every Wednesday afternoon in the House of Commons, the Prime Minister spends half an hour answering questions from Members of Parliament. Prime minister's questions (PMQs) is regarded as a political barometer within Westminster and the media due to the level of coverage it receives. PMQs is an effective ways of getting profile for an issue, which can often lead to raising the priority of an issue inside government – not necessarily the same thing as a change of position. The prime minister's brief is still provided by the relevant department dealing with the issue.

Parliamentary Questions enable MPs to hold the Government to account through either oral or written questions to the relevant Minister. Questions to ministers – parliamentary questions – cost you nothing; you can ask any sympathetic MP to ask them for you. They not only solicit information but also draw ministers' and officials' attention to an issue, as ministers have to personally sign them off and have to appear in parliament to answer oral questions.

Prime minister's questions
In 2008 during PMQs, Malcolm Bruce MP asked whether the Prime Minister, Gordon Brown, would meet a delegation of sign language users to discuss current failings in providing deaf people with British Sign Language interpreters. It would have looked churlish to refuse this simple request and so the delegation gained a meeting with the Prime Minister. Once in the door this led to considerable contact with officials from government departments responsible for provision of the interpreters as well as with ministers that attended the meeting.

The government had to be seen to take action and additional money was committed to funding interpreters and support for school-age children. Not bad for a one-minute question, but the secret to success was in then having a very clear agenda to follow.

Source: Third Sector 30 July 2008[24]

[22] www.parliament.uk

[23] www.parliament.uk/about/mps-and-lords/members/apg/

[24] Lamb B.(2008) If you don't ask you don't get. Third Sector. 30 July. 2008. Available online: www.thirdsector.co.uk/news/archive/834807 (accessed December 2010).

[25] www.parliament.uk/business/news/2008/12/private-members-bill-ballot

Private members' bills

Private members' bills provide backbench MPs with the opportunity to introduce their own bills through a yearly device known as the private members' bills ballot. The topics are restricted and they cannot impose any serious cost to the public purse. Only the top 20 MPs in the ballot have the slightest chance of their bill proceeding to become law and without government backing, or at least benign neglect, they cannot succeed.

However, proposing a private members' bill can be a very useful way of influencing policy, even if you cannot get your issue through the entire process. If you want any hope of it becoming legislation, you need a very specific issue, one that can be that contained in a short bill, one that does not radically challenge government policy and an issue that is likely to gain cross-party support.[25]

The 2010 Autism Act started as a private members' bill, when the National Autistic Society and a coalition of 15 other organisations successfully mobilised supporters to put pressure on MPs. By having a bill ready for an interested MP they just had to ensure that when the ballot was drawn they could persuade one of their supporting MPs near the top of the ballot to take their bill through parliament.

The role of officials

The most important relationship you can have is with the policy officials in any department as they drive and respond to the implementation of the government's agenda. While it is MPs and lords who will table and promote amendments, it is policy officials who will make recommendations to ministers about what government should accept or reject based on the overall position of government policy.

There are other ways that you will come into contact with officials. Most crucially when working on legislation you need to ensure that you have a strong relationship with the relevant bill team and policy team. The bill team will be led by a bill manager who will be responsible for co-ordinating across the department on the policy content of the bill and turning this into legislation with help of the parliamentary council who will draft the legislation. The bill team become the vital conduit between all sections of Whitehall and the minister's office and, to some extent, the government whip's office who control the timing and pace of the bill. Never forget, however, that it is the policy team not the Bill team that ultimately guides and delivers ministerial intentions.

If you are seeking meetings about particular concerns it is often helpful to contact the relevant policy teams very early on in the process and also ensure that the bill team is then aware of how you are planning to proceed, tabling amendments, and which ones you seriously hope will make progress as opposed to those where you are simply seeking a reassurance from a minister. Many organisations brief bill or policy teams about their intentions before a debate.

Special advisers

Special advisers play a contested but crucial role within Whitehall. Most cabinet ministers will have two or three special advisers, normally one who might focus more on presentation of policy and the others on overseeing and liaising between the minister, officials and the party around the department's work. At best they can be an essential conduit between the minister and officials about the minister's thinking and expectations. They are also the minister's political weather vane with department stakeholders – such as you. As such, they are also a crucial target for campaigners who need to put issues on the map for the minister and you can use the special adviser to keep channels of communication open and hopefully head off potential public conflict when behind the scenes negotiation would help.

Influencing
government (continued)

Devolved governments

Unless your organisation covers England only, your political campaign strategy could be UK wide, taking account of the devolved governments. UK-wide organisations without a devolved presence are unlikely to have legitimacy and access as an organisation to influence devolved administrations.

Devolved powers differ across the three administrations in Scotland, Wales and Northern Ireland. What has been devolved has been changing and evolving as the devolved administrations take on additional functions.

Do your homework on the devolved administrations' powers on your campaign issue and find out who's who and who does what – each parliament has its own particular procedures. Assess where your issue sits within their priorities and how they are positioned on the issue. Because the devolved administrations are relatively small it can be much easier to have a dialogue with elected representatives and officials than within the UK Parliament in London.[26]

Local government

The drive towards greater regionalisation and local involvement may provide growing opportunities to influence local government.

Elected local councillors are responsible for making decisions for the community about local services such as planning, land use, social care and leisure. Local councils exist at different levels – parish, district, county or unitary – and have different areas and levels of responsibility. First, identify which council and what level of administration you need to influence for your campaign.

The role of councillors and the structures at a local level have changed over the last few years, with many councils now having an 'executive system', with a leader or mayor and a cabinet, rather than the old committee system. Councillors in a cabinet have responsibilities for certain areas, such as housing, children's services and social care. Councillors not in the cabinet have a scrutiny or oversight role, as well as representing the needs of their local ward, and can be useful for bringing issues from their ward to the full council. Most councillors are also members of political parties and will be constrained by their party line on an issue.

Paid staff, in the form of officers, are accountable to elected councillors, but in reality councillors rely hugely on the officers for advice. Get officers on your side or at least ensure that they are well briefed on your issue. Some committees have extensive powers; others have only authority over limited particular areas. Check out the scope of any committee you are dealing with.

Winning the support of individual councillors is important but in local politics the real political power rests with the leader of each political grouping. Where the council is in no overall political control you will need cross-party support. Most major local authority decisions today are made by the cabinet – the key committee chairs and leader of the council. Some local authorities are run by an elected mayor – make sure you are aware of the structure and key decision-makers in your local authority before you plan your campaign.

Political, administrative or legal?
At local government levels an issue is not always political. Do not address an administrative problem as if it is political. If, for example, the local authority is failing to provide a service properly, this is an administrative problem; if you want to challenge the allocation of budgets or the authority's policies, this is a political question. If the local authority has acted outside its remit or been negligent, then there are potential legal remedies.

Redress for local authorities' failings may take you to the Local Government Ombudsman. Local authorities are also required to plan for equal access to their services The Equalities and Human Rights Commission monitors these plans and advises on individual complaints.

The European Union
There are many opportunities to influence decisions in the European Union (EU), but the sheer size and reach may make it feel distant and it can seem difficult to know where to begin.

Lobbying at the EU level can mean that you are campaigning right at the source of decision-making, as legislation often begins in the EU before it is amended and passed as law in member countries. Organisations may not have the resources to campaign in the EU.

By leaving things until they devolve to a UK level you may lose the chance to affect legalisation that originates in the EU, so if you can it is worth keeping an eye on what is happening at the European level, especially to check if any new proposals might affect your campaign.

The EU is founded on the principle of conferral of competences, this means there are:
- Certain policy areas where the EU alone is able to make laws or has exclusive competence, such as agriculture, employment conditions and trade.
- Areas in which power is shared between the EU and member states known as shared competence, such as culture, environment, foreign affairs, transport and social policy.
- Areas where the EU has no scope, such as defence, education, tax and welfare.

Find out what scope the EU has to make decisions about your campaign issue. The European Commission website has detailed information on EU policies and initiatives. There are numerous guides for voluntary bodies to help you find your way through the EU, its laws and its institutions.

About two-thirds of laws made in the EU are made through the co-decision procedure where legislative power is shared equally between the parliament and the council. Both institutions must agree for a new law to be passed. The commission's proposal for new laws are first looked at and scrutinised by the parliament.

Working with partner organisations across the EU can help you to influence decision-makers within these countries and can get their constituents involved in lobbying too. If you are new to the EU or a smaller organisation with limited resources, linking up with pan-European umbrella organisations can give you the advice and support you need.

A coalition representing views from across the EU has more chance of lobbying successfully in the European Parliament than an organisation on its own. Alliances with organisations, such as trade organisations, trade unions and professional bodies, can demonstrate widespread support for your campaign. Finding allies from other states can pay big dividends for a small amount of effort.

---

[26] For more on what you need to think about, see: NCVO (2009) In Focus: Working with Devolved Governments. London: NCVO.

Influencing
government (continued)

Example

One woman's campaign in the EU

In July 2000 Louise McVay was diagnosed with multiple sclerosis (MS) and was turned down for disease-modifying medication by her local health authority – the effect of the infamous 'postcode lottery'. Louise complained to her MP and to the then Prime Minister, Tony Blair, about this unfairness but received only standard responses.

Undeterred Louise decided to take her case to the European Parliament and through its website found the address of the then EU President, Nicole Fontaine, who sent Louise a personal response saying that her case had been forwarded to the European Parliament Committee on Petitions.

Louise's arguments about unequal access to medication were compelling and by July 2003, supported by the UK Multiple Sclerosis Society, she addressed the Committee on Petitions in Brussels.

After hearing Louise's petition, along with speeches from representatives from the UK, Belgium, German and Italian MS societies, the chair of the Committee agreed to look at access to medication, services and employment for people with MS across Europe and work with the European MS Platform to look at how the European Union can help support more European research into MS.

In 2002, under a new NHS scheme, Louise received the medication she needed but she continued the campaign to push for people across the EU to receive equal access to drugs and therapies. Louise's petition has contributed to closer links between MS societies across the EU and demonstrates the opportunities of targeting the EU where, in this case, the views of people with MS can be taken into account in decision-making.

Source: NCVO web resource www. ncvo-vol.org.uk/why-bother-brussels-ms-platform

The Council of Europe

The Council of Europe was established in 1949 to promote human rights, democracy and the rule of law. It currently has 47 member countries from across Europe, represented through elected officials and parliamentarians of the various member countries. The Council of Europe is distinct from the European Union and seeks to develop common and democratic principles based on its conventions, the main one being the European Convention on Human Rights.

The Council of Europe plays an important role in promoting human rights and social justice through a number of conventions that have been adopted by the member states; its key areas of focus are children's rights, discrimination, violence against women, the death penalty and protection of social rights. As with the European Union, it is important to assess what areas it is working on that might be relevant to your issue and the ways that you can lobby the various institutions.

Influencing private sector targets

Collectively the private sector employs the majority of the world's workforce, owns much of the world's assets and, and has a huge effect on the environment, society and politics. Campaigning focused on the private sector can bring results not only to shareholders but to individuals and to wider society; largely through effecting changes to the ways companies and individuals operate in securing a profit.

What has strengthened campaigners hands over recent years is number of investors and companies that are now actively engaging in environmental, social and corporate governance issues and the growth of Corporate Social Responsibility (CSR) policies providing standards which can be used to hold companies to account to their own stated standards.

Conversely private sector companies are often sophisticated at managing their public profile, framing their issues and using their huge marketing and PR budgets to sustain that approach. This can often make it difficult for campaigns to directly take on large companies in the public arena outside of the more obvious "disaster" scenarios of oil rigs that fail, breaks that malfunction on cars and product defects that cause serious injuries. Even the largest companies can be vulnerable especially when reputation is at stake. Consistent campaigning pressure on the multinational corporation McDonalds over the years has achieved results and changes in practice. For example, in 2006 after revealing that McDonalds had been implicated in the clearance of Amazon rainforest to grow soya as animal feed,

Greenpeace encouraged its supporters to lobby the company to change it's practice, following a successful campaign the two organisations are now working together in partnership on the issue and McDonald's is one of the leading company in the campaign to halt deforestation for the expansion of soya farming in the Amazon and working in partnership to change the food industry's attitude towards the issue.

As with all campaigns the approaches and tactics that you will take will depend on how your issue is positioned and how receptive your targets are to the proposed change, involving a mixture of persuasion and pressure.

Influencing private sector targets (continued)

Activity can range from boycotts of particular company's products or services, holding companies to account to industry wide or regulatory standards, targeting specific stakeholders or shareholders of a company or mobilising public support into action.

Influence mapping is a useful way to identify which stakeholders have influence over the decisions made in the particular organisation, industry or sector you are targeting; to scope out the individuals to target for dialogue and communication. If you do not have any existing contacts it is important to think creatively about which other bodies you may be able to work with and through.

It is important to consider not only who makes decisions in a particular company but who sets the agenda – which financial, social and political actors have influence on the wider market, political and social environment in which companies operate.

Source: Adapted from NCVO In Focus Guide Campaigning and the private sector (2011).

Example
What is the most effective route your target?

In 2006 Greenpeace embarked on a campaign to get Apple to be at the forefront of green technology. Greenpeace realised that the best route to influence Apple's business practices was through their existing customer base and cleverly tapped into both the creative talents and brand loyalty of Apple users.

The message was pitched perfectly, playing on all the right angles:

'We love Apple. Apple knows more about "clean" design than anybody, right? So why do Macs, iPods, iBooks and the rest of their product range contain hazardous substances that other companies have abandoned? A cutting edge company shouldn't be cutting lives short by exposing children in China and India to dangerous chemicals.'

Existing Apple users were targeted and encouraged to get involved with the campaign by sending on personalised messages of support to Apple's CEO Steve Jobs. Greenpeace established a website that mimicked Apple's brand and provided a range of campaign materials and graphics to make it easy for people to take a photo of themselves hugging their Mac 'hug my Apple' or to create mock up adverts or 'pro creations'.

Nine months after the campaign began Apple posted on their website 'A Greener Apple' and linked to an open letter from CEO Steve Jobs which stated: 'want us to be a leader in [becoming greener], just as we are in the other areas of our business. So today we're changing our policy.'

---

[27] Fawcett Society (2008) Sexism and the City: The Manifesto (London, Fawcett Society): http://www.fawcettsociety.org.uk/documents/SATC%20manifesto%20public.pdf

[28] NCVO In Focus Guide: Campaigning and the private sector (2011).

Example
The Fawcett Society 'Sexism and the City'
In 2008 the Fawcett Society embarked on a campaign highlighting women's experience of sexism in the UK workplace, with a particular focus on the City of London.

"Only when Government, businesses and individual employees finally come together to effect changes will we see an end to the divisions between women and men at work."[27]

At the same time the Fawcett Society launched the Gender Equality Forum which brought together diversity practitioners from politics and business in a space for debate and leadership and act as recognised policy group to achieve legislative change to the way lap dancing clubs are licensed

The campaign focused on the resurgence in 'sex-object culture' in workplaces and on exposing corporate entertainment in lap dancing clubs as well as lobbying government to reform legislation around the licensing of lap dancing clubs.

The Fawcett Society undertook research into 'discreet receipts' (receipts which disguise the name of the venue) building up the confidence of a few key businesses in the FTSE 100 they encouraged them to spread the word businesses to audit expense, introducing a competitive element.

They also initiated targeted meetings with employers and a Chatham House discussion and raised the media debate on lap dancing through coverage in the London press – raising public awareness of lap dancing as a cultural question. As part of this work they also launched the Fawcett Charter representing a coalition of progressive employers – who joined to promote an inclusive work environment challenging the objectification of women – signatories include household names such as the BT Group; the Olympic Delivery Authority and Barclays Wealth.[28]

Influencing private
sector targets (continued)

Shareholder activism

Shareholder activism – targeting companies and corporations through leveraging the power of shareholders to exercise their right to know how their money is being used, has been growing over recent years as people realise that investments can bring financial as well as ethical returns.

Shareholder activism can involve motivating existing shareholders to hold an organisation to account or becoming shareholders yourselves. It can be comparatively cheap approach to take as to qualify as a shareholder you need only buy one or more shares in a company. Shareholders are usually entitled to attend, vote and speak at Annual General Meetings or other meetings and with enough support put forward resolutions of their own.

Example

The Tar Sands: Counting the Cost campaign, launched by FairPensions, supported by Greenpeace, The Co-operative and others took a targeted approach encouraging their supporters to contact their pension funds and other shareholders to express concern over decisions taken by oil companies to invest in tar sands (or oil sands) development. The concerns relate to huge increases in greenhouse gas emissions, financial risk, pollution, wildlife disturbance and threats to indigenous communities.

The campaign successfully secured from 150 shareholders to table resolutions at the 2010 meetings of Royal Dutch Shell plc and BP plc, together with a coalition of NGOs – between 1/10th and 1/7th of investors defied company management.

Alongside this approach the campaign also raised the issue in mainstream newspapers and the investment press, providing both a business and ethical case for the campaign. It also secured an Early Day Motion raised in Parliament by a cross-party group of MPs.[29]

---

[29] NCVO In Focus Guide: Campaigning and the private sector (2011).

Changing people's behaviour

Change often takes place within a context of shifting public beliefs, opinion and behaviour. Behaviour-change campaigns can involve tackling long-held attitudes and values that inform and are linked to behaviours or they can try to change behaviour directly. They can also tackle the underlying perception of particular issues, which can make people more likely to accept certain laws, policies and practices.

Campaigns may also want to link changes in legislation to part of a wider aim of changing behaviour on issues from climate change to obesity. The right combination of legislation and attitude-changing campaigns can change really longstanding difficult issues over time. Heavy taxes on tobacco products, bans on smoking in public places and general health campaigns have followed different and sometimes complementary routes, making it more difficult for people to smoke; over time they have also shifted social perceptions of smoking, making it less acceptable.[30]

There is vast array of social marketing theory to draw upon if you are embarking on this type of campaign and some of the main concepts are summarised here. Recent additions to the debate have raised the questions of how much you need to change attitudes to affect behaviour or how much behaviour can be changed irrespective of what people think.

Attitude or behaviour change?

'If social psychology has taught us anything during the last 25 years, it is that we are likely not only to think ourselves into a way of acting but also to act ourselves into a way of thinking'[31]

So where is the best place to start to change people's behaviour?

People may get used to behaving in a certain way and change attitudes to fit with the way they behave. We wear seatbelts in cars not just because law requires it, but because this has become a socially accepted norm that no longer needs advertising or the threat of prosecution to enforce it. Many people recognise that they need to eat better diets and have positive attitudes to exercise, but their behaviour does not necessarily change unless they are supported by others and the environment supports that choice.

---

[30] Knott et al (2008) P81. Knott, D with Muers, S. Alderidge, S. (2008) Achieving Culture Change: A Policy Framework. Strategy Unit Discussion Paper. Cabinet Office.

[31] Myers D. (2006) Exploring Psychology (8th edition). New York: Worth Publishers.

[32] However this is not the same as saying attitudes make no difference – a recent report identified that there were over 700 studies demonstrating the link between attitudes and behaviour. The challenge is to not assume that by focusing on attitudes, behaviour change automatically follows. Knott D. with Muers S. and Alderidge S. (2008) Achieving Culture Change: A policy framework. Strategy Unit Discussion Paper. London: Cabinet Office.

Changing people's
behaviour (continued)

The idea that changing someone's attitude automatically leads to changing their behaviour is a simplistic one; the causal relationship is much more complicated than this. As behavioural economists and psychologists have argued we can also change behaviour directly – presenting people with an incentive to change by making desired behaviours easier or cheaper and making undesired behaviours more difficult or illegal. If campaigning is about creating change and having an impact, then focusing only on a change in attitudes should not be an end in itself, it is possible to also look first at supporting behaviour change.[32]

Campaigns to shape behaviour indirectly

'Behavioural economics... It rejects "rational choice theory" or "rationality" – the dominant theoretical paradigm in economics. When we say rationality, we mean the idea that a person balances the costs against benefits before taking an action and will make the decision that is in his or her best interests.'[33]

The rational theory model that presented with the right information people are motivated to change they way they think or act because it benefits them to do so has been challenged for not being nuanced enough to account for how people actually respond to information and make decisions.[34]

There has been a huge amount of interest around what has variously been termed 'behavioural economics' or 'nudge' theories. This approach has been taken up by politicians with both the Obama administration in the US and Cameron's Conservatives in the UK setting up behaviour analysis and change units in the heart of their administrations; these are looking at different ways of affecting change where governments wish to structure people's choices differently without necessarily resorting to legislation.

Behavioural economics or nudge theories rest on the distinction between two kinds of thinking – one that is intuitive and automatic, the other is reflective and engages the more conscious and 'rational' thought processes.

Thaler and Sunstein, the leading advocates and popularisers of a behavioural economics approach, argue that intuitive or automatic thinking takes shortcuts to make decisions, resting on previous experience and emotions. The implication of this is that decisions are not all made in the 'rational' calculating mode that we might assume. The reflective system, based on deliberation and rational thought, often only kicks in when we have time and where the decisions are not 'clouded' by other emotive factors.[35]

The automatic part of our brains (which we share with lizards) developed long before the more rational, reflective part, and tends to rule much of our everyday decision-making. As Thaler and Sunstein note, people may go with the reflective system (if they have time), 'but humans sometimes go with the (automatic) lizard inside...

---

[33] Allingham M. (2002). Choice Theory: A very short introduction. Oxford: Oxford University Press.

[34] Dawnay E. And Shah H. (2005) Extending the 'Rational Man' Model of Human Behaviour: Seven key principles, New Economics Foundation Briefing for the Environmental Agency. London: New Economics Foundation. Available online: www.neweconomics.org (accessed November 2010). As they point out following the study of blood donations (Titmuss RM (1970) The Gift Relationship. London: Allen and Unwin.) this model has never stood up to all the evidence about how people actually behave.

Think of Mr Spock whose reflective system is always in control... in contrast, Homer Simpson seems to have forgotten where he put his reflective system.'[36]

People will often rely on those reflexive responses and mental shortcuts – know as heuristics – influenced by pre-existing assumptions and reinforced by friends, family and others around us. Nudge theories also build on the fact that people are strongly influenced by peer pressure and expectations about what others are doing, or what they think others are doing, or even what they think is expected of them. People's self-expectations also influence how they behave – they want their actions to be in line with their values and their commitments.

Social norms have an enormously important role to play in motivating people to take action. Christakis and Fowler, two American professors, who conducted a major study of how social networks influence our decision-making showed:

'Social influence does not end with the people we know. If we affect our friends, and they affect their friends, then our actions can potentially affect people we have never met. We discovered that if your friend's friend's friend gained weight, you gained weight. We discovered that if your friend's friend's friend stopped smoking, you stopped smoking. And we discovered that if your friend's friend's friend became happy, you became happy.'[37]

There has been much interest in how you structure the choices available through the social and political context to nudge people into making better choices without necessarily prescribing how they should behave with dos and don'ts or regulation. This has been referred to as 'choice architecture'.

For some issues, structuring people's choices differently, rather than large-scale awareness campaigns or bringing in new policies can have a big impact.

Nudge theories suggest that we need to alter the triggers and default choices available to influence people to behave differently – making 'good' decisions easier and 'bad' decision harder – tapping into people's propensity to make practical shortcuts in thinking or follow what others do, nudging them the way we want them to choose.

[35] Thaler R.H. and Sunstein C.R. (2008) Nudge Improving Decisions about Health, Wealth and Happiness. New Haven, CT: Yale University Press. Pages 19–33 lay out the basis of the psychological theories behind this idea.

[36] Thaler R.H. and Sunstein C.R. (2008).

[37] Christakis N. and Fowler J. (2009) Connected: The surprising power of our social networks and how they shape our lives. London: Little Brown and Company. Cited: in Taylor M. (2010) Twenty-first Century Enlightenment. London: RSA. See also: Christakis N. and Fowler J. (2007) The spread of obesity over large social networks. New England Journal of Medicine 357. This showed that risk of being obese increased by 57% if a friend was obese.

Changing people's behaviour (continued)

Small changes can make a difference. Research into the behaviour of guests of a hotel in Phoenix reusing towels revealed that small changes in wording can dramatically alter people's behaviour. When a notice in hotel rooms asked guests to reuse towels, only about 38% of people complied. When the wording changed to say 'most guests reuse their towels' the reuse rate went up to 48%.[38]

Thaler and Sunstein cite the 'Don't mess with Texas' advertising campaign that promoted people to look after their environment and not drop litter through a positive 'nudge', rather than additional legislation, achieving a 72% reduction in litter.[39]

The provision of more information by itself may not lead to people changing the way they do things, you also have to look at the context in which that behaviour occurs and the framework people are presented with.

Nudge theories also recognise that trying to change attitudes to then change behaviour is often complex, so they focus on achieving behaviour change by altering the signals, prompts and structures around decisions to get people to choose differently. The implication of this thinking is that how you structure choices is key – providing clear information to make decision-making easier, making the choice you want them to make the default option, using peer pressure in positive ways or providing examples of what positive action has or can achieve.[40]

Some have criticised the paternalist assumptions behind this approach but used its insight to help construct a more transparent decision-making context, making people more aware of the way less conscious decisions are made and give people the tools to change.[41] Whichever approach you favour, such insights point to a different way in thinking about the construction of successful behaviour-change campaigns.

Social and community marketing

Campaigners have also found insights from social marketing theory helpful in exploring behaviour change through this complex and ever-growing area.[42] Campaigns seeking to change behaviour need to identify specific behaviour(s) to promote or change, such as turning lights off, picking up dog litter or eating more healthily.

Many social marketing approaches start from the individual and their perceptions, to identify what is driving their responses and behaviour.[43] Alternately, approaches can be based on systems of intervention – the methods that are going to be applied. For both types of approaches identifying the behaviour change you are seeking is essential.[44] Social marketing is usually focused on the mechanisms of getting individuals to make different choices and to remove the barriers (internal or external) they face in doing so.

---

[38] Cialdini R.B. (2005) Don't throw in the towel, use social influence research. Observer, Available online: www.psychologicalscience.org/observer/getArticle.cfm?id=1762 (accessed December 2010) and Cialdini R.B. (2001) Influence: Science and practice (4th edition). Needham Heights, MA: Allyn and Bacon.

[39] Thaler R.H. and Sunstein C.R. (2008) Nudge Improving Decisions about Health, Wealth and Happiness. New Haven, CT: Yale University Press. Pages 19–33.

[40] For some early attempts of how to use this theory on campaigning and behaviour change campaigns in the Obama administration see Grunwald M. (2009) How Obama is using the science of change. Time Magazine (April 2). Available online: www.time.com/time/magazine/article/0,9171,1889153-1,00.html (accessed November 2010).

[41] Taylor M. (2010) Twenty-first Century Enlightenment. London: RSA.

There is a set of general insights that now inform social marketing approaches which are summed up by Knott as:

- Individuals have 'bounded rationality' – there are often large gaps in information available to us and we respond to choices only to the extent of our knowledge and abilities
- Individuals have 'cognitive complexity' – we make decisions in highly complex and nuanced ways that cannot be reduced to simple laws of behaviour. See more on behavioural economics page 106.
- Individuals respond to incentives and information in a more 'ecological' manner than previously thought – responses largely depend on the environmental and psychological circumstances in which people operate including values and anticipating other people's behaviour.[46]

Persuading people to adopt behaviour(s) that many might rather avoid is challenging. Social marketing theories have explored barriers to behaviour change.

There may be a low desire to change and unwillingness to take action unless the incentives to change are significant. It can be more difficult to motivate people to take action where they do not personally benefit unless it is framed within a broader imperative.

People tend to be averse to loss. Efforts to convince people about what they will lose tend to be more successful than those that outline what they will gain, even when the outcome is the same.[47] People are also poor at calculating their own interest even when they try – they overestimate risk, underestimate the importance of other factors in their decision-making and jump to conclusions.[48] People also respond to subconscious cues, including words, sights and sounds that alter the choices they make. Therefore, how decisions are framed is crucial to what choices people make.

Applying social marketing techniques to campaigns can focus on a range of methods to encourage change:

- Start or adopt new behaviour(s) – including taking action on your issues.
- Stop doing something damaging to themselves or the community or place in which they live.
- Prevent the adoption of a negative or harmful behaviour.
- Change or modify an existing behaviour. [49]

Change can be focused at a range of levels from the individual through to interpersonal levels such as regulatory or legislative change or at the community level through building social capital or consensus to change behaviour.

[42] It is only possible to scratch the surface here in highlighting some of the potential implications of social marketing approaches. Over 60 different theories and approaches have been identified by Darnton A. (2008), GSR Behaviour Change Knowledge Review. Reference Report: An overview of behaviour change models and their uses. London: HMT Publishing Unit. Darnton promotes a nine-point, systems-based approach that maps all the factors influencing a particular issue. For a useful introduction to some of the current most used approaches illustrated with government behaviour change campaigns see: Lund M. (2009) Communications and Behaviour Change. London: COI..

[43] French J. and Blair Stevens C. (2005) The Social Marketing Pocket Guide for the National Social Marketing Centre and the Department of Health. London: The National Social Marketing Centre.

[44] 'Alongside identifying the audience groups, the intervention design process must begin by specifying the behaviour to be changed. This is fundamental to designing effective interventions, whether or not they are based on behavioural models; however, the task of model selection particularly requires clarity about the target behaviour.' Darnton. A. (2008) GSR Behaviour Change Knowledge Review. Reference Report: An overview of behaviour change models and their uses, HMT Publishing Unit, London.

Changing people's behaviour (continued)

When looking at individual behaviour change you need to consider:

- The potential impact of the proposed behavioural change on the individual.
- The barriers specific to this behavioural change.
- What resources are required to overcome the barrier – personal and in the community.
- What the overall context within which those decisions take place is and whether this could make it easier or harder to achieve.

Better information at best can only be seen as helpful in beginning to point people towards a course of action, not the intervention itself. Research has shown that overloading people with facts often has the opposite effect to that imagined, leaving people confused, disempowered or uninterested. Research shows that what generally motivates people is:

- Knowing and understanding what is going on; not feeling disoriented or confused.
- Learning, discovering and exploring – people prefer acquiring information at their own pace and answering their own questions.
- Participating and playing a role in what is going on around them, not feeling incompetent or helped.

People are more likely to act when provided with an opportunity to do so, when it is clear to them that it is their responsibility, when they believe their action will make a difference and when the means to action is there as well as the call to action. The more public the commitments an individual makes are, the more chance that the behaviour will change and that the person will stick with it. Research shows that when commitments by individuals are written, made in groups and are freely given, they have more chance of being sustained.[51]

Tim Jackson, professor at Surry University who focuses on social, psychological and structural dimensions of sustainable living, sees community-based change focuses on a different aspect of how to bring about change he notes: 'Community-based social marketing looks for psychological insights into the importance of social norms and community engagement in changing behaviours.'[53]

Building up cultural capital – shared perceptions within a whole community on behaviour – has been seen a vital third step to compliment focus on individual change. It is only by building up the overall capacity of communities, and the consequent impact this has on changing the overall framework in which people make decisions, that lasting social change can be supported at the individual level.[54]

[45] Kahneman D. (2002) Maps of Bounded Rationality: A perspective on intuitive judgement and choice. Nobel Prize Lecture, 8 December 2002.

[46] Slightly abridged summary from Knott et al (2008) p61. Knott, D with Muers, S. Alderidge, S. (2008) Achieving Culture Change: A Policy Framework. Strategy Unit Discussion Paper. Cabinet Office.

[47] Dawnay E. And Shah H. (2005) Extending the 'Rational Man' Model of Human Behaviour: Seven key principles, New Economics Foundation Briefing for the Environmental Agency. London: New Economics Foundation. Available online: www.neweconomics.org (accessed November 2010).

[48] Dawney E. and Shah H. (2005) Behavioral Economics: Seven principles for policy makers. London: New Economics Foundation. This gives a very helpful comparison of some of the key differences between classical economic theories of behavioural economics.

[49] For an extended discussion of this see: Halpern D., Bates C., Mulgan and Aldridge S. with Beales G. and Heathfield A. (2004) Personal Responsibility and Changing Behaviour. London: Prime Minister's Strategy Unit, Cabinet Office. On social capital approaches see also: Knott et al. (2008) Cabinet Office. Knott, D with Muers, S. Alderidge, S. (2008) Achieving Culture Change: A Policy Framework. Strategy Unit Discussion Paper. Cabinet Office.

This approach is very much evident in the way social movements and groups actually approach change for example, London Citizens, where community development has gone hand in hand with building towards larger campaigning aims.

Campaigns should explore how messages and the overall narrative, or campaign concept, can help motivate people to take action. They need to deploy the insights from these approaches and not assume that simply providing the right information or 'challenging' attitudes will bring about change.

Modbury modelling behaviour change

The campaign in 2007 to make Modbury, a small town in South Devon, plastic bag free proved to be the catalyst for similar campaigns across the UK and a shift of policy by some retailers who now no longer provide plastic bags or now charge a nominal amount for using them.

Led by Rebecca Hoskins, a resident of Modbury who had been inspired to campaign after witnessing the effects of plastic bag pollution first hand on a recent wildlife film she had worked on, succeeded in making Modbury the first plastic-bag-free town in Europe. The campaign intuitively exemplified some of the key insights of behaviour change – providing people with information about the change and why they should change and providing a different standard of behaviour, a simple action that was easy to follow. Once a new habit is set this becomes the norm for others.

The information being imparted in the campaign was compelling; a plastic bag – used for a few minutes – takes hundreds of years to degrade and in the UK we are using billions of them a year. It also suggested a sound practical case for how behaviour could change.

The campaign focused on a small group of early supporters within the trading community to champion the campaign. Once they helped to bring in others through a mix of moral support and community spirit, momentum became unstoppable; nobody wanted to be left out.

Source: Adapted from Power and Social Change, NCVO[52]

[50] Mayne and Coe (2010) p60. Mayne R. and Coe J. (2010) Power and social change. London: NCVO. Available at www.ncvo-vol.org.uk/influencingsocialchange (accessed December 2010).

[51] McKenzie-Mohr D. and Smith W. (1999) Fostering Sustainable Behaviour: An introduction to community-based social marketing. New Society Publishers.

[52] Mayne R. and Coe J. (2010) Power and social change. London: NCVO. Available online: www.ncvo-vol.org.uk/influencingsocialchange (accessed December 2010).

[53] Jackson T. (2005) Motivating Sustainable Consumption: A review of evidence on consumer behaviour and behavioural change. A report to the Sustainable Development Research Network. London: Policy Studies Institute.

[54] Knott, D with Muers, S. Alderidge, S. (2008) Achieving Culture Change: A Policy Framework. Strategy Unit Discussion Paper. Cabinet Office.

Changing people's
behaviour (continued)

Example
Changing behaviours

ENCAMS is an environmental charity campaigning directly to the public to change behaviour and improve the local environment. Over recent years ENCAMS adopted more and more sophisticated approaches to getting its messages heard utilising techniques already widely used in the private sector such as segmentation and targeting.

Running over many years ENCAMS campaign against dog fouling proved to be one of their most successful to date. To inform the campaign ENCAMS conducted extensive market research to create detailed profiles of public attitudes and behaviours towards dog fouling and picking up dog litter. Collecting information on the types of magazines people read, tv programmes they watched as well as attitude and awareness surveys enabled ENCAMS to segment audiences by their attitudes to dog litter and formulate relevant targeted messages that would appeal to that specific group.

The segments were:

Beautifully behaved – people brought up not to drop litter and would be embarrassed if someone caught them littering.

Guilty – people who will litter when nobody is around to watch them, in the car or public gatherings.

Life's too short and 'Am I Bothered?' – people who have a disregard for the consequences of littering, and would not care.

Blamers – people who blamed their littering on the council for their inadequate bin provision.

Justifier – people who would justify their behaviour by saying 'everyone else is doing it' and also blamed lack of bins.

Central to the campaign was the understanding people will not change negative or undesirable behaviour unless a positive and simple solution is made available – in this case providing people with plastic doggy bags to collect the litter in.

For certain segments, having tested messages on samples, ENCAMS decided the only way to get the target to change was by using shock tactics shock them into change and focused on an advertising campaign of posters very strong, powerful, images of dog mess and health hazards associated with simple messages alongside them 'Bag it, Tie it, Bin it' displayed in public places close to the parks and open spaces such as bus shelters.

The campaign also worked with local authorities to combat the problem as well as providing education packs to dog owners and conducting a media campaign to raise the profile of the campaign.

The campaign built in regular monitoring processes to help access whether or not they were on track and messages where reaching the right people, at the right time and in the right place to change their behaviour. ENCAMS also monitored sales of doggy bags in pet shops and chose ten specific areas which were surveyed for dog fouling prior to the campaign and then following the launch to help assess its impact.

Source: based on presentation from ENCAMS

---

[55] See for example Crompton, T. Common Cause, The Case for working with our cultural values (2010) WWF. London. www.wwf.org.uk/change. p31 for an interesting example of segmenting audiences by motivational similarities based on a typology from Schwartz, S, H. (2006) Basic human values: an overview. The Hebrew University of Jerusalem. Available at: http://segr-did2.fmag.unict.it/Allegati/convegno%207-8- 10-05/ Schwartzpaper.pdf (accessed November 2010).

[56] See, for example of a basic template: www.socialmarketing-toolbox.com/toolbox-getting-started.html.

[57] Adapted from templates provided by Professor Jeff French of Social Strategic Marketing.

Audiences

Segmentation – identifying subsections of your audience – and understanding individual motivations as finely as possible is crucial to producing tailored messages. Explore the underlying values and motivates held by each audiences – what will encourage people to change deeply ingrained ways of behaving? Are they rooted in social norms, personal identity and values?

You can segment audiences through simple marketing categories of age, lifestyle and consumption patterns. But more sophisticated models of segmentation now exist that look at people's affinities to issues and underlying values, from which you can identify target groups. Such approaches work with the issues raised in the section on framing page 76, about how people's underlying values and deeper motivational predispositions may affect the choices they make, providing powerful insights for campaigning.[55]

Example
Time to Change
Time to Change is a mental health campaign that aims to end discrimination against people with mental health. Time to Change states that: 'Discrimination is complex and deep-rooted and challenging it is not a simple task.
Evidence suggests that the best approach is to combine the enforcement of legal rights with work to engage the public, alongside grassroots projects that bring people with and without mental health problems together.

We can change public attitudes and behaviour towards mental health by:
• involving people with direct experience of mental health problems in all of our work
• combining national programmes with local, community activities
• sending out clear, consistent messages to specific audiences
• monitoring and evaluating all our work.'

Source: Time for Change Campaign materials[58]

This is a field littered with campaigns that failed or fell short. Focus on understanding the context and choice framework in which attitudes and behaviour is set and reinforced and be realistic about the resources, time and persistence you may need to make even small changes in people's behaviour but also be inspired by what changes you can achieve.

Changing people's
behaviour (continued)

A plan to influence individual behaviour

Here is a basic template for producing a social marketing plan to help pinpoint the behaviours you will target, and with what interventions.[56] While it follows some of the basic structure of producing any plan, you need to think much more specifically about what change in behaviour you are seeking, by targeting what audience and what intervention you are making to achieve the change desired.

The rationale

- Set out why action is needed on the identified social issue, the target audience(s) and why they have been selected. This will also set the action in the relevant context and within the overall strategic objectives.

Situation analysis

- Use SWOT and force field analysis to identify and weigh up factors influencing the behaviour change – both positive enabling factors and barriers to change.

- Look at what has gone before – what do you already know about how to tackle the issue. Scan for similar policies or programmes focusing on similar efforts, the activities and lessons learned.

Asset mapping

- List what resources you already have and what resources are already in the community that you wish to work with, such as social networks, community groups and assets. Stakeholder analysis can be used but keep the focus on behaviour and how it will change.

Target audience profile

- Pinpoint the size of target audience. Identify those who you want to reach and those who can be reached.
- Collect relevant information of current behaviour, which could include existing service take up as well as demographics such as age, sex, location.
- Use target audience insight developed from qualitative and quantitative target audience research and plotting – key psychological aspects by which you might segment your audience, such as overall psychological outlook.

Intervention proposition

- Set out how and why the behaviour change will be positioned with the target audience(s) – how they could benefit and how this can be made easier for them to follow.
- Set out how you can structure the environment so that choices will be made – do you also need a change to policy or practices or a transformation in services?

Initial marketing objectives

- Set out aims and objectives for the work, establishing clear achievable behaviours.

Source: Adapted from a template provided by Professor Jeff French, Social Strategic Marketing.[57]

---

[58] http://www.time-to-change.org.uk/ Accessed November (2010) Based on Interviews with staff at Time to Change.

[59] Speech at Oberlin College 1964.

[60] Mayne R. and Coe J. (2010) Power and social change. London: NCVO. Available online: www.ncvo-vol.org.uk/influencingsocialchange (accessed December 2010).

'It is true that behaviour cannot be legislated, and legislation cannot make you love me, but legislation can restrain you from lynching me, and I think that is kind of important.' Martin Luther King[59]

Legal advocacy

Legal advocacy is founded on the premise that having laws is not always enough unless individuals can exercise their rights within the law and obtain redress when those rights are not upheld or violated. Test cases enable the law to be tested and refined. Using the courts can be a complex and sometimes expensive means of campaigning if you have to commission legal advice, but winning a case brings substantial gains – the change itself and the accompanying publicity.

If you have a case that is testing a legal boundary or seems to be a gross miscarriage of justice and therefore of interest to legal firms, they may supply free legal advice and representation see section on pro bono, page 72.

Example

Campaign for the Gurkhas' right to settle in the UK

A campaign for the Gurkhas' right to settle in the UK was fought for years in the courts, with well-organised support from the Gurkha Justice Campaign and the Gurkha Welfare Society. The government's case that they had no such right was challenged by the campaign's lawyers who claimed that they did.

Charismatic leaders can give campaigns a massive boost. Actor Joanna Lumley, whose father fought with the Gurkhas, was a very effective figurehead for the campaign. After years of struggle, the government gave in. Articulate and passionate, Lumley gave the campaign impetus and profile.

However, the campaign's success was also down to the efforts of a dedicated legal team (the campaign went to the High Court to fight its case). Gurkha Justice founder Peter Carroll used his contacts within the Liberal Democrat Party to excellent effect as the final Commons defeat for the government was on a Liberal Democrat motion.

Source: Power and Social Change, NCVO, 2010[60]

The prospect of a high-profile court case has a deterrent effect. Companies or public bodies may not want to enter into litigation, which could mean risking public embarrassment and a possible large fine. This can prompt an early resolution of the issues. After a company or public body has lost a case, you may be able to work with them to ensure that policies and procedures improve. This has been an especially effective approach in equalities legislation where companies routinely work with campaign organisations to improve their practices often following initial legal action which exposed flaws in how they were operating.

Individual cases should be carefully chosen because they potentially set precedents and test the interpretations of the law in question. While winning a case can have an extremely positive effect for the individual and your campaign, losing one can set you back and weaken the campaign. Engagement with legal advocacy gives campaigns a strong position in debates about the impact of specific legislation through the experience they gain of individual examples and the overall impact of the law.

Legal advocacy
(continued)

Judicial review

Judicial review is a special type of court case where a judge looks at the decision of a public body. It can only be used in situations where there is no other right of appeal and where you believe that the authority has acted unlawfully. Importantly, it does not challenge the merits of the decision, just the process by which it was made. So even if a judge does quash the decision, the remedy is that the public body goes back and makes the decision in the proper process so you could end up with the same outcome.

Although judicial review is a tempting route to go down, there are some important points to consider, which mean that in practice it is rare that judicial review cases are brought:

- A court case must be issued promptly and within three months of the date of the decision you are complaining about.
- It is expensive.
- It can only be used as a remedy of last resort.

However, when successful, a judicial review is a powerful tool: the ruling is binding on the public body and can set a precedent that other public bodies have to follow in the future.

Human rights

'Where, after all, do universal human rights begin? In small places, close to home... places where every man, woman and child seeks equal justice, equal opportunity, equal dignity without discrimination. Unless these rights have meaning there, they have little meaning anywhere.' Eleanor Roosevelt [61]

One of the major developments in campaigning over the last 10 years has been the opening up of possibilities offered by human rights legislation, both within UK law or internationally.

'Human rights are universal. They apply to all people simply on the basis of being human.

'Human rights are inalienable. They cannot be taken away simply because we do not like the person seeking to exercise their rights. They can only be limited in certain tightly defined circumstances, and some rights, such as the prohibition on torture and slavery, can never be limited.

'Human rights are indivisible. You cannot pick and choose which rights you want to honour. Many rights depend on each other to be meaningful – so, for example, the right to fair trial would be meaningless without the prohibition on discrimination, and the right to free speech must go hand in hand with the right to assemble peacefully.' Liberty[62]

Although the European Convention of Human Rights has allowed UK citizens to appeal to the European Court of Human Rights for many years, it was only with the introduction of the Human Rights Act in 1998 that its principles became directly enforceable in the UK. People who are resident in the UK could, for the first time, bring a case based on these rights to a UK court rather than having to go to European Court of Human Rights.

The rights set out in the UK's 1998 Human Rights Act are divided into absolute and not absolute; most rights that are not absolute are qualified rights. This is an important distinction because absolute rights, such as Article 3 (the prohibition of torture, inhuman and degrading treatment) can never be breached, regardless of any circumstances. Qualified rights can, in certain circumstances, be legitimately limited. For example, the state is able to legislate to restrict the freedom of speech so it cannot be used to incite racial hatred.

[61] Cited in www.ourhumanrightsstories.org.uk/about-our-human-rights-stories

[62] Liberty" www.liberty-human-rights.org.uk/human-rights/human-rights/index.php.

[63] Wadham J., Mountfield H. and Edmundson A. (2007) Blackstone's Guide to the Human Rights Act 1998 (4th edition). Oxford: Oxford University Press.

European Convention of Human Rights

Some of the key articles in the European Convention of Human Rights[63] are the right to:

- life (Article 2)
- not to be tortured or treated in an inhuman or degrading way (Article 3)
- be free from slavery or forced labour (Article 4)
- liberty (Article 5)
- a fair trial (Article 6)
- no punishment without law (Article 7)
- respect for private and family life, home and correspondence (Article 8)
- freedom of thought, conscience and religion (Article 9)
- freedom of expression (Article 10)
- freedom of assembly and association (Article 11)
- marry and found a family (Article 12)
- not be discriminated against in relation to any of the rights contained in the European Convention.

This does not mean that qualified rights can be breached at the whim of the state. Any infringement of a qualified human right must be lawful, for a legitimate purpose, necessary, and proportionate – a proportionate response to a problem is one that is appropriate in the circumstances that is not excessive.

The Act places all public authorities under a duty to respect it in everything that they do; they have a positive obligation to protect human rights, regardless of who or what is causing the harm. This means that, for instance, it is not enough for the state to be not actually committing the violation (ie. not torturing people) but it also has to ensure that everyone is protected from torture within its jurisdiction.

Human rights claims can only be brought against the state and public bodies, not against private individuals.

Human rights-based approaches

Using 'human rights-based approaches' means:

- Human rights principles and standards are an explicitly stated reference point.
- All key stakeholders are empowered and can participate in realising their rights.
- Accountability is clear.
- Prioritising the people who are most discriminated against, marginalised or excluded.

In practice this might mean:

- A mental hospital was routinely sectioning asylum seekers who spoke little or no English, without providing them with an interpreter. An organisation challenged this practice, arguing that it breached the asylum seekers' right not to be discriminated against on the basis of language and their right to liberty.

Legal advocacy
(continued)

• A parent and head-teacher challenged a local authority for failing to provide school transport for children with special educational needs living more than three miles from their school. They referred to the Human Rights Act, showing that the lack of transport was a disproportionate interference with a child's right to respect for private life (Article 8, European Court of Human Rights) given the failure to consider her specific circumstances.

A human rights-based approach is not a campaign strategy as such: it informs the overall approach of a campaign. The principles outlined in European Convention of Human Rights box on page 116 either underpin a campaign or more often are used to provide individual redress and enforce standards for public services and other providers. This means taking the spirit of human rights law beyond the courtroom, integrating into the way services are designed and using its principles to resolve disputes between different rights holders.

Many development agencies, community development groups and projects see very strong links between the notion of community empowerment and basic human rights have woven the human rights-based approach into their operations.

Human rights-based approaches have been used successfully to challenge attitudes in public service provision to mental health issues, in combating domestic violence and child abuse and in protecting patients from ill treatment that may be beyond the scope of other legal safeguards.

What happens when one person's or group's human rights compete with the rights of another person or group? The principle of proportionality provides a mechanism for weighing rights against each other. A human rights-based approach can help public bodies balance competing rights and can be used by campaigners to encourage public services to behave better towards service users.

Some organisations' sole aim is to uphold human rights, such as Liberty, Amnesty International and Human Rights Watch. Their work has promoted adherence – on both domestic and foreign policy levels – to international human rights.

For example, during the Queen's visit to Wakefield five protesters peacefully protesting and demanding fair pensions for all were arrested and detained so Liberty mounted a challenge. On behalf of the protesters it argued that the arrests were a disproportionate interference with the protesters' Article 10 rights (peaceful protest) and obtained damages for wrongful arrest and false imprisonment.

A husband and wife had lived together for over 65 years. He was unable to walk unaided and relied on his wife to help him move around. She was blind and used her husband as her eyes. They were separated after he fell ill and was moved into a residential care home. She asked to come with him but was told by the local authority that she did not fit the criteria. A public campaign launched by the family, supported by the media and various human rights experts and older people's organisations, argued that the local authority had breached the couple's right to respect for family life (Article 8). The authority agreed to reverse its decision and offered the wife a subsidised place so that she could join her husband in the care home.[64]

[64] For more examples and information see: BIHR (2008) The Human Rights Act: Changing Lives (2nd edition). London: BIHR.

Campaign activities

To reach each of your target audiences your campaign may require a wide range of activities. Your activities, however contrasting, should sit comfortably together and fit the overall concept of the campaign. This doesn't mean that organisations cannot use novel and innovative approaches and messages to communicate this concept. Organisations not typically known for their public campaigning can make very powerful interventions, which can in many ways be more powerful if they are unexpected.

Right tactic, right time, right audience

Campaigns can be planned around a defining moment, such as a major event, rally or demonstration, or a steady 'drip, drip' of small actions and activities or a combination of both approaches. But no matter how much you plan, be flexible enough to be ready take advantage of unexpected opportunities. Quick thinking and opportunism can deliver campaign success. The apparently luckiest campaigners are usually the best prepared ones.

There are perhaps only seven basic plots on which all novels are based. Campaign approaches and tactics may be similarly finite; the skill is to select the right tactic at the right time to address the right audience. Once a particularly innovative campaign theme or action has succeeded, its impact will not be as great next time round. You need to constantly create new ways to dramatise an issue as you build pressure for change.

A campaign may not achieve its ends, but can still make life very uncomfortable for the target if it succeeds in creating a serious public debate. This may make the target think twice before pushing a particular agenda on another occasion. Governments and others, when planning changes, calculate what level of opposition they may face, taking into account previous experiences. A campaign may curb them in a way that never becomes apparent, to the campaign or anyone outside.

Campaign
activities (continued)

Example
Campaign against fuel price rises

The campaign to blockade petrol and diesel depots in 2000, mainly led by a small number of road hauliers and self-employed lorry drivers and farmers, to stop a proposed petrol increase worked because of the way it was used.

There was nothing novel about a picket or blockade, except for the group that was doing it, but as it affected fuel supplies it brought many services to a halt, with very few people involved. It was this that caught the government off guard and made it initially difficult for them to shape a response.

The government was unprepared for the action and the extensive disruption it created, with supermarkets warning that they only had a few days' supply of many food items. The media was also hooked by the tactic's audacity and its effect.

Public opinion was behind the demonstration and it only lost public support as the impact on hospitals and other essential services become more obvious. The campaign led to the government introducing a raft of other reliefs for motorists, which mitigated the effect of the rise and effectively ended the fuel escalator, which has been the underlying cause of the rise according to the campaign.

When prices were about to go up again, the campaigners again threatened to take action. However, government largely brushed aside threats to repeat the blockade as it was much better prepared and the media were less interested, giving the protesters much less publicity and they did not achieve the same impact next time round.

Source: http://en.wikipedia.org/ wiki/Fuel_protests_in_the_United_ Kingdom

---

[65] This led some to argue that there was a failure by radical social movements to invest in 'countering of conservative social campaigns such as the British fuel price protests of 2000 – which arguably did more to retard the achievement of the UK's climate change targets than anything Friends of the Earth or Greenpeace have done since to support that goal.' Hilder P., Grice J.C. and Lalor K. (2007) Contentious Citizens Civil Society's Role in Campaiging for Social Change. London: Young Foundation. The campaign in some ways prefigured the Countryside Alliance campaigning that followed where conservative social movements took on similar tactics and organising that had traditionally been reserved for more progressive social movements.

How radical do you need to be?
You may come across mention of campaigns taking an 'insider' or an 'outsider' approach. This distinguishes between campaigns that work within the confines of the target they are want to influence – government or private or public body – to make change (invited spaces) and those willing to stand in outright opposition, putting pressure on a target through challenge or conflict (claimed or created space). In reality the insider/outsider distinction can break down quickly as many campaigns combine low-key lobbying with campaigning that seeks the glare of publicity.

A more helpful dividing line is to think about how far you want to be pushing at fundamental principles of the target or ameliorate certain aspects of a policy or the way it is carried out. Is being confrontational in public the only way you can make headway? How much room do you want to leave for quiet compromises at a future date? Clearly your campaign style will affect your relationships with target decision-makers and the possibility of success you may have. They way you choose to play may well depend on how your issue and organisation are positioned.[65]

What every activity you plan for it is not the action on its own that counts; it is the outcome of the action that is important. Go back to AIDA (see page 86) are you seeking to raise awareness of your issue with the action or transfer awareness into action?

Campaign
activities (continued)

Table: types of campaign activity

Activity	Advantages	Need to consider
Marches, demonstrations or smaller protests	Can be useful for demonstrating a depth of feeling for an issue and for motivating supporters. Can trigger media coverage and therefore all put pressure on a key target or demonstrate public will for change. Best combined with some element of novelty about venue or style and tone or at a particularly sensitive moment for the target. For example Cafod used unexpected 'messengers' to demonstrate widespread support for the Make Poverty History campaign. In 2005 on parliament's first day, after a general election, a group of nuns and monks protested outside parliament to lobby MPs. The pictures were very powerful.	Rarely effective on their own, but should be used as one element in a much wider strategy. Can be very resource heavy and can be ignored by politicians and the media unless part of a wider story. The potential risks – do you need permissions to demonstrate, liaise with the police before hand etc.
Stunts	At their best when underpinned by evidence. Humour can be a vital weapon if delivered with purpose when the situation is right, think Mark Thomas.	Need to ensure that you comply with charity regulation and the law. Think through how its linked to the strategy how will you turn awareness into action.
Public meetings and rallies	Can be very effective at community level and nationally, depending on the issue. Allows face-to-face interaction and accountability. Can be linked into other campaign actions or build towards them. Probably most useful when trying to hold officials to account or motivate members and often used together with marches.	Needs to be integrated in wider strategy or could be confused with the end result. Can be expensive and if not well managed and focused only exposes that the campaign is not cohesive.

Activity	Advantages	Need to consider
Symbolic association with the cause	Wearing of armbands, badges campaign pledges, signing up to Facebook groups etc. These can all be useful ways both to raise money for the campaign and create the impression of momentum and broad-based support. The more on trend a message is the more it becomes the common sense of the day.	Need to ensure that this does more than raising awareness by giving people more substantial follow on activities that have the prospect of building towards changes in the targets of the campaign.
Online actions	Getting supporters to take action by email, join Facebook groups, use Twitter, complain to MPs or companies about issues.

Virtual marches such as the Beat Bullying march on Westminster in 2010 or the End Child Poverty march that was then linked to recruiting for a live rally in 2009.

Online polling to demonstrate support for or against issues, which can then be used to focus pressure on the targets of the campaign. | Some risk of lifestyle politics unless followed up to ensure that real action is taken to put pressure on the target of the campaign.

Need to ensure that there is an end focus or aim that either builds pressure on a target or steps towards it. |
| Modelling change | Starting up the change you want to see and then encouraging others to do the same. For example, the 2010 campaign to get people to change one small part of their behaviour to save 10% of their energy consumption.

Once people have taken action they demonstrate this by also wearing a wristband.

Demonstrates an effective way of showing that you are supporting change. | Very powerful when it works and can be easily implemented at a local or individual level. Sometimes hard to find something that is simple enough for people to easily do and can be criticised for not addressing the root causes of issues just their symptoms. |

Campaign
activities (continued)

Direct action

'Direct action is prefigurative, what is desired must also be involved in the methods of reaching that aim... It stands as a practical response to a given situation, but also as a symbol of the larger vision of societal change.' (Benjamin Franks, 2003)

'Direct action: The use of strikes, violence or protests as a way of trying to get what you want, instead of talking.' Cambridge dictionary definition.

Definitions of direct action are diverse holding vastly different meanings depending on your view point. Direction action can take the form of anything from marches, boycotts, and stunts. Some campaigning groups have also undertaken activity to achieve political aims outside of normal social or political channels. Direct action, targeting people, groups, or property can be non violent (legal or within the law) or violent (always illegal).

History is full of examples of social movements that have challenged the status quo with direct action – both legal and illegal – from the suffragettes fighting for the right of women to vote in the UK, the civil rights movement in the US in the 1960s to more contemporary examples, such as stunts by Plane Stupid and the Women's Institute asking its members to leave excessive food packaging in supermarkets.

Non violent and legal direct action activities, such as public demonstrations, for all their particular risks, are an important part of a campaigner's repertoire and give people opportunities to work together and exercise their rights to free speech. You do need to be very careful to align your methods with what is best for the campaign and those you are representing or working with and what fits with your organisational positioning and legal status.

If you are a charity the situation is crystal clear: you cannot break the law or tell anyone to do so. Make sure you know both what is legal and the potential risks of alienating either your target audiences or your supporters, or both. Public demonstrations are directly covered by the Serious Organised Crime and Police Act 2005 (SOCPA), the Protection from Harassment Act 1997 and the Public Order Act 1986 and you should check this legislation before undertaking public demonstrations.

The main areas you need to think about are:

- Ensuring you have the correct permissions if demonstrating near parliament – the definition of demonstration is very widely drawn in the legislation and can cover almost any type of activity.
- Ensuring that if picketing is involved, demonstrators are not harassing individuals, especially if at their home rather than place of work, or where the two places are likely to be close to each other.
- Ensure that the organisation is in full control of the demonstration and you have liaised with the police and other authorities. Ensure that those taking part are clear about the aims of the event and requirements to have a peaceful demonstration.[66]

---

[66] For more guidance on the law around this see Charity Commission (2008) Speaking out: Guidance on Campaigning and Political Activity by Charities (CC9). Available online: www.charity-commission.gov.uk/Publications/cc9.aspx (accessed December 2010).

[67] Shimming S. and Coles G. (2007) Campaigning in Collaboration. London: NCVO.

Working with others

Change cannot happen without the active involvement, support and co-operation of others. Here we explore ways of working with others, such as your beneficiaries, supporters and allies.

Working collaboratively with other organisations

Many of the challenges campaigners face – from climate change to tackling poverty – cannot be solved by organisations acting alone. Strength in numbers can give better leverage, and a coherent and co-ordinated voice is much easier to negotiate with and will increase your chances of not being picked off. Change cannot happen without the active support and co-operation of others. Collaboration therefore often lies at the heart of successful campaigning and influencing and can be central to achieving lasting change.

What makes for a successful collaborative working? Organisations can campaign together in a range of ways, from loose networks to more formal structures.

- **Networks** are informal associations of individuals or organisations that sometimes have a co-ordinating secretariat or individual. Rather than joint working the emphasis is often on sharing information and ideas. Members can invest as little or as much time as they wish and leave as they wish. Often these can come together around discussing particular a problem or issue where there is perhaps not enough consensus to make a more formal commitment.

- **Coalitions** consist of joint working ventures between what can be diverse organisations, around a single event, issue or campaign. Members invest resources and co-ordinate their messages, strategies and activities. Different organisations divide the tasks in the most appropriate ways, but the structure tends to be formal and to work well often requires a high level of trust between participants. Everyone recognises the coalition has a limited lifetime.

- **Alliances** are more long-term, formalised groups with agreement on common ideals among trusted partners. Alliances require regular consultation between organisations and investments of time in order to make them work. Alliances are usually long term. Strategies and plans may be jointly developed and implemented.[67]

There are some very good reasons why organisations want to join together in some form of collaboration. Some of the more memorable recent campaigns have mainly been driven by coalitions or alliances. The most obvious is that for some issues even the largest of organisations are seldom in such powerful positions in relation to national governments, and certainly not internationally, to be able to afford to go it alone. Nor do they always individually have the resources and capacity that working together can bring.

Working with others
(continued)

If several organisations are working in the same field there is always a risk of a target playing them off against each other and sowing division. There is nothing that suits decision-makers better than a divided sector as an excuse to take no action. The public can also be very unforgiving at the spectacle of different organisations saying slightly different versions of the same thing and irritated at being asked to donate to each and every one in the name of fighting for a good cause. Diverging messages can simply confuse the public about what you all really want causing uncertainty where you need clarity.

The rise of the internet and social media means there is a growing space for a different kind of network campaigning that does not depend on formal alliances between organisations but rather on dispersed networks based around particular places, interests and causes.

Deciding when to go into a partnership what ever form it may take can be a complex decision – you need to strive for a balance between the considerable costs of working across a range of organisations and the increased benefits that it can bring.

You need to consider the following questions:
- Is this the most effective way of pursuing your aim?
- Do the other organisations share the same aim?
- If not, what compromises can you accept for the advantage of greater leverage?
- If you do not co-operate, will this damage your capacity to achieve your goal with your target or create conflicting or competing public messages?
- Do you have the capacity to be an active and equal member of the partnership?
- Can the required level of trust and co-operation be created between the organisations? It helps if there is also trust between the individuals involved.

When collaborations fail and their members fall out it is often because of hastily made arrangements, without clear agreement about their purpose, scope and members' obligations. Working in collaboration can bring up difficult questions about branding and organisational profile. There is often a balance between achieving your aim and being able to claim credit for the success. Successful collaborations have good, clear management structures in which members can come together and discuss issues, agree a common position and allocate work. The clearer the structure and lines of responsibility, the more likely it is that the coalition will last. Working in collaboration is not necessarily about all getting on well; it is about clarity of purpose and responsibility for decisions.

Be clear about the overall aim

Be very clear about the collaboration's overall aims and what scope there is for disagreement. Is there only one clear solution that all the members must be required to sign up to, or is there consensus about the problem but organisations might be more relaxed about potential solutions?

Be clear about the risks

Especially if you are a charity you need to be aware of risks that formal collaborations could bring. Is being part of the coalition a reasonable means of achieving your charitable objectives? You also need to ensure that you have effective control over the messages and positions the coalition takes so that you cannot be brought into dispute or your independence questioned by being inadvertently associated with a political party, lose your independence or inadvertently fund a cause that is not relevant to your purposes.

Think through whom you work with

Are you leaving key organisations outside of your arrangements that may weaken the coalition? What is the critical mass you need to be effective that sufficiently represents the campaign issue? Conversely, having too many, or the 'wrongly positioned' organisations in the coalition can lead to failure to agree, disproportionate transaction costs in managing the relationships and being pulled to a very broad aim at the expense of focusing on specific changes. If you have not worked with some of the organisations before, hold meetings to explore whether they are feasible partners for you.

Take your supporters with you

You need to think about how and who will manage any relationships with supporter networks, especially in more long-term collaborations in which the alliance is building new networks of supporters.

Balancing smaller and larger partners

You might need to think about how you structure contributions from partners of the coalition to ensure that everyone has an equal stake or how smaller organisations can be supported to contribute by those with more resources.

Structures

How far do you need to go in formalising the structure of the group? A campaign designed to work over several years, involving many partners and multiple activities is going to need a much more formal structure than a group brought together to work on a particular bill or stop a new supermarket being built or local service being closed.

Planning

You will need to agree how formal or otherwise planning needs to be. Ensure that there is a clear aim, strategy and plan with agreed objectives to both ensure focus and so that you can monitor progress. Planning within a consortium is in principle no different from organisational planning – just more complex given the number of partners.

At a minimum you must agree what the sign-off mechanisms are going to be for communications, who the spokespeople are going to be, or if there will just be an agreed line that individual organisations then work with. Decide this at the start so everyone is clear. The more that all organisations share the profile that arises from the campaign and take part in activities, the more they will feel committed to working through the coalition.

Working with others
(continued)

Brand and profiling issues

Think through how the coalition will be presented – what are the expectations? How prominent do organisational brands need to be? How do partners need to be acknowledged? Does this apply to all communications? Produce clear agreements that everyone is happy with and agrees to.

Different cultures and operating styles

When working with commercial partners, professional associations and trade unions, everyone will need to adjust to the implications of different cultures and operating styles. Business, for example, may make decisions quickly and expect others to do so; trade unions may expect much more extensive consultation with members; professional associations will be sensitive to how they are positioned on standards issues.

Legacy

As with all campaigns you need to think about what happens if you are successful or even if you are not. Will the partnership continue to exist promoting and monitoring the implementation of the change you seek? Do you want to share learning with the wider sector?

If the partnership is formal with joint resources, what happens to the remaining resources, who is responsible for staff and who controls any future ownership of any brands or campaign identities that you have established or lists of supporters? This can become very important if some members wish to continue and others do not.

Leaders

Look into most successful collaborations and you find a strong leader. Campaigning often produces leaders more than other areas of endeavour, partly pushed by the media's demands for a spokesperson and for meeting decision-makers. In some campaigns leadership is shared among several individuals, each bringing different qualities and skills to the consortium. The danger with relying too much on one organisation or charismatic individual is that they can become the campaign's public face. When leadership is shared things can fall apart unless there is a high level of co-ordination. As relationships are negotiated during the planning stage coalitions sometimes stumble and even crumble if leadership is contested.

Inspiring supporter action

Mobilising and involving supporters can enhance the credibility of a campaign amplifying real-life experiences or authentic voices; it can also help demonstrate to decision-makers that public opinion is behind you. Campaigns are successful when the target is morally persuaded or is pressured to the extent that there is no alternative. Mobilising supporters can be a way to achieve change through both of these routes.

Working with supporters is not confined to mass mobilisation but can range from hundreds of thousands marching in support of a major global issue to a small number of people making targeted actions to decision makers unused to being lobbied.

Sometimes it will be more appropriate to use methods other than mobilising supporters to achieve your campaigning aim, for example if you are negotiating with government on the finer detail of a policy it is possible that an avalanche of emails could do more to irritate than influence. Supporter action therefore needs to be part of your overall campaign strategy and targeted to achieving your ultimate campaign aim. The focus should always be to try and get the right amount of people to achieve the particular objective of the campaign – in doing so the emphasis may shift from sheer numbers, to authenticity, to access they have or the status of relevance of those you are mobilising.

Example
FairPensions

FairPensions joined up with Oxfam to prevent legal action by the pharmaceutical company Novartis which would result in restricting access to life saving medicines for millions throughout the developing world. FairPensions used its expertise working with investors such as pension funds and pension managers to lobby larger investors who own Novartis to put pressure on the company to change its policy Working with Oxfam they were able to mobilise their supporters to take joint action, creating a website to enable individuals to write to their pension providers expressing concern over their investments and exercise influence.

Despite having mobilised thousands in the Novartis campaign, FairPensions says " As far as pension schemes, pension funds, pension providers and fund managers are concerned, very small numbers of people can have quite a big effect. Those sorts of organisations are not used to large numbers lobbying them. We have seen instances whereby a pension scheme has received two letter and has then taken up an issue. A small amount of supporters can be very valuable."

Source: Inspiring Supporter Action guide jointly produced by Bond and NCVO.

Working with others
(continued)

Whom will you recruit and why?
Depending on the campaign you will need to decide on which audiences you need to focus your resources on and motivate to take action. Do you need to target people with an existing interest in the issue or target groups of people because they are best placed to demonstrate influence on the campaign targets, or both?

Remember the analysis around framing and what motivates people to take action. One of the main reasons why people get involved is that an issue affects them personally in some way. Make your issue relevant to their personal experiences and ensure they have the opportunity to talk about their experiences. Service users of the charity Leonard Cheshire Disability were asked to reflect on issues that affected their everyday lives as disabled people and these examples were used in campaigns at a later stage.

Try to avoid recruiting only from the small group of people you are comfortable with who are already drawn to the issue; try to broaden your supporter base to include people who have not campaigned before or belong to communities that are underrepresented in your campaigns. It is too easy to always be going to the 'usual suspects' and overuse of the same spokespeople can lead to a lessening of their impact as they start to represent the 'professionals' they were meant to be working alongside with.

With any targeting of audiences you need to think carefully about how to tailor your communications and other recruitment channels used to reach different groups. To recruit, consciously tap into people's likely motivations. Identifying a problem is important but it must be accompanied by belief that change is possible. People may be interested in your campaign but hesitate to get involved. When deciding whether or not to join in or take an action people will be influenced by how easy it is for them to do so.

You need to make it as easy as possible and not structure in involvement that introduces unnecessary barriers or bureaucracy. You also need to be aware that there may be conflict and debate between groups of beneficiaries about the type of campaign and what you should be aiming for. Debate is healthy, but may also need facilitating well to bring about consensus or manage dissent. You need to allocate time to work these issues through.

---

[68] See: Grimm K. (2006) Discovering the Activation Point: Smart strategies to make people act. Spitfire Strategies and the Communications Leadership Institute.

How to organise

There are many ways to organise your supporters that range from individuals through to formal local groups, which could be campaigning at local level, regional or national level. Some supporter networks take the form of formal membership-based organisation, others take the form of a loose network. You should think through what kind of support is required for your campaign and what resources you have to facilitate this. Even if you have informal supporter groups, different levels of activism should be offered to match diverse interests and experiences of supporters as well as the time they have to campaign.

Aim to offer actions that cater to each level on the activism pyramid and supporters can be encouraged to move up the pyramid if 'escalators' are provided. Supporters need to be aware that higher levels can be reached and need to be provided with feedback and opportunities to build confidence, skills or sense of a movement.

Although organising and labelling supporters can be a useful way of managing activity it is important to understand that audiences hold their own identities. It is tempting to think that people who support a cause consider themselves advocates or activists, but approaching the target audience in this way may actually create distance. Campaigns audiences may be concerned parents, responsible homeowners or pet lovers for example and this is how they are likely to identify themselves emotionally (though perhaps not literally), not as 'activists' or 'advocates'. 'Activist' may not be the label your audience responds too.[68]

Diagram: Activism pyramid

A
few
people
dedicating
time and
energy to
activism –
coordinating local
groups, attending
meetings, contacting
decision makers directly etc.

Less people regularly taking part in
easy actions such as signing a petition,
emailing their MP, might forward on
actions to friends. From time to time they
will get involved in more demanding actions
such as lobby of parliament or a march.

Bulk of supporters feel connect to a campaign, read a
newsletter or email but will rarely, if ever, do more than take
part in quick, easy actions, such as click through petitions.

Working with others
(continued)

Providing support

All supporters regardless of experience may require some kind of support. You need to consider what kind is needed (including paid staff time) and how you will provide it. Do your resources allow you to offer intensive one-to-one support to relatively few high-level activists or develop a national network of individuals who occasionally take action or a combination? The kind of support you provide will depend on available resources. However, you should provide these basics:

- Accessible information about the issue and campaign such as campaign packs, briefings etc.
- Explanation of who or what the target is and why you are approaching them.
- Template actions to make it easy to campaign, such as example letters and emails, press releases etc.
- Signposting or information on regulations and legislation that affect campaigning.
- Feedback on results of actions, from meaningful 'thank yous' to following up actions or updates on the campaign.
- A culture inside the organisation that values and works with involving beneficiaries rather than seeing them as an add-on to your activities.

Inspiring action

There's no exact science that will guarantee success every time; what works for one campaign may not necessarily work for another, but there are some general methods that could increase your chances.

Recruiting support

Try to reach your audience in at least three different ways, for example a news story, community group meeting and newsletter email. Focus most of your energy on people who are likely to have most sympathy with your cause and people who might become interested. Utilise 'warm' networks; many people already involved in your organisation are likely to campaign if asked, such as donors, fundraisers, service users and members. If you have existing supporters ask them to link up with others with an interest in the issue to encourage involvement, for example Plane Stupid started an 'Adopt a Resident' scheme to partner with local people living near Heathrow to work together and exchange tactics in the campaign to stop a third runway being built.

Talk to opinion leaders in community groups who might share your concerns – ask if they will recommend your campaign. Online activity can put you in touch with people who already share a similar view or who want to join in rather than converting those with different views. Make use of online tools such as Twitter to take your message to a wider audience and target Facebook groups that share an affinity with your issue.

**Make the most of social media
The Children's Food Campaign,
Coco Pops and Twitter**
The Children's Food Campaign
is part of Sustain, an alliance for
better food and farming. A
recent Children's Food
Campaign action harnessed
widespread anger among lots of
parents about a poster by
Kellogg's (a partner in the
government's Change4Life
health campaign) advertising
Coco Pops, which asked children
'Ever thought of Coco Pops
after school?'

The poster featured the Coco
Pops monkey in a school
uniform. The Department of
Health deems Coco Pops too
unhealthy to be advertised on
children's TV and they are
banned from schools.

Children's Food Campaign used
Twitter to search for people
talking about the issue by
searching for relevant hashtags
and contacted the users directly
through Twitter with details
about the campaign. This
provided a receptive new
audience to tap into for the
campaign's efforts to improve
children's food. As well as
encouraging supporters to write
directly to Kellogg's, the Sustain
website also ran an inventive
competition for supporters to
compose their own slogan for
the poster.

Sustaining supporter action
The more supporter action is
integrated into the campaign
strategy, the more likely it is that
actions will be meaningful and not
invented to keep people busy or
remind them of the issue.

Educate and inform your
supporters about the issue. Explain
how their actions can help achieve
the aim of the campaign. You may
need to manage expectation of
what needs to be done, and what
is realistically achievable. Change
can be long term and milestones
will therefore need to be clearly
explained to demonstrate how
each action is leading towards a
larger end result.

Provide feedback after each
action, from 'thank yous', to more
information, to further action. If
there is no further action required
explain why or find alterative ways
of involving people, such as
shaping the direction of campaign
or evaluating the process so far.

As well as developing welcome
strategies for new supporters, you
may also need to develop
strategies to reactivate dormant
supporters or simple provide
people with the opportunity to
exit the campaign.

For more on communicating with
audiences see *Framing the campaign*
page 76 and *delivering the campaign*
page from 41.

*Source this section is based on
Inspiring Supporter Action guide
jointly produced by Bond and NCVO
(2010).*

Working with others
(continued)

Beneficiary involvement

Involving those who you represent or are directly affected by an issue you are working on and placing them at the heart of your campaigning is not only positive and desirable but a can be a source of legitimacy and accountability that strengthens your campaigns.

Beneficiary or user involvement can strengthen campaign effectiveness by:

• Increasing the campaign's legitimacy and moral case.
• Increasing the campaign's credibility with decision-makers by being demonstrably supported by those affected.
• Changing a target's knowledge or insight of an issue through having it articulated by those most affected.

Example
Ban Advocates

As part of the Cluster Munitions Coalition, Handicap International Belgium established a project to ensure that victims of cluster munitions from around the world help influence the international negotiations to ban cluster bombs.

The 'Ban Advocates' advocate for a ban on cluster munitions and the full application of the rights of survivors and affected communities and were directly involved in planning and implementing advocacy activities including presentations at international conference, meeting diplomats and media work. Handicap International Belgium provided the Advocates with training and tools to enable them to most effectively lobby decision-makers and opinion formers as well as with the practicalities to attend conferences, e.g. providing an interpreter as well as through training, briefing reports and support networks.

The Ban Advocates have been able to influence discussion on all major topics and successfully lobbied government delegates at the Dublin Conference, where a draft treaty to ban the use of cluster munitions was agreed. In Dublin, Advocates focused their lobbying on the countries which wanted to weaken the treaty, meeting with over 30 different delegates and speaking at the opening ceremony.

Because of their direct knowledge of the issue the Ban Advocates helped strengthen the text of the convention, particularly on victim assistance. Their involvement also helped secure high profile media coverage for the campaign. An independent evaluation showed that the Ban Advocates helped increase the legitimacy and moral case for an international ban on cluster munitions, and influenced the views and, in some cases, positions of diplomats. As one respondent said 'their' capacity to move people was important. It was quite difficult for diplomats to keep their humanity in check in order to represent institutional positions. The Ban Advocates brought their humanity to the fore – and were very powerful in doing so.

[69] Case study adapted from the Presentation to Beneficiary Voice Peer Exchange by Stan Brabant and Stephanie Castanie Handicap International, and Independent Evaluation of the Ban Advocate Initiative, Ruth Mayne, forthcoming)

[70] Chapman & Fisher, The Thoughtful Activist Also as Schuler argues: 'Hard won gains can be dissipated unless there is constant vigilance over the law's application and interpretation. Legal reform strategies work best, after all, when the social value base is in concordance with the desired new norms. As long as the old regime of values is in effect, the tasks of making the new norms operative, or activating the educative function of law to change values, will be difficult and require action on many fronts.' quoted in: Chapman J. and Wameyo A. (2001) Monitoring and Evaluating Advocacy: A Scoping Study. London: ActionAid.

"The Ban Advocates were experts in the human effects of cluster munitions ... they brought specific experience which helped elaboration of Victim Assistance clause ... I learnt a lot from them as they could tell me how things work on the ground and they raised several things I hadn't thought of". Diplomat quoted in Independent Evaluation of the Ban Advocates Initiative.

Handicap International Belgium summarise its learning from the project:

Go at people's own pace, take the time to explain the project and build relationships with your beneficiaries based on mutual trust.

Help build confidence, through training, briefings and support networks.

Help foster a group dynamic for people to exchange experiences and help each other.

Most importantly leave the Advocates to speak in their own words.

Sources: adapted from webresource NCVO http://www.ncvo-vol.org. uk/count-me-in/banadvocates and Beneficiary Voice in campaigning joint guide produced by Bond and NCVO.[69]

Beneficiary and user involvement can help to make hard-won change sustainable. Research on effective campaigns has shown how 'long-term grassroots involvement is essential to ensure real change of any type even after policy changes have been achieved... the essential links between policy and project work.'[70]

At the strategy and planning stages of a campaign beneficiary involvement could tap into the specific knowledge and personal experience that different groups can bring to provide vital insight and background into the campaign targets. Beneficiaries could also be integral to informing appropriate indicators of success or milestones for your campaign, for example, shared intelligence on any adverse effects that achieving a particular campaign objective may have on their lives or the lives of others.

Your beneficiaries or users may be able to identify areas of concern and provide valuable insight into important issues but it might not always be possible to provide specific solutions to a problem. In such cases 'experts' could be invited to provide background on particular issues and answer questions to inform choice to ensure realistic and consensual decision-making is achieved.

When planning how to involve beneficiaries in campaign decision-making it is useful to distinguish between whether they:
- Have formal powers to make decisions and sign off plans and objectives etc.
- Have authority to make decisions on their own.
- Are consulted about decisions – if so how, when, how are different voices managed?
- Are informed about decisions.

Working with others
(continued)

Tips on how to involve people

There are similar issues to consider around how you involve people in your campaigns.

To ensure you have a representative group, explore creative ways to involve those people who can't or don't get involved in your work. Think about when and where you are holding meetings – time, location and agenda – make them as accessible, convenient and un-intimidating as possible. Think about the language that you use – remove the jargon.

It is presumptuous to assume that people will want to get involved, spare the time and invest emotional energy into a campaign. To develop best practice you should move to their terms – ask people what support they would like in exchange for their experience, knowledge and time they are sharing with you. It is worth thinking creatively about building a mutually beneficial relationship with people you wish to involve.

If you or your organisation are regularly involving the same people in your work it is important to consider the benefits of longer-term investment in developing the learning and skills of the people you are working with. This approach can demonstrate the importance and value being placed on involvement and lead to deeper engagement through developing skills and potential to participate more fully in campaigning as well as enhance beneficiary retention in terms of involvement.

Different kinds of involvement can co-exist in the same organisation, or at different stages of the campaign. Whatever level of involvement you are developing, be clear about the terms on which you are involving people. Key is managing expectations about involvement and what is realistic and achievable, as well as the parameters of the relationship. Organisational documents or protocols could be produced in partnership with the groups you are working with, that clearly specify roles and responsible. You can also produce guidelines for people on how they can share their experiences with you.[71]

Going off message

Organisations may have concerns about using their beneficiaries, supporters or volunteers as this opens up the possibility of people not sticking to the view or line of the organisation and 'going off message'. You can always manage these concerns by putting in place more formal arrangements and with risk assessments. Ensure that people are properly briefed about your issues. But also think hard about what 'control' is really necessary and how far you can give people basic messages and guidance but then let them develop and enrich your campaign with their experience.

---

[71] See Amnesty Internationals guidelines on this which are simple but effective. http://www.amnesty.org/en/library/info/POL41/001/2008/en (Accessed November 2010)

Campaign action groups

Leonard Cheshire Disability (LCD) aims to change attitudes to disability and seeks to ensure that disabled people are central to campaigning and their voices are heard. In 2005 LCD agreed a 10 year organisational vision to change public attitudes to disability. A key element of the strategy to achieve this is a renewed emphasis on campaigning – devolving power from the centre to individuals campaigning in their own localities. Disabled people will be involved at all stages of campaign development and implementation.

To do this the organisation has invested heavily in creating Campaign Action Groups (CAG). These are not 'Leonard Cheshire Disability' groups, but independent, individually named groups of disabled people that set their own agendas and methods of working. LCD acts as a facilitator and support to these independent groups.

Pilot group success

To see if the concept was viable LCD decided to establish three pilot groups within six months – so starting small and aiming for motivating quick wins. The first CAG members went into action with energy and passion. For example the Battersea based group in London, frustrated by accessibility problems on London buses and apparent poor staff training, met with Transport for London to voice their concerns. The outcome of their campaigning saw Transport for London filming a new training DVD at Channel 4 studios where CAG members and bus drivers were separately interviewed then came together to discussed the issues. Within the next two years all 22,000 plus London bus drivers would see the DVD as part of their training.

From the success of the pilots the CAG model rolled out across the UK during 2007 with a huge variety in the type of group and membership. Groups usually start small with less than 10 members and are supported from dedicated staff at LDC. LCD produces a newsletter every three months to help groups keep in touch and exchange news.

Source: Count me in webresource NCVO http://www.ncvo-vol.org.uk/count-me-in/campaignactiongroups

Working with others
(continued)

Recognise the limitations of involvement

Whilst involvement is important, organisations should also recognise the barriers to their work; your beneficiaries or supporters may be geographically dispersed, politically at risk or, for legal or confidentiality reasons, be unable to be directly involved. If this is the case you will need to think more creatively about how to represent people.

The empty chair

One organisation developed a creative solution when – for confidentiality reasons – beneficiaries could not participate in public meetings. They turned this into an opportunity to make a deliberate statement that these individuals are vitally important to the debate but that their situation means they cannot speak out publically in this way.

Leaving an empty chair around the table during a meeting, or on a speaker's panel at an event, and explaining the reasons why they could not attend in person, highlighted the issue and made an effective impact.

This tactic was also used to great effect to point out the absence of the 2010 Nobel Peace for winner Liu Xiaobo who was refused permission to pick up his prize by the Chinese Government. This led to the photograph of the empty chair at the awards ceremony being shown around the world by the media.

[72] Charity Commission (2008) Speaking out: Guidance on Campaigning and Political Activity by Charities (CC9). Available online: www.charity-commission.gov.uk/Publications/cc9.aspx (accessed December 2010).

[73] For more advice consult the Electoral Commission: www.electoralcommission.org.uk and the Charity Commission: www.charitycommission.gov.uk.

Charity law – some key points

If you are a registered charity you will need to ensure that you are aware of and follow the Charity Commission's guidelines on campaigning.[72] Trustee's have a key role and the ultimate responsibility for ensuring that your organisation stays within the law so you need to ensure that they are fully involved in strategic decisions on campaigning and kept aware of progress of a campaign so they can discharge their duties in charity law. Further, keeping trustees informed and engaged in your campaign provides an invaluable resource for contacts and wisdom and you should be thinking about how you can ensure they are appropriately involved in campaigns.

Charities and political parties

Charities can have policies that coincide with those of a political party as long as it is made clear that the policy is in support of the furtherance of their charitable aims. As a charity you can also contribute to the development of policy by a political party by commenting on policy documents or draft manifestos.

It is also acceptable to work with political parties by appearing on a joint platform with them, for example at party conferences. However, when doing so you need to ensure that the organisation is managing risk properly. This includes ensuring you are even-handed between the political parties and that you can demonstrate that your activity is in the furtherance of your charitable objectives.

Elections

Charities can campaign during elections and the election period often provides a good opportunity to promote your views and raise your profile. However, more care needs to be taken to ensure you maintain political neutrality and independent. In the run up to and during an election a charity may promote its views but must not explicitly compare these views with those of the political parties or candidates taking part in the election and they must leave the electorate to draw their own comparisons between the parties' candidates and policies. Charities are free to approach candidates and ask for opinions and invite them to meetings – you need to ensure that you are not treating one candidate or party with preference over the others however.

For example, if you have planned for your local MP to attend an event and then an election is called, and your event takes part in the election period, you should invite the other main candidates too. There is guidance on hustings at elections from the Charity Commission, which you should consult if planning this type of activity. At all times charities must strive to maintain a balance between the parties if you do so.

Publishing materials during an election period could mean that your organisation also has to register with the Electoral Commission, depending on a certain level of expenditure.

You need to be vigilant about activities undertaken during an election period, especially in ensuring you maintain your independence. If in doubt, ensure that you have sought advice about what actions are permissible. The Charity Commission produces specific guidance on elections, as does the Electoral Commission.[73]

Charity law – some key points
(continued)

Party political activity

Political activity is permitted but must not be confused with party political activity, which is expressly forbidden by charity law.

A charity cannot:
- Support a political party or allow the charity to be the vehicle for political views (personal or party political) of any trustee or staff member.
- Financially support or give support in kind to a political party.
- Have a political activity as its main charitable purpose – this would include, as a purpose, a change in law or policy decision of government or furthering the interests of a political party.

Charities derive part of their trust from the public from the assurance that they are not acting in a party political way or are the surrogate for other political interests and therefore the trustees of your charity have a duty to ensure that the charity does not undertake any activity that exposes you to accusations of political bias, as this will affect perceptions about your independence.

Balance of activities

Charities do not need to have campaigning mentioned in their constitution to allow them to campaign. Governing documents can also refer to campaigning or political activity as long as it is clear that these are in the furtherance of the charity's purpose.

There is no set amount of resources that charities are allowed to devote to campaigning or political activity. Trustees are ultimately responsible for ensuring that campaign activity is only a means of supporting or contributing to the achievement of your overall charitable purposes.

This means that there could be situations in which it was reasonable to apply most or all of the organisation's resources to a campaigning or political activity if they judged that this was the best way of achieving your organisations charitable purpose. However, this situation could only apply for a specific and limited period of the overall life of your charity.

This requirement may be more difficult to achieve if you are small community-based organisation than if you are a large charity, given the disproportionate resources involved but it is not impossible. A small community charity for the preservation of the local countryside could campaign for a bypass to the village as its sole activity for a period of time if it felt that best achieved its objectives.

Trustees have a duty to ensure that the organisation stays within the scope and implications of the definition of campaigning and political campaigning by the Charity Commission. These are very broad and only party political activity is expressly prohibited. Trustees also have a duty to ensure that the activity you undertake is in line with achieving your purposes. Over time you must ensure that this activity is a means to an end and does not become the reason for your existence.

Complaints and the Charity Commission

Complaints against charities for inappropriate campaigning are a very small part of the Charity Commission's work. This suggests that rather than this being an area of exceptional risk for charities, it is a relatively low one. However, if you are the subject of a complaint you need to be aware that the Charity Commission will investigate and that if you are found to have breached the guidance they have extensive powers to address any failings. Normally the first action would be simply to ask the charity to remedy the particular problem.

Delivering
your campaign – making it happen

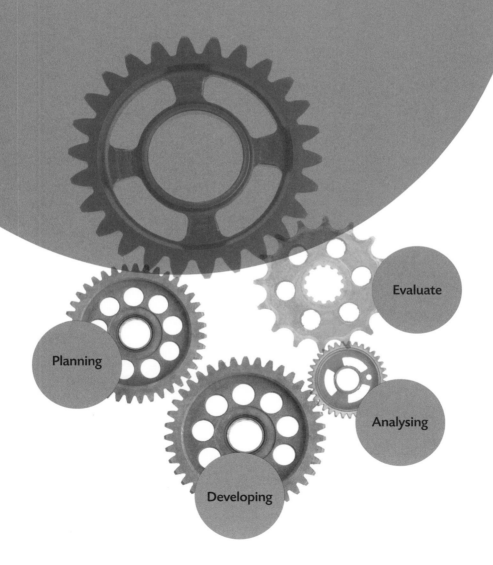

Planning

Evaluate

Developing

Analysing

Contents

Understanding your audience
• Positioning and shock tactics
• Messages and messengers

Bringing the story to life
• Using images
• Film

An integrated communications strategy
• News media
• Online/offline blurring
• Citizen journalism
• Letting go of the message

Using online communications
• Websites: a campaign's hub
• Email
• Using social networking sites
• Twitter
• Crowdsourcing

Keeping legal
• Advertising standards
• Defamation
• The Communications Act

Some of you may have opened the book here, eager to get on with the actual campaign. However, the most effective campaigns are meticulously planned before being carefully executed. By this stage you should have:
• Developed your issue and a theory of change.
• Have clear aim and objectives.
• Know who or what the target is.
• Know the best routes to influence them.

You should also have a clear concept for the campaign that projects your vision of change; this will bring your issue to life and make it easier to communicate. Crafting the messages of your campaign should be the end result of your strategy, not the starting point. See more on campaign concepts, page 77

The most effective campaigns mix the right ingredients in a logical order. You need to:
• Understand your target audiences.
• Pitch the message appropriately for those target audiences.
• Develop campaign actions to attract attention and stimulate action.
• Communicate with your audience through appropriate channels.

Once this is all in place you will be in a position to decide how you are going to communicate your campaign to the audiences you have identified ensuring that how you do so reinforces the understanding and framing of the issue.

Understanding your audience

Your stakeholder analysis (see page 36) and influence mapping (see page 85) will have identified priority target audiences – that may be allies, neutrals and opponents – that you will need to target with tailored communications. To make best use of your resources you need to build a profile of each target audience that you need to reach. Consider:

- How might the audience react to your view of the issue?
- What frame of reference are they likely to be using in relation to the issue, and how could you tap into that or disrupt it? (see section on framing, page 76.)
- What are their values and how are you going to relate to them?
- Do you have the capacity and resources to do this?

Next you will need to build up a deeper understanding of which channels your target audience receives and how they digest information.

- What sort of information would be most persuasive for the different audiences (case studies, plans, results, learning)?
- What type of communications do the respective audiences use most (websites, short reports, detailed reports, letters, emails, meetings, phone calls, posters, cards)?
- Which newspapers do they read?
- Which magazines do they buy (specialist publications or journals)?
- Do they listen more to local or national news?
- Which social media sites are they on? etc.

Unless you divide up or segment your target audiences in this way you will lack focus and will not be using your resources efficiently. A broad message – to anyone who just might be listening – will not go far. Once you have an understanding of your target audiences and the most effective routes to influence them you will be ready to create appropriate campaign messages to fit both the audience you want to meet and the medium you are using.

Positioning and shock tactics

Depending on how your target audience is positioned in relation to your campaign issue you will need to devise a strategy to recruit them, win them over to the campaign's way of thinking or neutralise/decrease the effect of their arguments. Are you facing an open door or a brick wall? The style of your campaign may well affect your relationships with your target audiences. They way you choose to work will depend on what your organisation is like and how your issue is positioned.

When used effectively shock tactics can have a powerful effect – bringing home the real impact of an issue and stimulating action. However, there is a danger that shock tactics can be used as the quickest route to provoking a reaction without thinking through the potential consequences, such as backlash from potential supports or the people you are representing in the campaign.

Understanding
your audience (continued)

Research suggests that sensitivity of the public to strong or challenging messages has been overestimated. Public polling has[1] found that almost 80% of those asked thought it was justifiable for charities to use 'shock tactics' especially if it was appropriate to the seriousness of the issue being raised. The findings also showed that just over a third of people had taken action, while only two per cent of responses had been negative, resulting in cancelling a subscription or making a complaint.

The Charity Commission has guidelines on potential risk to reputation by charities associated with using shock tactics to encourage donations or raise awareness of an issue .

Messages and messengers
What do you want people to do? The outcome of the action that you want people to take is more important than the action itself. What do you want your target audience to do as a response of your communication? Remember AIDA (see page 86). Are you seeking to attract attention, generate interest, encourage a desire to respond or prompt an action?
You may need a series of communications combining a mix of persistence and opportunism to achieve the ultimate action you want.

Although you will tailor your messages to the medium you are using – it's obvious that an article in a specialist journal is requires a different approach to a tweet – the essence of your messages should communicate your campaign concept consistently.

Tips for successful messages
- Keep it simple, even if the context is complex. Jargon will put people off.
- Have a clear ask – spell out what you want people to do and what could happen as a result of their action.
- Make it compelling – explain why action is needed now.
- Be consistent – in both your overall campaign concept and in the wider organisational style.
- Keep repeating the same message.

Your campaign messages need to fit with your organisation's overall tone and style of communication. There may already be guidance about how the organisation depicts the issue or the people involved in it. Does your campaign fit with this? Are there organisational brand guidelines that specify ways of describing your work – ways of presenting the issue – that you need to follow or develop? Do you need to deliberately change your style and presentation to break new ground with a new audience? If so have you thought through the implications for other parts of the organisation? Who do you need to work with to achieve a style that suits both the organisation and the campaign targets?

Think especially hard about how you represent people on whose behalf the campaign is being conducted or you are campaigning with. Do the messages match up with the way you actually conduct the campaign? Have the people you represent or are campaigning with been involved in the process? Joint working and sign-off procedures can guard against this.

Who is the messenger?

Who your message comes from can be as important as the message itself. People are more likely to respond positively to a message if it comes from a source they trust. There are ways you can boost the credibility of your messages:

- Personal testimony is the most potent way of getting the public sympathy or interest and providing a hook for your story. Real stories bring an issue to life. For more on meaningfully involving people see *Bringing the story to life* page 145 and *beneficiary involvement* page 134.
- Unlikely allies and unusual messengers will get attention and bolster the argument: CAFOD used nuns and monks to lobby parliament during the Make Poverty History campaign in 2008 and the images had a big impact in the press. The Rain Tax campaign in 2009 against Ofwat's change in charges for surface water drainage that resulted in a huge rise in water bills got noticed in parliament because it was a coalition of unlikely bedfellows such as the Scouts, the Rugby Football Union and members of the Church of England all affected by the issue.[2]

- Use someone whom people trust – someone who is seen as being above the fray will add weight and public profile to your cause.
- Find an impartial endorsement or trusted voice that has credibility in your area to pre-empt any opponents' accusations of bias or 'they would say that' accusations.
- Work with a respected expert and use the evidence – someone with credibility will be trusted even if they are clearly working on your behalf.
- Enlist a personality who is trusted by the public and has a talent for communicating. But choose someone who is already involved in the issue or will stay the course. The actor Joanna Lumley's involvement boosted the profile of the Gurkhas' campaign.

Bringing the story to life

You also need to think about how you can illustrate your issue and capture the attention of your target audience(s). How you illustrate your issue or the story you tell may differ for each target audience and the medium you use and depend on the story itself. Personal stories are the most effective means of attracting publicity for an issue especially in broadcast media but there are other ways you can present your evidence. Images can resonate emotionally and can encapsulate a whole issue or idea. Good photographs and video, well deployed, can bring stories alive and reach huge audiences; they have no language barriers. Special care must be taken to ensure you are portraying and representing people in an appropriate way.

Start by asking the questions:
• Are you stereotyping?
• Are you showing people as victims and dependants or positive actors?
• What is the relationship you are portraying between staff and beneficiaries?
• Who has sign off?

Using images

There is truth in the cliché that a picture is worth a 1,000 words. Images can resonate emotionally and can encapsulate a whole issue or idea.

Pictures can be a very effective alternative for people whose stories you want to tell sometimes cannot do so directly themselves because they lack confidence, find it too painful. Because of the potential impact of an image, extra care needs to be taken to ensure you are not putting people at risk or misrepresenting them. It is vital that people in the images you use have control over how they are used or have given informed consent for their use. Some organisations have guidelines requiring that any image of beneficiaries must carry information saying who they are, where the picture is taken, and their relationship to the campaign. Think though:

Collecting images can be built into your campaigning work by training in-house staff or supporting people you are working with in your campaign to take and produce their own photographs.

Example
PhotoVoice
PhotoVoice is an international charity that seeks to empower disadvantaged groups by providing them with photographic training so they can express themselves, advocate and make some money. PhotoVoice works with refugees, street children and orphans, as well as with people affected by HIV/Aids.

The PhotoVoice training workshops allow people, who are traditionally the subjects of photography, to become its creators – and gain some control over how they are perceived by the rest of the world. In a partnership project with a local women's centre in London's Bethnal Green PhotoVoice ran weekly photograph workshops with women involved in prostitution providing people with the opportunity to express themselves and reflect upon their lives. With the women's consent a targeted postcard campaign was run in the area and an exhibition held.

Evaluation into PhotoVoice's work shows that the training helps participants gain confidence and speak out about their lives. They have copyright of their images, and all photos are accompanied by a brief, which outlines the conditions of use.

Source: Presentation by Matt Daw, PhotoVoice to Beneficiary Voice Peer Exchange, Bond 2009)

Film

Film or video provides another way of telling stories. Be clear about what you are aiming for: do you want to inform people or inspire them to take action?

Basic interviews with people sharing their opinions on a campaign can be recorded and distributed quite cheaply and easily – you can often just use a mobile phone with a video camera to do short 'vox pops' style interviews with people.

Don't be put off by costs; basic digital video cameras are relatively cheap, as is editing software, or you could just find someone willing to lend you a mobile phone that contains a video camera. You may be surprised by how many people in your organisation have skills and are willing to help, or how many budding film students will lend a hand. If you have a clear concept of what you are doing and keen volunteers, a relatively high level of production can be achieved.

If you want to capture attention and mobilise new supporters you may need to think more creatively and involve specialists. Pro bono (see page 72) support might be useful here. If you want a video to 'go viral' think about what might motivate someone to pass it on to their friends. Humour helps if your campaign issue is suited to it, or there may be other simple ways to dramatise the issue.

Consider the following points when you are thinking about how to use film in your campaign:

- Use video to get across emotionally engaging, personal elements of your story. Treat interviews like news stories – what is the 'human' interest? Where possible let people use their own words.
- You need to get permissions. Anyone appearing in the video must understand the film's aim, how it will be used and where it will appear. Get them to sign informed release forms (samples are widely available online) and keep copies. Be careful you do not accidentally include people in the background who might not want to be included or are at risk if they are included. Be especially careful if your film uses or shows children (or vulnerable adults); get their parent or guardian's permission.

- To make sure you have the right tone for the campaign, test the product on a sample of your intended audience.
- Keep it short. The average news item is three minutes long; you will lose attention if you go on too long.
- As well as planning the content of a film you will also need to plan for how you will distribute and promote your film.

Example
Dying Matters, a campaign that aims to change public knowledge about, attitudes to and behaviours towards death, dying and bereavement, used a video – A Party for Kath – to help people to have difficult conversations about death and dying. This is now being used through their network to help make difficult conversations easier and supporting people to able to talk more about the end-of-life care they want.[3]

[3] See: www.dyingmatters.org.uk.

An integrated communications strategy

You will need to integrate both your online and offline communications – there is a growing integration between them; people get news from websites, personal blogs and tweets as well as from conventional news channels. An integrated communications strategy will have considered what the advantages are of using one medium over another or when to use both. It will also consider how these need to be different to best take advantage of the route you are following.

Once you have a detailed picture of your intended audience, you will be in a more informed position to decide which communications channel will reach that audience best. This may involve a range of communications through different channels so to keep on top of this activity it helps to keep a communications grid that records the type of message, phases of activity and timescales. This will help you avoid duplication and show who has contacted whom and in what way. It should be an ever-evolving document which should make your life easier.

News media

We are bombarded with information from hundreds of media outlets. Media work can be an extremely cost-effective means of conveying your messages, either directly or indirectly, to your target audiences. The way in which news media positions an issue (along with the questions it poses and assumptions it makes) will have a big impact on your target audience's understanding of your issue. Policy-makers and politicians often see the media as a surrogate for public opinion. Many politicians' reaction to an issue or event is determined by the prominence and type of coverage that issue is receiving in the media. How the media frames stories will dictate how much your issue is covered. See more on framing page 76.

Analysis of the media has shown that there are three main but different ways in which the media structures the type of discussions and focus that takes place which can inform what approach you take:

Agenda setting – The media doesn't instruct what people think, but acts as a gatekeeper of information, determining what is important. The more often issues appear in the media, the more salient they become with the public. Campaigns will need to focus on channelling that awareness into action.

Framing – The media provides the frame of reference for how people think about and interpret issues, in particular how they think about solutions to problems. Campaigns can focus on trying to fit the issue into existing frames or challenging the framing of an issue completely.

Persuasion – The media influences how people think about attitudes and behaviours they need to adopt in order to enhance their own lives. Campaigns need to focus on providing specific actions or simple alternatives to change behaviours.[4]

The news media however is not monolithic; researching and segmenting media outlets is time well spent. If your story clashes with the way a particular outlet portrays your issue, or there is a risk that it will turn your story on its head, there may be other routes to go down. Always try to anticipate how the media outlet will respond to your issue – have they been supportive or hostile in the past? Don't use jargon and focus on one clear message.

If your campaign seeks to challenge a prevailing 'frame' or public perception or is open to challenge, think carefully about how to communicate your message in the face of potential media hostility. Negative media coverage can provide opportunities for you to get your message across, as long as you are prepared to cope with being attacked.

What story do you have?

What kind of feature would your story make? Your issue may be news or may be better suited to the lifestyle, personal interest, health or finance pages of a newspaper or magazine where more detail can be added. Can you offer an opinion item or a letter? The letters page is one of the most read in newspapers and sometimes can then spark off further coverage.

You stand more chance of having your issue covered if the journalist already has some knowledge of you and your issues, and your organisation has a reputation for being able to deliver what they need. Journalists may want to know about:
• What the issue is.
• How many people are affected.
• The impact of the issue.
• Why it matters now.
• Your solution and how much it will cost.
• What you want decision-makers to do.
• What decision-makers say they will do.
• The names or names of people affected by this issue whom they can interview.

Online/offline blurring

Will your story work online and offline? Online you may be able to include more detail and start an interactive discussion. Many news websites use material from blogs, either commissioned pieces or users' contributions. Your communications strategy may include ways that you can pitch for content or respond to the latest thought pieces on your issues.

Blogs are the regular online publishing of comment and articles usually from a personal perspective. Blogs provide an opportunity to present more detailed information about an issue or regular updates that others can then comment on and contribute to further debate. It's worth researching and making contact with existing blogs that cover your issue or are read by your target audiences they may well be looking for content.

[4] Adapted from Susan Beals S. and Gilliam F. D. Jr. (2004) Communications for Social Good. Foundation Center; Goffman J. (2002) Public Communication Campaign Evaluation. An Environmental Scan of Challenges, Criticisms, Practice, and Opportunities. Prepared for the Communications Consortium Media Center Harvard Family Research Project. Cambridge, MA: Harvard Family Research Project.

An integrated communications strategy (continued)

Citizen journalism

New technologies have had a profound effect on news reporting. Images captured on people's phones or video cameras have been used to expose human rights abuses across the globe – from political protests in Iran to Burma – and to record live footage of demonstrations in the UK. Social media tools such as blogs, commentaries, Twitter, YouTube etc provide spaces to capture and document issues and share breaking news in real time and provide opportunities to challenge or bypass existing media coverage or highlight new issues. Whilst specialist citizen journalism websites can feature your news or even broker stories on your behalf to media buyers. The potential for campaigners to tap into this is massive providing opportunities to gain more control over the news cycle and media agenda, bringing new issues to light and providing opportunities to bypass traditional media channels.

Letting go of the message

Developments in new technologies, the internet and the growth of social media are rapidly altering the way people access information and communicate with each other, facilitating instant two-way communication.

Social media is inevitably having a transformative effect on campaigning, offering more and more opportunities to reach and engage directly with wider audiences in a different form of conversational activism.[5]

Engaging with social media can open you or your campaign to wider and more visible public reach; it can also allow easier access for people – members, supporters, beneficiaries or other stakeholders – to get involved and make their opinions known and be acted on. But to get the most out of it involves 'letting go' and listening, joining in or starting your own conversations providing real conversation or observation about an issue rather than talking at people or broadcasting messages from the organisational line.

This may involve a shift in the way some organisations are used to working – from campaign control centre to more part of a movement – and gaining buy-in from across the organisation to support the shift. It could involve supporting and being involved in campaigns in different ways – by offering a meeting space, making introductions to key decision-makers or helping promote others' work on a relevant issue.[6]

Using online communications

New technologies and social media provide opportunities for campaigners in all stages of the campaign cycle; this next section explores some main aspects of online communications that can be incorporate into the delivery stage of the campaign.

[5] The Obama presidential campaign has become something of a template for online campaigning; see for example: Delany C. (2009) Learning From Obama. Lessons for online communicators in 2009 and beyond. Available online: www.epolitics.com.(accessed November 2010) and D. Raymond (2009) How to Campaign Like Obama. Fairsay website: http://fairsay.com/obama-howto (accessed December 2010) for the implications of how the Obama campaign used the internet but also looser messaging.

[6] Adapted from NCVO Future Focus: What will campaigning be like in five years time? (2009) Third Sector Foresight.

The benefits of online communications

Reach – the internet provides you with the potential to reach millions of people across the world in a wide variety of ways. This holds out major opportunities for campaigners, no matter what size of resources they have behind them to extend their footprint.

Speed and flexibility – as the pace of news and information increases campaigners and others are using text (SMS) messages, Twitter updates and email alerts etc to respond to news as it happens, keeping supporters up to date and mobilising them into action.

Levelling effect – to get up and running with an online campaign you may need no more than an internet account, a website and time. Many online resources are free, giving individuals and small organisations as much clout as larger ones.

The age barrier myth – A recent study into on and offline participation shows that age is not necessarily a barrier to digital engagement of those polled the age group who were most likely to contact an elected representative online was the 55–64 age range.[7] There's a wealth of research out there – look closely at the audience you want to talk to and find out how and where they spend their time on the internet.

Getting the most out of it
It's about people not technology[8]

Online activity should be an extension of linking people together offline, building on existing relationships or making new ones by starting two-way conversations. The more personalised the communication, the more likely people are to read and act on it. Involving people in the process of selecting the issue or creating content for the action means it will be more likely to strike a chord and be taken up by your audiences.

Avoid a frenzy of inactivity

Virtual virtuousness may have little to do with virtual effectiveness. 'Click-through activism', as it has become known, can have the opposite effect diluting pressure. With some commentating that some online gestures give people a false sense of having taken action which can deter them from doing anything more, much like the wearing of cause-related wristbands. As with any action, online action needs to be about value and impact rather than numbers reached.

Keep focused

The best communication strategies combine a strong message with clear calls to action. Start simply, gain expertise and build your relationships with social networks that are relevant to your cause.

Internet time vs human time

Thinking of 'internet time' as fast or instant can be misleading – you still need to plan and work around 'human time', allowing the project to grow. Adding an artificial expiry date to a project so it fits into a project plan can restrict time put aside for people to get involved or take ownership.[9]

[7] 'Whilst it is true to argue that the younger age groups are more likely to participate online than offline, age is no barrier to digital engagement; the highest users of online engagement are in the 55–64 age bracket.' Williamson A. (2010) Digital Citizens and Democratic Participation. London: Hansard Society. Available online: www.hansardsociety.org.uk ' (accessed October 2010).

[8] For more ideas about the use of the internet in campaigning see: Fairsay, Advocacy Online, Oxfam (2008) eCampaigning Resource Pack . Available online: www.fairsay.com/insights (accessed November 2010).

[9] Raymond D Fairsay e-seminar Campaigning futures Available online: www.forumforchange.org.uk/forum/topics/the-role-of-cocreation.

Using online communications (continued)

Websites: a campaign's hub

Most campaigns now have a campaign home: usually your organisation's website or a specific campaign website. Websites often act as the core of your online presence from which you can link both online and offline activities.[10]

Think about how you are segmenting the website to appeal to different audiences – journalists, politicians (especially those who work for them) through to your members and activists, and the curious. Any website should be easy to find, navigate and read. Information on the campaign and what you want people to do to support it should be clearly visible. Make it easy: start with top-line information and link to more detailed information such as case studies, reports, news coverage, short films or images to build a fuller picture of the issue/ campaign. Be clear about what you want people to do. The 2009 Ecampaigning review noted:

'Campaigners are perhaps concerned to get the maximum number of people down a narrow funnel to take action, without 'distractions', but failing to properly inform people taking the action may undermine a campaign's credibility.'[11]

Does your website allow you to change from 'broadcast mode' to online conversation and activity? If not, does it link to other places where interaction is possible?

Once the campaign is over update your website to reflect this. Campaign pages can be archived and linked to show past successes, but whatever you do, don't leave it gathering dust.

Email

'We [the Obama campaign] used so much social media during the presidential campaign, but the initial relationship that allowed it to work was email, it was the text-heavy, narrative-based emails that kept people engaged. Our mantra has been, invest in your relationships online via email.' Thomas Gensemer, Blue State Digital[12]

Obama's campaign for the US presidency in 2008 relied predominantly on email communications with supporters for reach, campaign co-ordination and fundraising. Despite the often-predicted decline of email in favour of other forms of online communication, most people still use it and a new generation of mobile phones provide instant access to it.

---

[10] Raymond D Fairsay e-seminar Campaigning futures Available online: www.forumforchange.org.uk/forum/topics/the-role-of-cocreation.

[11] Ecampaigning review 2009, Jess Day and Duane Raymond, http://www.advocacyonline.net/resources/ecampaigningreview

[12] Interview with Thomas Gensemer (managing partner of Blue State Digital who built Barack Obama's online presidential strategy) 17 September 2009. PR Week. London.

'The most successful actions... provided users with a range of levels of detail to support the case for action: simple, compelling action copy/ content, supported by straightforward, specifically-written background explanations/FAQs (linking clearly back to the action), plus further detailed research where relevant, usually presented as downloadable PDF documents.' Ecampaigning Review, Advocacy Online[14]

Email not only allows you to contact supporters quickly and cheaply but also allows you to keep track of whom you are communicating with, when you have contacted them and what they have done. This information is crucial as it enables you to segment audiences and further tailor communications to suit them. Managing email lists does not have to be complicated. You can monitor what actions people have taken, as well as when and how, contact them to say thank you for their support and update them on the progress of the campaign. Keeping track of who is doing what for you means you can identify those who might want a high level of engagement with the campaign.[13]

Email communications can track emails so you can see what is happening to your messages – who has opened them, forwarded them on etc. What subject lines are more likely to be opened and read and what calls to action generate the most responses? Does what time of the day the email is sent have an effect?

A big topic for contemplation will be the frequency of messages you should send. The key is to make actions meaningful – people will get put off if you invent actions to keep them busy. But if you have many campaign actions as part of your overall strategy don't be scared of telling people about them. The 2009 Ecampaigning Review found that it will be unlikely to bombard supporters with actions, rather you might not be able to satisfy their appetite.

Using social networking sites
Social networking sites such as Facebook, Mumsnet and Saga Zone offer great potential to tap into providing a potential supporter base for your issue and ways of engaging with them. Although cost may be low, or free, you will however need to invest time to make them work well.

It is always worth looking at what other groups exist first. They may already cover your interests; think about whether you want to duplicate their work, or instead join in with and tap into their existing and potentially captive audiences? Think through and plan the resources you may need to devote to this to keep the conversations going or respond to enquiries. If you do create your own profile for the campaign, make it engaging and keep it up to date – other social media channels, such as blogs, Twitter, online video, photos, articles and personal stories can be added to build up content around your issue.

[13] For more detail on use of email see http://www.helium.com/items/1017711-how emails-could-be-made-more-effective-in-political-campaigns

[14] Day J. and Duane Raymond D. (2009) Ecampaigning Review. Advocacy Online website: www.advocacyonline. net/resources/ecampaigningreview (accessed December 2010).

Using online
communications (continued)

Example
Facebook and Busts 4 Justice

At the end of 2007 Beckie Williams was fed up with Marks and Spencer charging up to £4.50 more for a DD cup bra than for smaller cup sizes. Her letter to the company only resulted in a standard customer service reply. But inspired by the Facebook group who lobbied Cadbury to bring back the Wispa chocolate bar, Beckie set up her own group, Busts 4 Justice, planning a coordinated letter writing campaign to Marks and Spencer.

Membership of the group grew steadily, but after a brief mention in the Evening Standard numbers dramatically increased rising to almost 8,000. Marks and Spencer were still ignoring the group but what had started as a straightforward single-issue campaign group quickly became more becoming a platform for women to share experiences and bombarded Marks and Spencer with complaints about poor fit, poor service and poor availability.

Marks and Spencer began engaging with the group but their interest dwindled and after months of silence and unreturned messages, a misdirected email revealed that the company had no intention of changing the policy and never had. Frustrated by the lack of progress Williams bought a Marks and Spencer share for £3.40, determined to bring the argument to the company's annual general meeting. Within three days of revealing her plan on Facebook the group had attracted 11,000 new members joined the campaign and gained huge media coverage on the issue. Within weeks of buying the share and attracting publicity Marks and Spencer backed down, dropping the extra charge and reduced the price of all bras by 25% in response to the amount of support for the campaign.

Williams recalls: 'It felt amazing to stand in Marks and Spencer the next day and see all bras costing the same... knowing that not only had we changed their pricing policy but encouraged them to retrain their 11,000 fitters too. One tiny little Facebook group had snowballed... and effected a real change. Even now, with the "bra wars" behind us, Busts 4 Justice is still evolving: remaining as a positive and supportive forum for women to share experiences and seek advice, a platform to campaign for better fitting standards and awareness, and a place to help raise money and awareness, championing bra recycling.'

Source: based on the article by Beckie Williams www.i-volunteer.org.uk/ beckie_williams/from-e-cup-to-e-campaigner-busts-4-justice

Twitter

Micro-blogging site, Twitter has captured the imagination of its users; messages or tweets are limited to 140 characters. It provides instant conversation with anyone who is following your tweets or hashtags, which group messages around key words. Twitter enables you to link to more information, such as webpages, photos and films as well as providing a 'leaderless' forum for ideas and messages to develop collaboratively among masses of people without formal co-ordination or leadership. One striking example of this was in 2009 when public outrage led to the first gag order of public reporting of parliament in 400 years, being overturned – a mere 12 hours after it happened.

Example
Trafigura

Trafigura, a British-based oil trading company, was under investigation in 2009 for the alleged dumping of toxic waste in the Ivory Coast, leading to a range of health problems for local residents. The Guardian newspaper had been following the story and in September had found itself the subject of a super-injunction by Carter-Ruck, lawyers specialising in media law. It could not write about Trafigura's activities in West Africa.

Normally the media can report issuing of injunctions, but with a super-injunction not even the court order can be publicly revealed. When questions about the gag on the Guardian were due to be asked in parliament, traditionally a place of free speech, Carter-Ruck secured the first gag order in 400 years (since 1688) against the reporting of parliament. This was on 12 October 2009 at 8:30pm.

As news of the gag reached the internet – initially via Twitter but soon being covered by blog posts, news stories and spontaneous protests actions – thousands of individuals began to attack the story and the act of gagging parliament's free speech untroubled by any legal boundaries of what the Guardian had been forbidden to say – the text of the question, the threat from the lawyers, and so on, was soon revealed.

By the next morning two of the country's leading political blogs, as well Private Eye magazine had published the full text of the intended parliamentary question, as well as a wealth of background on Trafigura's practices in the Ivory Coast. Among the most popular search terms on the Twitter was 'outrageous gagging order Trafigura dumping scandal'. Before 2:00pm Carter-Ruck caved in and the super-injunction was withdrawn.

Example
We love the NHS

In 2009 comedy writer Graham Linehan was angered by US right-wing attacks on the NHS. He took his anger to Twitter and his tweets about his experiences of the health service, tagged 'We love the NHS', snowballed into a full-blown Twitter phenomenon, with thousands of messages zinging back and forth. Linehan's campaign gave voice to tens of thousands of people who wanted to express their support for the NHS, but didn't know how.

The enthusiastic public response, facilitated by Twitter, turned the campaign into a major media event with online, print and broadcast media all reporting the campaign extensively. More importantly it changed the terms of the debate away from alleged failings in the NHS to a comparison with the American health care system.

Source: http://www.timesonline.co.uk/tol/news/uk/article6794585.ece.

Using online
communications (continued)

Crowdsourcing

Crowdsourcing is about outsourcing tasks to larger numbers of people, a crowd, through an open call to action, traditionally by an employee or contractor.[15] Crowdsourcing information, ideas and solutions has grown in popularity with the rise of the internet and social media channels for its reach, speed, flexibility and levels of participation. It has been utilised by campaigners from collecting information on an issue – monitoring what cuts are being made to services, gauging opinions to find solutions, to documenting events as they unfold.

Example
Kenyan 2007 elections – Ushahidi

Ushahidi (Swahili for 'testimony' or 'witness') was set up after the political crisis in Kenya after the controversial 2007 elections. Co-founder Ory Okolloh, a Kenyan activist and lawyer, proposed the site when she realised that ordinary people with mobile phones could report what was happening in their communities faster and more accurately than the mainstream media.

Using Google Maps, a free mapping tool, Okolloh and colleagues set about updating their custom map with information about political violence, sent to them by 45,000 people using simple SMS text messaging and email. This combination of 'crowdsourcing' of information combined with geolocation software, and the ease with which ordinary Kenyans could participate via mobile phones, proved highly effective at collecting evidence and holding the government and various parties to account for their actions.

The software the group developed was later used to document anti-immigrant violence in South Africa, collect eyewitness accounts of the Israeli invasion of Gaza in 2008–09, and is currently being used in Haiti to assist with the emergency work there. The group's aim is to create a platform that anyone can use to collect and visualise information.

Source: www.ushahidi.com.

---

[15] Adapted from http://en.wikipedia.org/wiki/Crowdsourcing

[16] http://asa.org.uk/

Keeping legal

Advertising standards

The Advertising Standards Authority (ASA)[16] is the UK's independent regulator for both broadcast and non-broadcast adverts, sales promotions and direct marketing, they administer the UK Code of Non-broadcast Advertising, Sales Promotion and Direct Marketing (The CAP Code) and the UK Code of Broadcast Advertising (The BCAP Code). All these codes set out what is permissible for advertising and broadcast media. The codes cover all marketing publications to the public, not just paid-for advertising. Any marketing material your organisation publishes could be referred to the ASA by a member of the public if they feel that you have breached the overall requirements to be 'legal, decent, honest and truthful'.

There are similar rules for broadcast and non-broadcast media and organisations also have to take account of the Communications Act 2003.

From 2011 the ASA's remit will be extended significantly to include online marketing communications on organisations own websites as well as non paid for space under an organisation's control – such as social networking sites. This will not extend to public affairs statements such as press releases, other public relations material and editorial content.

If you have followed the good practice outlined in previous sections these guidelines should not cause any difficulty. You do need to be careful that any claims you make can be substantiated. You also need to ensure that you do not unnecessarily cause distress. This latter element of the code has constrained several organisations who have wanted to publish powerful messages about issues such as rape, child abuse and bullying, but had permission refused or been asked to withdraw or alter adverts.

If a complaint is made the organisation will be investigated by the body concerned, which can be a rigorous process. If your organisation is found to have breached the guidelines the judgement will appear on the ASA website and you will probably be told to withdraw the offending claim and any material that reproduces it. Not only can this seriously damage your organisation's reputation but may also be very costly.

Persistent breaches of the code might be seen as implying mismanagement or maladministration of the charity's campaigning work. This could trigger an investigation by the Charity Commission. If you are unsure about any advert or item of material you can check with the ASA before hand.

Keeping legal (continued)

Defamation

The civil law of defamation includes both slander and libel. 'Slander' refers to the defamation by the spoken word and 'libel' to written defamation. Libel extends to statements that are likely to have a lasting impression, such as interviews on television or radio. Libel is a more significant concern as it reflects the damage someone does to an individual's reputation. You therefore need to ensure that any statements are factually based or honestly derived and that there is no malicious intent. It is seldom wise to personalise a campaign around attacks on one individual.

Making a compelling case using all communication methods is essential to effective campaigning; it raises no particular risks as long as the material is based on sound evidence.

The Communications Act 2003

The Communications Act prohibits the use of paid 'political' advertising in the broadcast media. The ban does not affect internet, cinema, SMS, telephone billboard or newspaper advertising, all of which are covered by the ASA rules. The legislation defines 'political' very widely and includes seeking a change to the law, government decisions or policy. It extends to prohibiting any advertisement from any organisations or individual constituted to achieve those ends.

It prohibits any attempt to influence public opinion on a matter that is the subject of public controversy. The most famous example of this has resulted in the banning of the Make Poverty History one-click advert in 2005, which was intended to highlight that a child dies every three seconds because of preventable poverty. The media ban ended up being adversely commented on the in the media and, in fact, generated significant coverage. These restrictions have hindered the activities of several organisations and have been challenged in the European Court of Human Rights for restricting freedom of expression.

Evaluate

– building on success – managing failure

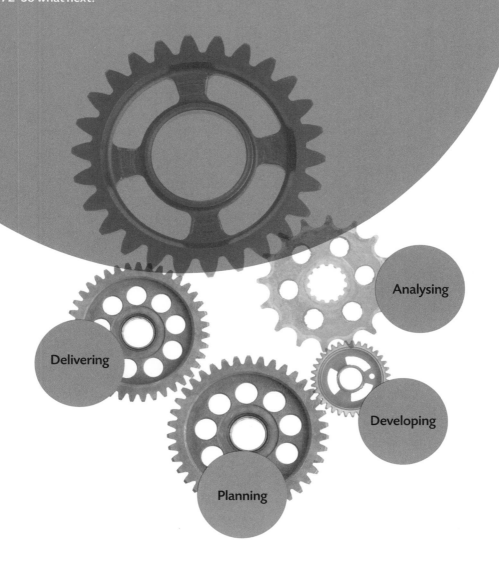

Analysing

Delivering

Developing

Planning

Contents

Building on success

Building on success
- You've won: now what?
- Sharing the credit
- Consider compromise?
- A lasting impact
- Partners in delivering change
- Attacks can be opportunities

Recognising failure
- Hindsight is a wonderful thing
- Lessons learned

Communicating success
- How did we do?

Organisational learning – building an effective campaign organisation
- Second time around

Anticipating future trends

If you have a clear aim and planned well your theory of change in advance you should have a very clear idea of the campaign's milestones and what will constitute success. While failure can be brutally clear, success is often more difficult to judge.

You've won: now what?

Your campaign has been successful but your work might not yet be over. Governments change, leaders move on, legislation can be changed or subverted, policy gets sidelined, people change their minds and habits, public attitudes and behaviour alter: all this can leave your gains high and dry. The price of success is, therefore, continual vigilance.

The fact you have needed to campaign to get to this point might suggest that there are powerful opponents to the campaign. They may be unlikely to want to give up and continue to try to undermine your success or redress the balance of change in a different way. There may be direct lobbying against your changes or attempts to undermine them. Further success can sometimes be preventing something happening or keeping the status quo. You also need to ensure that what you campaigned against is not slipped in via another route or mechanism.

Your organisation needs a plan for protecting the campaign's success. You also need to ensure that your organisation or campaign group is the one that gets consulted when any further work on the issue is undertaken.

Sharing the credit?

If you have been successful you need to think through who you need to attribute success to. Do ministers, MPs, company leaders, shareholders and so on need to be given credit for coming round to your point of view? Sharing the positive headlines with them because you have genuinely worked together is a good idea. Even if it has been a difficult a difficult relationship it's both wise and gracious to let them claim some of the credit too. It also allows for the option for you to work constructively with them as a partner in future work.

Sharing the credit can be difficult; your members, supporters or beneficiaries may worry about the campaign being co-opted. If the campaign has been oppositional, a seemingly sudden rapprochement may be misunderstood. It is important to ensure that those who support or benefit from the campaign are in step with what is happening, especially if a more lasting partnership is being offered.

'As with many rights issues, [maintaining this policy] is going to require consistent vigilance... almost a constant campaign.' Washington State Representative Ed Murray talking about legislation passed during the State's 2006 legislative session that banned discrimination based on sexual orientation.

Consider compromise?

Not all campaigns are complete victories. You may well have to be content with partial success. But is partial success better than none? If you compromise, what will you say to disappointed supporters who have campaigned alongside you with hopes that they would benefit or see success for others? And if you are not prepared to compromise, do you continue the campaign?

You may have to revisit your strategy. Would compromising be enough of a success, or do you need to explore a different track or campaign for another year to achieve success? Your strategy will only partly help with these difficult decisions – in the end you will have to make a judgement on the forces for and against you and further opportunities for change.

A lasting impact

Your task now is to ensure that your campaign achieves a lasting impact, making a real difference to people's lives. With success achieved, the more publicly you can get decision-makers to put their promises into practice, the less 'wriggle room' they will have.

One way to do this is to capitalise on the position you have established in the campaign as the key organisation that needs to be consulted about implementing the new policy or practice. If there has been a change in legislation you should be involved in advising on the follow-up regulations and practice guidance. Maintain relationships with the policy-makers and ensure that, as you move into implementation, you also develop new relationships with those tasked with taking the policy through to implementation; be aware of when responsibility shifts to bodies outside of government or to different parts of a company.

Assess whether you need to lobby government or implementing bodies to make sure that they make it a priority to promote the new policies and to find the resources to deliver them. This may not be an uphill battle – government departments may be very keen to have your backing and involvement at this stage, not merely because of your expertise but also because it bolsters their discussions across government about the priority of a policy they also want implemented. In interdepartmental power struggles a department may need to be able to point to active public support to ensure that the legislation does not sit on the shelf and resources are found for implementation.

You may be asked to publicly support the promotion of what you have campaigned for, perhaps appearing on platforms with ministers or company leaders. This is a very powerful position for a campaign to be in; take full advantage of it, unless you feel you will be seriously compromised in some way.

You've won: now what?
(continued)

Example

Early Support Programme

The Early Support Programme was established in 2002 following government commitments to ensure better early years support for disabled children were carried through and better support provided to parents by local authority services. The government agreed to the establishment of a delivery unit for the programme based outside of government in the voluntary and community sector with a joint management committee from central government, the voluntary and community sector and local government. The programme was funded through a £13 million fund established to deliver a transformation in the way parents with disabled children were supported at local level. This was achieved through training programmes and more co-ordinated support at local level and the programme ran over six years till 2008. Once the programme had proved its success after a major evaluation it was incorporated into the government's standard approach to early years and guidance was issued to all authorities.

Source: Lamb B. and Murdock A., Not a Curse to Live in Challenging Times?[1]

People's awareness and understanding is constantly shifting; behaviour may change as a result of your campaign but the effect may wear off. Until new habits of behaviour really take root you need to constantly and consistently reinforce your messages over long periods of time. Further success with one generation does not mean that the new behaviours are necessarily transmitted to the next. For example, campaigns around healthy eating are constantly coming up against new ways in which food is repackaged and sold, and changes in lifestyle that mitigate against the messages being received and acted on. This makes the focus on behaviour change through structuring decision making differently even more relevant as it holds out the prospect of sustaining changes without the same level of further interventions.

Do your supporters and beneficiaries know what the impact of the campaign's success will be on their lives, when it will happen and how many people will benefit? Provide as much information as you can – briefings and a website – ready to answer people's questions.

Partners in delivering change

You may be asked to provide the service that you have campaigned for. Providing a new service could affect the operation of all or part of your organisation which could result in significant changes for organisation as a whole. You need to carefully weigh up the potential opportunities of delivering services against the restrictions and implications that may bring.

In principle, VCOs should be safeguarding their independence; in practice, this can be a fine line to walk. It is a good idea to embed your relationships with the target to maintain influence; you could set up a joint 'implementation group' with the government department, public authority or company to see through a campaign gain. Planning the details of policy and guidance, or how delivery is going to work, puts you in a very powerful position. What gives you some leverage in the ongoing relationship is your potential to mobilise opinion if the change does not happen. However, you will have to weigh this up against the affect that potentially challenging and withdrawing from the relationship could have.

---

[1] Lamb B. and Murdock A. (2010) Not a Curse to Live in Challenging Times? Paper presented to the NCVO Researching the Voluntary Sector Conference. September, 2010.

Attacks can be opportunities

Having achieved success, you may find your organisation unexpectedly thrown onto the national stage. This may well provoke action from vested interests affected by your campaign, who want to reverse your changes or subvert or weaken the changes achieved.

Your proposals, or the implications of putting them into practice, may come under public attack. Such attacks generate increased public interest. Take advantage of the opportunity to explain your campaign's position and attempt to win new audiences over.

Attacks are often unfair; the media may misreport or deliberately distort your issue. Counter this by swinging the debate back to your frame of reference, and away from where your opponents are attempting to push it. You can list the myths and then, using your evidence base, counter them with referenced facts; enlist your allies to support this, especially if their support demonstrates widespread backing for your issue.

While attacks on your campaign – discrediting your claims or opposing the outcome – might be expected, you will not be able to predict all of them. Simply be ready to set out your case clearly and refute the attacks, usually point by point. Be careful that you do not inadvertently accept your critics' premise; continue to frame the issue in the way you feel is consistent with your overall messages and don't get drawn onto your opponent's ground. To recap on framing see page 76.

Try to treat critics as future potential allies – it can be more helpful to win them over rather than beat them into submission. Look for points of connection, not difference. Emphasising the principles behind your proposals you may have more chance of finding common ground. But be realistic: there may be only so much you can do in the short term to challenge those targeting you.

Recognising failure

Failure can be brutally clear – your amendment is rejected outright, your campaign does not resonate with public opinion, your great idea gains no traction with policy-makers who brush it aside as too complex or expensive.

There are degrees of failure; campaigning, like politics, is the art of the possible. You have three main options:

• Continue with the overall aim but adjust the strategy to take account of emerging issues: usually this will affect the timescale, and possibly scope of the aim.

• Adjust the campaign aim to what you now judge to be realistic and communicate this shift clearly to partners and supporters.

• Stop campaigning – either because the opposition is too strong compared with the forces you can mobilise or because your proposals have failed to stand up to public scrutiny or interest.

You cannot easily make judgements on any of these scenarios unless you have the yardstick of a clear theory of change and can evaluate your position in relation to your aim and objectives.

Clearly, pulling out of a campaign is a blow to morale for the organisation and its supporters. Learning from the failure, however, will help the organisation improve. Campaign failure may also damage your public reputation, especially if the campaign has come apart because it relied on poor analysis or implementation. On the one hand, if mistakes have been made it is better to admit them quickly – address them internally and with the targets of the campaign. On the other hand, if the judgement is that you have mounted an effective campaign but simply not been able to prevail, you may well have a strong platform for action at a later stage.

Working out why the campaign has not progressed will help you draw out learning and help you explain the situation to those who have supported the campaign. If you aren't keeping people informed it may be harder to set out why success is still possible in the future in other campaigns. Campaigns are rarely completely successes or failures; there will usually be something you can take back to supporters even if it is more about building your ability to campaign in future or small victories that can provide a launch pad for later efforts.

Hindsight is a wonderful thing
Campaigns usually fail for well-understood reasons. The main factor is often not having had enough focus at the right time.

You should think through the potential reasons for failure when planning you future campaigns or reviewing current ones.

Table: Lessons learned

What when wrong	Lessons to learn
The original analysis was over-optimistic about the level of support or the level of pressure that could be applied to decision-makers.	Test out the results of analysis and key messages early on in the campaign cycle to see how target audiences (sections of the public and decision makers) might react. Revise plans as necessary Conduct thorough stakeholder analysis and influence mapping to assess the most effective routes to influence the campaigns target audiences. Record campaign intelligence systematically both at the start and as the campaign progresses.
Solutions were unclear, unaffordable or could not easily be implemented.	Use tools such as problem and solution trees to breakdown the route causes of an issue and pinpoint achievable solutions. Test these with key target audiences are they palatable and achievable? Do you need to readjust your asks?
The campaign was well informed but, given the scale of the challenge, how long change would take was underestimated.	Be realistic about how long it takes to build support for change – build this into your theory of change. Does achieving change involve running a series of campaigns or several different types of campaigns (behaviour change and legislative) to get there?
Opposition was far stronger or more wide ranging than expected.	Conduct PEST and SWOT analysis to map out the environment your campaign will face. Conduct forcefield analysis to analyse the forces for and against the campaign – seek ways to address the negatives. Conduct stakeholder analysis to determine who will be affected by the campaign. Develop strategies to target both allies and opponents of the campaign.

Communicating success

Recognising failure (continued)

Some of the issues may be unknowable before you actually start to undertake the campaign, but you should at least be clear that this is the case. You can test the waters with your target audience(s) and have a planned escalation of the campaign if there are too many uncertainties. Also think about exit strategies for the campaign and review at key milestones to see if you are achieving your aim and objectives or if you are coming up against obstacles that cannot be easily overcome. While having audacious aims can be inspiring, routinely not achieving them does more than disappoint – it de-motivates supporters and can be misleading so make sure you are planning for realistic, if stretching, targets.

It is possible to run an excellent campaign and still not succeed. For example, it may be that the policy you were campaigning against was clarified which left your concerns unfounded. If so, then at least your campaign will have helped to clarify the issue and your interest in the area may have provoked adjustments you may not be immediately aware of.

Trying to bring about change is not an exact science. You may have good ideas that fail to gain support at that particular time. If so the learning would be you need to do more to change the overall context of the debate before your original campaign can be successful.

A campaign failure should be a spur to learning more about the constraints and opportunities in the external environment and also about scope for improvement within the organisation.

Organisations need a culture of honesty and trust so that people have the confidence to admit mistakes and learn from them. The high public profile of campaigning and its impact on reputation can make this difficult for staff and boards of trustees alike.

Campaigns will make mistakes, but should not to keep making the same mistakes. The key is being open about it within the organisation and learning from it for the future.

Your campaign may have been brilliant but unless you are telling the world its impact may not last. Celebrating the success is not only good practice it may be vital for attracting further support for your issue, holding onto existing support and ensuring the change you achieved is long lasting.

A successful campaign does not mean an end to your relationship with your supporters and funders; there may still be work to be done. Keep a sharp eye out for shifting support within the institution you targeted.

Is there political will to implement the policy you have campaigned for? The statute book is littered with legislation that is probably never going to be properly put into effect; it has conveniently been forgotten. You may need to remind decision-makers that you are still focused on the issue and ready to mobilise supporters again if the change is not seen through.

---

[2] See: Lamb B. (2006) Reporting on Impact. London: RNID.

[3] For three recent SROI approaches see: Wood C. and Leighton D. (2010) Measuring Social Value: The gap between policy and practice. London: Demos; Lawlor E., Nicholls J. and Neitzert E. (2009) Seven Principles for Measuring what Watters. London: New Economics Foundation; Cabinet Office, Office of the Third Sector (2009) A Guide to Social Return on Investment. London: Cabinet Office. Available online at www.thesroinetwork.org (accessed October 2010).

How did we do?

You will also need to communicate the impact of your campaign to stakeholders – the wider organisation, your beneficiaries, supporters, funders. How you do this may involve presenting your achievement in different ways for different audiences.

You may want to communicate the achievements of a complete campaign or just record the journey so far. How you do this can be as simple or as complex as your resources allow.

A simple way of reporting on your impact – assuming that the campaign still has some way to run – is to publish a plan stating:
• Aims for the year ahead in outcomes and desired impact.
• Activities you are planning.

At the end of the year you should report on your progress; everyone can see the impact you have had.[2] Gradually there will be a clear sense of progression towards the end aim. This general level of reporting works well for annual reports.

For individual campaigns you may want something that is focused on the needs of specific groups, for example, supporters who were most involved in the campaign, or funders. You may also want something that highlights lessons learned for your organisation's own internal use.

Social return on investment approach (SROI) is increasingly regarded as a 'gold standard'[3] for effectiveness in the eyes of funders or government. It is difficult, however, to apply SROI models to all campaigns and may well not be what a campaign supporter, as opposed to a funder, needs to hear.

As long as you can compare activities with outcomes – for example, 'we put down amendments to the Bill, which changed it; this will lead to enhanced rights' – you are showing that your campaign is on track. See more on building evaluation frameworks page 60.

Table: Example of a simple 'distance-travelled' reporting

Aim last year	Activities	Outcomes	Impact
	... research report, media coverage, meeting with decision makers...	... influence decision maker on the decision, build the capacity of beneficiaries to campaign, build links with key partners....	.. people's health improved by having access to clear information about food, decrease in incidence of drunk driving lives are saved etc....

Building an effective campaigning organisation

To be an effective campaigning organisation or group it is important to step back and look at the overall capacity needed to achieve the aim you have set. By focusing on the essential inputs and capacity to campaign in a more systematic way, you are going to give yourself more chance of success.

Organisational learning

The most successful campaigning organisations create a learning culture. Unless you build learning into your procedures – making it part of 'the way we do things around here' – you, or those who work with you, will make the same mistakes all over again. Ensuring a vibrant and learning culture will be both more effective and more enjoyable to work in. Look at the various elements of your inputs and resources to ensure that you have the right skills, processes, resources and leadership in place to ensure success.

The more you can demonstrate a learning culture that is also good at assessing risk, the better you will be able to justify taking some risks. This will help senior management and your board understand more about what campaigns entail and will create spaces for you to develop your work.

Effective campaigning organisations understand the context in which they operate and appreciate how they can achieve impact by gathering intelligence systematically. Building up and recording systematically well-resourced campaign intelligence will enable you to gather and keep up to date information that is relevant and necessary to guide your campaigning work and make your life easier. You will need to develop ways to build up your own campaign intelligence resource in a way that suits your organisation and is shaped to your own needs, rather than relying on information sources that aren't tailored to your requirements. See more about campaign intelligence page 91.

Second time around

Just because a campaign plan worked last time, don't assume it will work again. Things may well have changed – use your theory of change model on each situation as it arises and assess the external environment.

Don't always go for the easy wins; look for the big win and the smaller ones along the way that lead to this. Using the tools in this guide will help you constantly revaluate your practice. The more you can build teams that are prepared to work in this way, the stronger you will be individually and as a group.

Sometimes it is also good to have outside feedback and criticism (both positive and negative). This can be done formally – setting up mentoring programmes within or outside the team – or through more informal arrangements such as mutual support with colleagues in other organisations that have similar roles.

Following this approach will ensure that you are also looking at what makes your organisation more effective at campaigning and ensuring you have the resources and capacity to underpin your campaigning activity in the future.

Anticipating future trends

All organisations or campaign groups can increase their chances of success by spending some time analysing and understanding the potential impact of changes in the external environment on your work.

Whatever plans are made, changes in the external environment will have a knock-on effect – reduced funding, changing government priorities, shifting social attitudes, new technologies, and so on. Time spent understanding likely future trends and external pressures that could influence your organisation and its work can make you more effective as you will be more prepared to take advantage of opportunities or anticipate challenges.

Future foresight work can focus on both the organisation and the issue(s) you are working in.

Future foresight

One simple way of looking at drivers is to list what you think are some of the key trends that will impact on your area of work and evaluate their importance to what you are trying to do. Looked at them will help you address any implications of those trends or drivers.

You can identify drivers that will influence the development of campaigning generally in your organisation as well as specific areas related to your issue. It will be useful to regularly scan areas of interest with the process known as horizon scanning.

Horizon scanning

1. Scoping: setting out the broad parameters of interest. Scope of the area you want to examine.

2. Information: gather information, from a wide range of sources, about current and future trends that might affect the issue. Think broadly at this stage.

3. Look for emerging patterns: you will begin to see patterns in the information gathered during stage 2, which will suggest emerging trends or developments.

4. Watch trends: start to track some of the most important emerging trends to get a clearer picture of how these are developing.

5. Analyse: explore what the emerging trends mean for development of the campaign and its relationship with the organisation as a whole.

6. Agree the response: decide if the response needs to be part of your strategy now or integrated into future planning.

Source: Third Sector Foresight, NCVO

Anticipating future trends
(continued)

Drivers
How important are the trends that you have identified (the drivers) going to be for your own campaign over the coming five years? Some trends may be marginal, some crucial. You can grade them – low, medium or high priority – to think about what response your organisation might have to make. Doing this will give you a picture of the future context for your campaigning and help you identify actions to take to maximise opportunities and minimise risks and challenges. It can be helpful to think about three kinds of opportunity:

• **Improve** – what opportunity do the drivers give you to improve what you do?

• **Innovate** – what opportunity do the drivers give you to do different things?

• **Improvise** – what opportunity do the drivers give you to manage risks and threats?[4]

You could take this analysis further by building scenarios around several drivers and plotting what response you may need to make. This could be specifically on the subject of your campaign or more generally on the context in which you are campaigning, such as development of beneficiary activism, use of social media and so on.

Stakeholders are people who have an interest in or affected by what you do. Don't forget to consider how these drivers may impact on them and how this may then influence your relationships. Consider your workforce, both paid and voluntary, your beneficiaries or users, your funders, other players such as your competitors and collaborators as well as the media and policy-makers.

Diagram: *Working out how key drivers affect your campaign*[5]

	How could key drivers affect your campaign?					
	EXTERNAL					INTERNAL
Your key drivers	Users and their needs	Funders and their priorities	Relationships and influence (media, policymakers and other players etc)	Workforce (paid, volunteer and trustees)	Your organisation's work (services and activities)	Governance including accountability and evaluation
Driver one						
Driver two						
Etc						

Scenario planning

You can use scenario planning to assess the importance of key drivers and enable you to explore possible scenarios in more detail. You can plot these scenarios on a matrix to prompt further analysis[6] into their likeliness or unpredictability and the impact they could have (high and low).

One of the key uses of this scenario planning is to look at what is likely to happen and where your campaigning strategy and organisation needs to develop over the next five years.

Once you have a better understanding of how some of the key drivers may affect your work over the coming years the next step is to turn this information into choices about future action. Analysis could leave you with some of the following options for your campaign:

- The gains look secure and we only need to monitor progress.
- The gains need further development with target such as developing guidelines, pilot projects or services being embedded.
- The gains look insecure and likely to change because of opposition or poor levels of commitment.
- The gains look insecure but it's difficult to see what further action could be taken.

Future foresight work can be built into your existing research and monitoring work for a campaign. You could also seek to embed it as part of the change you are campaigning for – for example government research or the target setting up publicly available monitoring mechanisms.

Information and analysis on future intelligence combined with that from campaign monitoring will also allow you to make more informed decisions about your work – such whether to move on to different issues, exit from the campaign, or keep an eye on developments.

Future foresight is not the same as crystal ball gazing – it can be fun to try and predict the future but it will be a much more useful exercise if you focus on identifying key trends that could affect your work and make informed decisions about how to respond.

---

[4] NCVO Foresight team has a comprehensive list of drivers at www.3s4.org.uk/drivers

[5] Adapted from Third Sector Foresight http://www.3s4.org.uk/

[6] Adapted from NCVO Future Focus: What will campaigning be like in five years time? (2009) Third Sector Foresight.

So what next?

As we have seen as key themes throughout this guide, we need to retain the vibrant dissatisfaction of campaigners, increase meaningful involvement of beneficiaries and communities in our work and meld this with the best thinking about how to run effective campaigns.

Having reached the end of the campaign it may feel that you are back at the beginning of the campaign cycle. You will have learnt much by now and the world and your issue will also have moved on. You may be back at a similar point in the process but you will be looking down with an enhanced perspective gained from the campaign and looking at a changed landscape and a developed or resolved issue.

While you do not have to agree with Malcolm Gladwell or Richard Sennett that to become a genius at something takes 10,000 hours of practice,[1] by building in the time to reflect on the learning from your campaign and the tools in this guide you will be able to both run more effective campaigns and be better prepared for whatever the future holds. It may only take a small group of committed people to change their world, but the better organised and insightful they are the quicker the world will change for the better.

[1] Gladwell, M. (2008) Outliers. The Story of Success. Little, Brown and Company. Sennett, R. (2008) The Craftsman. Allen Lane. Both use the common measure that the key to success in any discipline is to have practised the tasks involved for around 10,000 hours.

Quick finds

How do I develop aims and objectives?
See Setting the campaign aim page 52, Setting objectives page 87.

How do I work out targets of the campaign?
See Targets and influences section page 84, Stakeholder analysis page 36.

How to I build meaningful beneficiary involvement to our campaigning?
See Involving people page 40, Deciding who to involve page 41, Beneficiary involvement pages 42 and 134, Bringing the story to life page 146, Tips in how to involve people page 136, Example Campaign action groups page 137.

How do I get funding for my campaign?
See online campaigning and fundraising page 68, Trusts and foundations page 71, Pro bono: a different way of giving page 72.

How do I work out any potential risks of running the campaign?
See Managing and mitigating risk page 89.

How do I work out what are the right tactics to use?
Campaign activities page 119, Example What is the most effective route to your target? page 102, How radical do you need to be? Page 121, Direct action 124, Understanding your audience page 143.

What exactly are resources, activities, outputs, outcomes and impact?
See Theory of change – how to plan for impact page 53.

What types of evaluation models are there?
See Table: Evaluation models page 62, In more detail page 64.

What sources of research are out there to tap into?
See Tapping into government research and knowledge page 19, Freedom of Information requests page 20, Other sources of evidence page 21.

What tools are there to turn problems into solutions?
See Tools for policy development page 26, Problem and solution trees page 27 Fishboning page 28.

How do I map out all groups that are affected by our issue or have an influence over it?
See Stakeholder analysis page 36.

How do I try to change people's opinions or frame of reference on our how they see the issue?
See Facts are not enough page 77, Placing the right frame on the issue page 79, Connecting with your audience page 80, Presenting your issue page 81.

We have all this useful information on the campaign how do we store it?
See campaign intelligence page 91, Building an effective campaigning organisation page 168.

What exactly should we monitor?
See What you can evaluate page 60, Measures page 61, Evidence page 65, Avoiding the pitfalls page 66.

How do we decide this is the right campaign to run?
See Analysing the external environment page 32, SWOT, PEST and Forcefield analysis pages 32-34, How to decided if a campaign is right for you page 39, Combining campaigning and providing services page 43.

What legal issues do I need to be aware of?
See Keeping legal page 157, Charity law – some key points page 139, Direct Action page 124.

How do we get inside the minds of our targets?
See Discourse analysis page 82, Influence mapping page 85, Audiences 143, Example Changing behaviours page 112, Connecting with your audience page 80.

Glossary

Aim a definition of the overall purpose of your campaign. This gives you an idea of where you are going and what you want to achieve. It should be SMART.

Activities what gets done in order to deliver your campaign, the tasks you do to make your campaign outputs happen – planning, recruiting supporters, campaign actions etc.

Analysis understanding the issue and examining the external and internal environment that affects your campaign.

Attribution being able to point to a specific change was brought about as a direct consequence of the actions in your campaign. Direct attribution can be hard to demonstrate in campaigning.

Beneficiaries those whose lives will be improved by the successful achievement of your campaign aim.

Many people object to the term beneficiaries because it can imply that beneficiaries are passive subjects, rather than active agents, rather than active agents of change. There are a range of alternative terms from users, stakeholders, partner, rights holder.... However few are applicable in all contexts and all have pros and cons. While recognising its short comings we use the term beneficiaries in this guide because it's short and simple.

Capacity is the time and resources to do something.

Campaign actions are the activities which are undertaken in support of your campaign – often what you may ask your supporters to do for the campaign.

Your campaign actions should sit comfortably together and fit with the over all concept of the campaign.

Campaign concept is the big picture or vision for your campaign. Through this you will be able to develop conversations with your audiences and motivate them to take action. It will exemplify and bring your issue to life and bring coherence to your campaign and how you communicate it.

Campaigns are organised actions around a specific issue seeking to bring about changes in policy or behaviours of institutions and/or specific groups. The word campaign can be used to describe election campaigns and fundraising campaigns, but in the context of this guide we are looking at achieving social, political, economic change.

Campaigning is the mobil¬ising of forces by organisations or individuals to influence others in order to affect an identified and desired social, economic, environ¬mental or political change. You might call it influencing, voice, advocacy or campaigning, but all these activities are about creating change. But what is important is campaigns are created to produce a change. The impact is the real change created by a campaign – the difference it makes to people's lives or environment.

Campaign cycle a model/framework for visualising and managing the different processes in the lifetime of an issue campaign.

Civil society is a contested term NCVO's working definition is that it is about people acting together, independently of the state or the market to make a positive difference to their loved and or the lives of others. Within civil society there is a range of organisations that are a vehicle for collective action – including VCOs, co-operatives, housing associations, trade unions and political parties.

CSOs Civil Society Organisations.

Clicktivism is a form of digital activism that usually requires a small online action such as signing up on a website, adding your name to an e-petition or forwarding an email. Subject to large debate recently the term can have negative connotations about the impact of such activity.

Contingency planning is planning devised for a specific situation when things could go wrong. In the case of your campaign you should think about what the potential risks could be and what potentially could go wrong in your campaign and your contingency plan should look at how you would respond and what actions you would take should something go wrong.

Crowd sourcing is the outsourcing of tasks to larger numbers of people, a crowd, through an open call to action. (Adapted from Wikipedia definition.)

Direct action can be difficult to define and holds different meanings depending on your position, but is generally activity undertaken by individuals, groups, or governments to achieve political goals outside of normal social/political channels. Direct action can include nonviolent and violent activities which target persons, groups, or property. It can take the form of marches, boycotts, stunts, blockades, destruction of property and violence against a target.

Drivers are major forces of key trends that will impact on your area of work – either positively or negatively.

Evaluation using monitoring information to assess the performance of your campaign, the impact it has made.

Framing the way your issue is packaged and presented. Our own framework of values and beliefs structures the way we see the world and what 'facts' we find convincing or don't.

Indicators a sign which shows whether something is happening, evidence to measure progress towards objectives. Indicators should be measurable, representative, feasible and reliable.

Impact the difference your campaign makes. The impact is the real change created by a campaign – the difference it makes to people's lives or the environment.

Impact chain is model for planning change that breaks down the process of a change into different stages and in doing so makes a distinction between different levels of change.

Impact reporting the process of reporting back to your organisation or funder on the impact you have made.

Influence mapping is a process of identifying targets, individuals and groups, with the power to affect decision making. Looking in detail at their motives, positions and channels through which to influence them.

Inputs resources used in delivering the campaign – people, money, office space etc.

Key messages the core messages that you will use to get your campaign aim across, derived from your campaign concept.

Logic model a basic planning tool that looks at the process of identifying resources through activities, outputs, outcomes and impact as logical change of event to form a project plan.

Mission the reason an organisation exists; a summary of the overall difference it wants to make, to who or what, and where; the particular contribution the organisation hopes to make to its vision.

Monitoring the ongoing process of gathering information on the progress of the campaign towards the achievement of its objectives

Objectives are defined milestones that guide you towards achieving your campaign aim. Setting objectives involves making explicit your thinking to reach the aim and helps you to both target your campaigning and yardstick to asses your progress.

Outcomes the benefits or changes that happen as a result of your campaign.

Some people use outcomes and impact interchangeably others don't.

Outputs the campaign actions you undertake to achieve the desire change

or what is generated by your activities – marches, meetings with ministers etc.

PEST analysis is a planning tool to help explore the external environment under a series of headings – political, economic, social and technological.

Public campaigning a process of creating and mobilising demonstrable public concern, in order to influence wider public behaviour or the policies and practices of public and private bodies.

Public policy how government addresses (or doesn't address) issues that affect public, this could be through regulation, legislation, funding priorities or other actions.

Policy development process through which an organisation identifies and articulates the change it wants to see in the world.

Glossary

Resources everything a campaign or organisation draws on to carry out its activities. These will include the people, equipment, money and services you need. They may also include intangible elements, such as time, morale and knowledge. Also referred to as inputs.

Risk analysis a crucial part of the planning process involves assessing and analysing the kind of risks that may occur along the course of the campaign or result of the campaign so as to make informed decisions about hoe to handle and mitigate them.

Segmentation identifying subsections of your audience to target.

SMART objectives are a formula for setting objectives – Specific, Measurable, Achievable, Realistic and Time-related.

Social return on investment (SROI) essentially this involves allocating a financial value to a social outcome and comparing this with current practice or future investment. Campaigners have applied SROI methods to demonstrate that an intervention will deliver greater social benefits than continuing with the current practice.

SWOT analysis an assessment technique looking at strengths, weaknesses, opportunities and threats to help inform strategic decisions.

Stakeholder person, group or organisation that has an interest in your work or might be affected by your actions – this could include your beneficiaries, funders, supporters.

Stakeholder analysis the process of identifying who is affected by your issue and prioritise voices.

Strategy provides an effective route for you to achieve your aim. A campaign strategy should include selecting a solution, setting an aim, framing your campaign and identifying routes to influence and steps to influence your targets.

SWOT analysis a planning tool used to asses strengths, weaknesses, opportunities and threats.

Target audience(s) the individual or groups who needs to change in order for the campaign aim to be achieved.

Theory of change is an extension of basic planning tool. It defines all building blocks required to bring about a given long-term aim but puts more emphasis onto drawing out what particular activities will deliver the impact you are seeking to make.

VCO voluntary and community organisations.

VCS voluntary and community sector.

Vision the ideal state a project or organisation wants the world to be in. What the world will look like if the project or organisation is successful in achieving its mission.

Work plan your plan of activities for the campaign outlining who will be doing what and when.

Further reading

General reading on campaigning and the sector

There has been a growth industry in analysing both the changing face of political and civic involvement, the voluntary and community sector role generally and how campaigning fits within it. Below is a selected reading list of those that have informed the overall approach to this guide.

Atkinson, K. (nd) The political campaigning role of registered charities and 'campaigning organisations': a submission to the Inquiry into the Future of Civil Society in the UK and Ireland

Brazier, A., Kalitowski, S., & Rosenblatt, G. (2007). Law in the making: A discussion paper. London: Hansard Society

Bubb, S. (2006). Choice and Voice: The Unique Role of the Third Sector. ACEVO

Clark, J., Dobbs, J., Kane, D., & Wilding, K. (2009). The State and the Voluntary Sector Recent trends in government funding and public service delivery. London: The National Council for Voluntary Organisations (NCVO).

Etherington, S. Cass Lecture. Building a Better Society. 3rd November 2010.

Fox, R, Gibbons, V. and Korris, M. (2010) Audit of Political Engagement 7. The 2010 Report with a focus on MPs and Parliament. Hansard Society.

Future Focus: What will campaigning be like in 5 years' time? (2009) NCVO.

Grant, W. (1995) Pressure Groups and British Politics, Politics and Democracy In Britain. 2nd Edition.

Healey, J., Gill, M., & McHugh, D. (2005). MPs and politics in our time. Dod's Parliamentary Communications

Kendall, J. (Ed.). (2005). The third sector and the policy process in the UK: ingredients in a hyper-active horizontal policy environment. London: TSEP Network

Kingham, T., and J. Coe. (2005) The good campaigns guide: campaigning for impact NCVO.

Knight, B., & Robson, S. (nd) [paper] The Value and Independence of the Voluntary Sector

Lamb, B. (2005) Adding value to public services: London: RNID

Lattimer, M. (2000) The campaigning handbook. 2nd ed. Directory of Social Change

Leat, D. (2007) Just Change Strategies for Increasing Philanthropic Impact. Association of Charitable Foundations

Lloyd, J. (2001) The Protest Ethic, Demos London.

McNeill, K. (2007) "The pressure's on: the lessons from how NGOs engage with the public." Participation Nation. Reconnecting Citizens to the Public Realm. Creasy, S (ed) Involve

McHugh, D, Parvin, P. (2005) Neglecting Democracy. Hansard Society

Machiavelli The Prince. Penguin Books. Translated George Bull, 1975 ed.

NFP Synergy poll (2007) quoted in Parvin, P. Friend or Foe? (2007) Lobbying in British Democracy, Hansard Society

Office of the Third Sector The future role of the third sector in social and economic regeneration: final report. (2007)

Parvin, P. (2007). Friend or Foe? Lobbying in British Democracy: A discussion paper. London: Hansard Society

Power Inquiry. Power to the People. The report of power, an independent inquiry into Britain's democracy. (2006)York: Joseph Rowntree Foundation.

Raymond, D. (2010) How to Campaign Like Obama. Fairsay.

Rose, C. (2005) How to win campaigns Earthscan

Rosenblatt, G. (2006), A Year in the Life: From member of public to Member of Parliament, Hansard Society, London

Survey of Campaigning Activities and Charity Commission guidance (CC9). (2006). Commissioned by: People and Planet and the Sheila McKechnie Foundation

UK Workforce Hub (2009) National Occupational Standards for Campaigning, developed by Pye Tait Consulting

Further reading for each sections

Analyse the Issue

The most useful work around the interface between policy and research issues have been developed by the Overseas Development Institute, Hovland and Pollard and Court are good places to start but also explore their website at http://www.odi.org.uk/ which has a wealth of material on policy development the relevance of which goes well beyond development issues. While a little old now Young and Quinn (2002) covered most of the bases in thinking through the relationship between research and policy and they typology's still form the underpinning for much that has been developed since.

On participation the best starting place are Involves materials – Andersson (2010) is a good starting point on current thinking. The Cabinet Office also has material both for an insight about how sophisticated Government is becoming on consultation methodologies but also to pick up some useful tools.

For more on commissioning research the NCVO In Focus guide is the best place to start and work you way outwards to Start and Hoveland (2004).

Andersson, E., Burall, S., & Fennell, E. (2010). Talking for a Change: A Distributed Dialogue Approach to Complex Issues. London: Involve.

Better Together Improving Consultation with the Third Sector, (2008) Cabinet Office

Brock K, Cornwall A, Gaventa J, (2001) 'Knowledge and political spaces in the framing of poverty policy', Institute of Development Studies Working Paper October

Cabinet Office (2008) Better Together Improving Consultation with the Third Sector

Cairns, Hutchison and Aiken (2010) 'It is not what we do, it is how we do it' managing the tension between service delivery and advocacy., Voluntary Sector Review Vol 1, No 2

Court, J., Hovland, I. and Young, J. (2004) Bridging Research and Policy in International Development: Evidence and the Change Process, ITDG.

Coe, J. and Kingham, T. Tips on good practice in campaigning, NCVO.

Communities and Local Government's Departmental Annual Report 2008. House of Commons: Stationery Office

Crutchfield, L & McLeod-Grant, H. (2008) Forces for Good: Six Practices of High Impact Non Profits

Davies, P. (2004) Is Evidence-Based Government Possible? Jerry Lee Lecture, presented at the 4th annual Campbell Collaboration Colloquium, Washington DC.

Hovland, I. (2005) Successful Communication: A Toolkit for Researchers and Civil Society Organisations. London: Overseas Development Institute

Jones, N., & Walsh, C. (2008) Background Note: Policy briefs as a communication tool for development research. London: Overseas Development Institute

Making Policy that Matters (2005) National Government Office

NCVO In Focus Making sense of the external environment (2009)

NCVO, In Focus Guide, Commissioning Research (2010)

NCVO In Focus Guide Making sense of the external environment

Mulgan, G. (2003) Government, knowledge and the business of policy-making, Prime Minister's Strategy Unit, Conference paper for Facing the Future conference Canberra available at www.odi.org.uk

Perkin, E. and Court, J. (2005) Networks and Policy Processes in

International Development: a literature review. Overseas Development Institute

People and Participation. How to put citizens at the heart of decision-making. (2005) [Brochure] Involve, London.

Pollard, A., & Court, J. (2005) How Civil Society Organisations Use Evidence to Influence Policy Processes: A literature review. London: Overseas Development Institute

Public Administration Select Committee Public Services and the Third Sector: Rhetoric and Reality Eleventh Report of Session 2007–08, House of Commons.

Stachowiak, S. Pathways for Change: 6 Theories about How Policy Change Happens, Organizational Research Services.

Start, D., & Hovland, I. (2004) Tools for Policy Impact: A Handbook for Researchers, Overseas Development Institute.

Stone, D. Policy Paradox: (2002) The art of political decision making. New York: W.W.Norton & Co.

The Policy Project. (1999). Networking for Policy Change: An Advocacy Training Manual. Washington, DC: The Policy Project.

Rarer Cancers Forum (2008) Exceptional England: An investigation of the role of Primary Care Trusts in making cancer medicines available through exceptional cases processes (Canterbury, Rarer Cancers Forum). Available at: http://www.rarercancers.org.uk/news/archive/winter_2008_12_03/exceptional_england_new_report_from_rarer_cancers_forum

Sumner, A., Ishmael-Perkins, N., & Lindstrom, J. (2009). Making Science of Influencing: Assessing the Impact of Development Research. Brighton: Institute of Development Studies

Sutcliffe, S., & Court, J. (2006). Toolkit for Progressive Policymakers in Developing Countries. London: Overseas Development Institute.

Viewfinder, Cabinet Office, Collection of the main methods of public consultation, again primarily focused on officials in Government. www.policyhub.gov.uk/

Voicing your right to know: A guide to using Freedom of Information in campaigning, NVCO. (2010) available at http://www.ncvo-vol.org.uk/yourrighttoknow

Young, J. and Mendizabal, E. (2009) Helping researchers become policy entrepreneurs. How to develop engagement strategies for evidence-based policy-making. ODI Briefing Paper 53

Warburton, D., Wilson, R., & Rainbow, E. Making a Difference: A guide to evaluating public participation in central government. London: Involve

Young, E. and Quinn, L. (2002) Writing Effective Public Policy Papers A Guide for Policy Advisers in Central and Eastern Europe. Budapest. LGI documents

Further reading

Developing a strategy for change

Understanding power

On power the central reference point is John Gaventas at IDS by following this through it will take you to some of the broader debates. Beetham et el (2008) provides a really helpful overview that links the discussion of power back into current institutional issues while Mayne, and Coe (2010) give a comprehensive and useful overview that locates the issues within a voluntary and community sector framework.

Beetham, D., Blick, A. Margetts, H., & Weir, S. (2008) Power and Participation in Modern Britain. by Democratic Audit for the Carnegie UK Trust Democracy and Civil Society programme

Bachrach, Peter and Morton S. Baratz. (1962) "Two Faces of Power," American, Political Science Review 56(4)

Eyben, R., Harris, C., & Pettit, J. (2006). Introduction: Exploring Power for Change. IDS Bulletin Vol 37 (6), 1-10

FENTON Communications. (2009). Now Hear This: The 9 Laws of Successful Advocacy, New York

Gaventa, J. (2006). Finding the Spaces for Change: A Power Analysis. IDS Bulletin Vol 37 (6), 23-33.

Gaventa, J., (2007) 'Levels, Spaces and Forms of Power: Analysing opportunities for change' in Berenskoeeter and Williams, eds., Power in World Politics, Routledge

Lukes, S. (2005) Power a Radical Analysis, 2nd Edition, Palgrave, London

Mayne, R, Coe, J. (2010) Power and Social Change, NCVO

Making Change Happen: Concepts for Revisioning Power for Justice, Equality and Peace. Washington, DC: Just Associates

Mulgan, G. (2005) People and participation: how to put citizens at the heart of decision-making. London: Involve. Available at www.involve.org.uk

http://www.powercube.net/ powercube and supporting materials.

Power to the People (2006) The report of an Independent Inquiry into Britain's Democracy, Joseph Rowntree Reform Trust.

VeneKlasen, L. and Miller, V. (2002) A New Weave of People, Power and Politics: the Action Guide for Advocacy and Citizen Participation, Oklahoma: World Neighbours

VeneKlasen, L., & Miller, V. (2002). Causes, consequences, and solutions. PLA Notes, 43

VeneKlasen, L., & Miller, V. (2002). Power and empowerment. PLA Notes, 43, 39-41

Strategy and evaluation

Stachowiak's typology of different approaches to change is worth exploring in full, especially if you are going to follow a TOC model.

As we have seen strategy and evaluation are intimately linked and much of work in this area has been driven mainly through the development of theory of change approaches in the North American context. If you want to follow up these approaches the best place to start is with Coffman's work, ideally in chronological order so you can see how the thinking around linking to TOC to evaluation has developed, then consult Guthrie et el. That explores the different approaches that have been developed using theory of change. For a practical approach that will give you a number of models and tools then go to Reiseman et el, and the Organisational Services Material. For further approaches Innovation Network has collected a fairly comprehensive range of approaches to evaluation. Chapman, J., & Wameyo, A. Paper is helpful and still influential looking at how often it's referenced.

If you want to look at some of the more general theories around evaluation

from a different perspective Collins (2005) is helpful in translating from a business perspective which has been applied to non profits in the USA and is broader than just evaluation and not campaign focused but helpful in thinking about what makes organisations do better and all has application to campaigning issues.

For reporting start with Wood and & Leighton for Demos which strongly promotes an SROI approach but also helpfully reviews others.

A Guide to Social Return on Investment (2009) [Brochure] Cabinet Office.

ActKnowledge and the Aspen Institute Roundtable (2003) SCOPE: How Much Should a Good Theory Account For?

Alinsky, S. Rules for Radicals, Vintage Books, New York

Anderson, A. A. (2004) Theory of Change as a Tool for Strategic Planning: A Report on Early Experiences. New York: The Aspen Institute Roundtable on Community Change

Breeze, B. (2006) UK Philanthropy's Greatest Achievements a research based assessment on philanthropic success, Institute of Philanthropy

Broach, S. Coleman, B. and Franklin, L. (2009) Winning a new priority for disabled children: the every disabled child matters campaign Steve Broach, Ben Coleman and Louise Franklin. J. Public Affairs 9: 1–6

Burns, S., Graham, K., & MacKeith, J. (2006). The Outcomes Star. London: The London Housing Foundation available at www.lhf.org.uk

Campbell, M., & Coffman, J. (2009). Tools to Support Public Policy Grantmaking. commissioned by The James Irvine Foundation www.irvine.org.

Center for Nonprofit Strategies. (2005) Advocacy for Impact: lessons from six successful campaigns. Commissioned by: Global Interdependence Initiative a Program of the Aspen Institute

Chapman, J., & Wameyo, A. (2001). Monitoring and Evaluating Advocacy: a scoping study, ActionAid.

Coffman, J. (2002) Public Communication Evaluation: An Environmental Scan of Challenges, Criticisms, Practice, and Opportunities. Prepared for the Communications Consortium Media Center, Cambridge, Harvard Family Research Project available at www.hfrp. org.

Coffman, J. (2003). Lessons in evaluating communications campaigns: Five case studies. Cambridge, MA: Harvard Family Research Project

Coffman, J. (2008). Foundations and Public Policy Grantmaking. Commissioned by the James Irvine foundation www. irvine.org

Coffman, J. (2009). A User's Guide to Advocacy Evaluation Planning. Cambridge, MA: Harvard Family Research Project

Collins, J. (2005). Good to Great and the Social Sectors: A Monograph to Accompany "Good to Great". [Electronic version] Random House Books.

Cottingham, M. (Ed.). (2009). Seven principles for measuring what matters: A guide to effective public policy-making

Cupitt, S. (Ed.) (2009) A guide to Social Return on Investment. This guide was produced by Society Media, www. societymedia.co.uk

DeMilto, L. (2007) Evaluating Communication Campaigns, Research and Evaluation Conference

Eikenberry, A.M. (2009) The Hidden Costs of Cause Marketing, Stanford Social Innovation Review Summer

Ellis, J. (2007) Building on Success: How to cope when you achieve your campaign goal, NCVO

Egbert, M., & Hoechstetter, S. (2006) Mission Possible: Evaluating Advocacy Grants. Foundation News and Commentary www.foundationnews.org.

Flatt, K. (2005) Ten campaigning tips for lobbying MPs, London, nfpSynergy.

Gould, D. (2004). Writing a Media Analysis: Prepared for the Communications Consortium Media Center, Washington

Griffiths, M., (2009). ACF Guide: How charitable trusts can support campaigning activity, London, Association of Charitable Foundations

Guthrie, K., Louie, J., David, T., & Foster, C. (2005) The Challenge of Assessing Policy and advocacy activities: Strategies for a Prospective Evaluation Approach, funded by and prepared for The California Endowment. San Francisco: Blueprint Research & Design, Inc.

Guthrie, K., Louie, J., David, T., & Foster, C. (2006) The Challenge of Assessing Policy and Advocacy Activities: PART II—Moving from Theory to Practice, The California Endowment. San Francisco: Blueprint Research & Design, Inc.

Innovation Network, Inc. (2009) Pathfinder: A Practical Guide to Advocacy Evaluation, Commissioned by The Atlantic Philanthropies

Lamb, B. (2005) Impact Reporting. RNID

Lamb, B. (2010) Supporting Campaigning a Funders Guide, NCVO

Lamb, B. (2010) Campaigning for Change: learning from America, NCVO

New Economics Foundation (2009) Seven Principles for Measuring What Matters. A Guide to Effective Public Policy Making

NCVO array of materials on strategy and planning http://www.ncvo-vol.org.uk/strategy-impact

Ten Considerations for Advocacy Evaluation Planning: Lessons Learned from Kids Count Grantee Programme (2009) ORS for Anne E. Casey Foundation

Ranghelli, L. (nd). Strengthening Democracy, Increasing Opportunities Impacts of Advocacy, organising and Civic Engagement in New Mexico. National Council for Responsible Philanthropy.

Reisman, J. and Gienapp, A. Theory of Change: A Practical Tool for Action, Results and Learning. (2004). Organisations Research Services www. organizationalresearch.com

Reilly, M., (2007). An Agenda For Change In The USA: Insights From A Conversation About Assessing Social Change In Washington, DC, Washington: Just Associates.

Reisman, J. Gienapp, A., & Stachowiak, S. (2007) A Guide To Measuring Advocacy and Policy, funded and prepared for Annie E. Casey Foundation, Prepared by Organisational Research Services www. aecf.org

Reisman, J. Gienapp, A., & Stachowiak, S. (2007) A handbook of data collection tools: Companion Guide to "A Guide To Measuring Advocacy and Policy". Funded and prepared for Annie E. Casey Foundation, Prepared by Organisational Research Services www.aecf.org

Theory of Change: A Practical Tool For Action, Results and Learning (2004) Prepared for the Annie E. Casey Foundation.

Tuan, M. T. (2008). Measuring and/or Estimating Social Value Creation: Insights Into Eight Integrated Cost Approaches. Prepared for Bill & Melinda Gates Foundation Impact Planning and Improvement

Further reading

Weiss, H. (2007). The Evaluation exchange: a periodical on emerging strategies in evaluation. Cambridge, MA: Harvard Family Research Project

W.K. Kellogg Foundation. (2004). Logic Model Development Guide. http://www.wkkf.org/knowledge-center/resources/2010/Logic-Model-Development-Guide.aspx

Whelan, J. (2008). Advocacy Evaluation: Review and Opportunities

Wood, C., & Leighton, D. (2010). Measuring social value: the gap between policy and practice. London: Demos

Planning your campaign

Framing
On framing theory the best place to start is with Susan Bales Framing Public Issues which is a good introduction to the whole issue and then follow the genesis of her and Institutes work. For an introduction to the thinking around emotion and framing in campaigning start with Westen's Political Brain (2007). While some of the comments about the positioning of the Democrat party may now be outdated the principles throughout are not. Then for a more trenchant views from more of linguists angle on the same approach read Lakoff (2009) and then (2004) who has much greater stress on the functioning of metaphor and how that relates to deep frames in political debate. See Nunberg (2006) for a fascinating if sympathetic critique of some of Lakoff's theories. You don't have to agree with everything he thinks about the power of metaphor to see the usefulness of his ideas for campaigning.

Planning
For a very practical yet powerful short planning guide see Grimm just enough planning guide for Spitfire Strategies which while produced for an American context is fully relevant for the UK, as is their Discovering the Activation Point (2006) guide which is very helpful on some of the issues around persuasion and motivation

that links well with the themes around motivation and framing developed in this guide.

Allingham, Michael (2002). Choice Theory: A Very Short Introduction, Oxford University Press

Mauss, A. and Wolfe, J. eds., (1977) This Land of Promises: The Rise and Fall of Social Problems, Philadelphia, PA: Lippincott

Auburn, A, Grady, J & Bales, S. (2004). Opening Up the Black Box: A Case Study in Simplifying Models. Washington, DC: FrameWorks Institute

Bales, S. N., & Gilliam, F. D. (2004). Communications for Social Good. The Foundation Center. New York

Bales, S.N. (2005) Framing Public Issues, Frameworks Institute, Washington

Bales, S. N. (2005). Wanted: Master Storytellers. Boston, MA: Nonprofit Information Networking Association

Bales, S. N. (2008). Framing issues for Public Consideration, Chamber Executive

Bales, S. N. (2009). Testing Frames, Talking Frames: Framing as Experiment and as Execution. Washington, DC: FrameWorks Institute

British Institute of Human Rights The Human Rights Act: Changing Lives (2nd Edition (2008)

Champan, J. Wameyo, A. (2001) Monitoring and Evaluating Advocacy, Action Aid

Dorfman, L., Ervice J., & Woodruff, K. (2002) Voices for change: A taxonomy of public communications campaigns and their evaluation challenges. Berkeley, CA: Berkeley Media Studies Group

Emerson, J. (2008). Visualizing Information for Advocacy: an introduction to information design, Tactical Technology Collective http://tacticaltech.org.

FrameWorks Institute (2005) Framing Lessons from the Social Movements Literature. Washington, DC: FrameWorks Institute

FrameWorks Institute. (2001). A Five Minute Refresher Course in Framing. Washington, DC: FrameWorks Institute.

Gilbert, C. Sarb, C. and Bush, M. (2010) Polls Apart 2010, Opening Elections to Disabled People, Scope

Grimm, K. (2006) Discovering the Activation Point: Smart Strategies to Make People Act, Created for the Communications Leadership Institute by Spitfire Strategies

Grimm, K. The Just Enough Planning Guide: A Roadmap to Help Nonprofits Reach Their Campaign Goals, Spitfire Strategies

Grunwald, Michael. (April 2, 2009). How Obama is Using the Science of Change, Time Magazine

Heath, C. and Heath, D. (2007) Made to Stick: Why Some Ideas Take Hold and Others Come Unstuck, Random House

Hilder, P. Grice, J C. Lalor, K. (2007) Contentious Citizens Civil Society's Role in Campaiging for Social Change. Young Foundation

Lakoff, G. (1995) Metaphor, Morality, and Politics, or, Why Conservatives Have Left Liberals In the Dust

Lakoff, G (2004) Don't Think of an Elephant! Know your Values and Frame the Debate, White River Junction, VT: Chelsea Green Publishing

Lakoff, G (2009) The Political Mind: A Cognitive Scientist's Guide to your Brain and its Politics, London, Penguin

Lamb, B. (2008) 'Winning hearts as well as minds.' Third Sector, 13 February.

Lamb, B. (2008) 'If you don't ask you don't get.' Third Sector30th July.

Lipmann, W (1921) Political Opinion

NFP Synergy (2005) Ten campaigning tips for lobbying MPs

Nunberg, G. 'Frame Game' The New Rebpublic November 4th, 2006 http://www.tnr.com/blog/open-university/frame-game

Timmins, N. (2001) The Five Giants. A biography of the The Welfare State. 2nd edition. Harper Collins

Walter Lipmann (1921) Political Opinion

Wadham, Mountfield and Edmundson, (2007) Blackstone's Guide to the Human Rights Act 1998 (4th Edition), OUP

Westen, D. (2007) The Political Brain, The role of Emotion in Deciding the Fate of the Nation. Public Affairs, New York

Zetter, L. Parliamentary Campaigns see Lobbying: (2008) The Art of Political Persuasion Harriman House Publishing

Behavioural economics and social marketing

Social marketing is now a vast field that depends on psychology, sociology and economics for its main insights. Once past Thaler and Sunstein (2008) on Nudge theory, Cialdini (2003) is a good starting point and will take your further into some of the psychology behind the theory if you want to look further, and Compton (2010) provides a useful example of the how the approach is being linked with the insights from Western and Lakoff and applied to a campaigning context around climate change. Also see Anderson (2010) to see how some of the insights have been applied to fundraising including greater use of Homer Simpson metaphor.

For the impact of social marketing theories on social change start with Lund (2009) and then Danton (2005) while Knott et al is very useful on the broader approach that looks at social capital. See also French (2005) for an individual centred social marketing approach.

Andresen, K., McKee, A., & Rovner, M. (nd) Homer Simpson for nonprofits: The Truth about How People Really Think & What It Means for Promoting Your Cause. Network for Good and Sea Change Strategies

Bate, P, Bevan, H, Robert, G. 'Towards a million change agents' (nd) A review of the social movements literature: Implications for large scale change in the NHS, NHS Moderinsation Agency

Cialdini, R. (1993). Influence: The Psychology of Persuasion, New York: Quill

Cialdini, R. (2003). Crafting Normative Messages to Protect the Environment, Current Directions in Psychological Science, 12, 105–9

Christakis, N and Fowler, J. (2009) Connected: the surprising power of our social networks and how they shape our lives, Little Brown and Company

Crompton, T. Common Cause, (2010) The Case for Working with our Cultural Values, WWF

Darnton A (2008), GSR Behaviour Change Knowledge Review. Reference Report: An overview of behaviour change models and their uses, HMT Publishing Unit

Dawnay, E. And Shah, H. Extending the 'rational man' model of human behaviour: seven key principles, (2006) New Economics Foundation Briefing for the Environmental Agency. www.neweconomics.org

Department of Health. (2008).Healthy Foundations: A segmentation model. COI.

Department of Health. (2008) What is social marketing? COI

Ereaut, G. and Segnit, N. Warm Words (2006) How are we telling the climate story and can we tell it better? IPPR London

French, J and C Blair Stevens (2005). The Social Marketing Pocket Guide for the National Social Marketing Centre and the Department of Health

French, J and Blair-Stevens, C. (2009) Improving Lives Together Harnessing the best behavioural intervention and social marketing approaches, London

Grunwald, M. (April 2, 2009). How Obama is Using the Science of Change. Time Magazine

Kahan, DM (2010). Fixing the communications failure, Nature, 463, 296-297.

Personal Responsibility and Changing Behaviour. Prime Minister's Strategy Unit, Cabinet Office.

Jackson, T. (2005) Motivating Sustainable Consumption a review of evidence on consumer behaviour and behavioural change. A report to the Sustainable Development Research Network

Kahneman D (2002). Maps of Bounded Rationality: A Perspective on Intuitive Judgement and Choice, Nobel Prize Lecture, 8 Dec 2002

Knott, D with Muers, S. Alderidge, S. (2008) Achieving Culture Change: A Policy Framework. Strategy Unit Discussion Paper. Cabinet Office

Lund, M. (Forward) (2009). Communications and behaviour change, COI

McKenzie-Mohr D and Smith, W (1999) Fostering Sustainable Behaviour: An Introduction to Community-Based Social Marketing, New Society Publishers

Further reading

McKenzie-Mohr D (2000) 'Promoting Sustainable Behaviour: an introduction to community-based social marketing' in Journal of Social Issues 56(3) pp543-554

Myers, D. Exploring Psychology: (2006) Eighth edition, Worth Publishers.

'The spread of obesity over large social networks' (2007) New England Journal of Medicine

Oxera (2007) "When economics met psychology: rethinking incentives" (accessed November 2010)

O'Neil, Moira. (2007). Movement Building Not Marketing: Framing Lessons from the Social Movements Literature. Washington, DC: FrameWorks Institute

I will if you will – towards sustainable consumption, (2006) Sustainable Development Commission– available at www.sd-commission.org

Taylor, M (2010) Twenty-first Century Enlightenment. RSA. London.

Titmuss R, M. (1970) The Gift Relationship. London: Allen and Unwin.

Thaler, RH, and Sunstein CR (2003) Libertarian Paternalism is not an Oxymoron, Chicago Public Law and Legal Theory Working Paper No 43 (2003)

Thaler, R, H. and Sunstein C, R. (2008) Nudge Improving Decisions about Health, Wealth and Happiness, Yale University Press

The charted institute of marketing. (2009). Marketing and the 7Ps: A brief summary of marketing and how it works. Berkshire: The charted institute of marketing

Schwartz, SH (2006) Basic human values: an overview. The Hebrew University of Jerusalem

Sizzle. The New Climate Change Message. Futerra. www.futerra.co.uk

Human Rights

There are several organisations that specialise in human rights approaches to justice issues and provide extensive resources. See for example

New Tactics in Human Rights www.newtactics.org/ are an American based organisation but has much of relevance on their website.

Liberty http://www.liberty-human-rights.org.uk

British Institute of Human Rights www.bihr.org.uk/

More examples of how human rights have been used at http://www.ourhumanrightsstories.org.uk/

Delivering the campaign

Communications, tactics and media management

Evans, P (2009) Diversionary tactics – the imaginative campaigns protecting the countryside from developers. The Guardian, available from http://www.guardian.co.uk/environment/2009/apr/01/conservation-developers-countryside-uk

Trapese Collective (2007) Do it yourself, a Handbook for Changing our World, Pluto Press

Van der Zee, B. (2008) Rebel, Rebel. A protestor's handbook. Guardian Books

Online communications

There are a large number of sites online devoted to exploring online

communications. The Obama campaign has clearly been a catalyst and Raymond (2010) is an excellent starting place but see also Delany (2010) and Lutz (209) for other perspectives. For a general introduction to the impact of online communications on organisations and how to use more generally see Kanter (2010) who is an excellent starting point. NCVO have produced a helpful guide exploring where to use social media tools throughout the campaigns cycle see In Focus: social media in campaigning.

For peer support and insightful comments on ecampaigning join the ecampaigners forum http://fairsay.com/networks/ecampaigning-forum.

Brotherton, D., & Scheiderer, C. (2008) Come On In. The Water's Fine. An Exploration of Web 2.0 Technology And Its Emerging Impact on Foundation Communications, prepared for The Communications Network

Communication Consortium Media Centre: Guidelines for Evaluating Non Profit Communications Efforts. (2004) Communications Consortium Media Centre

Delany, C. (2009). Learning from Obama: Lessons for Online Communicators in 2009 and Beyond http://www.epolitics.com/learning-from-obama/

Delany, C. (2010). How Candidates Can Use the Internet to Win in 2010

Ecampaigning review 2009, Jess Day and Duane Raymond, Advocacy Online http://www.advocacyonline.net/resources/ecampaigningreview

eCampaiging Resource Pack (2008) produced jointly by Fairsay, Advocacy Online, Oxfam, (accessed at www.fairsay.com/insights. November 2010)

Julia Goffman (2002) Public Communication Campaign Evaluation. An Environmental Scan of Challenges, Criticisms, Practice, and Opportunities

Kanter, B. and Fine, A. (2010). The Networked Non Profit. Using Social Media to Power Social Networks for Change, Jossey-Bass

Lutz, M. (2009). The Social Pulpit: Barack Obama's Social Media Toolkit. Edelman

Raymond, D. (2010) How to Campaign like Ohbama. Fairsay. http://fairsay.com/obama-howto

Spitfire strategies. The spitfire strategies smart chart 3.0: An Even More Effective Tool to Help Nonprofits Make Smart Communications Choices. Spitfire Strategies.

Williamson, A., & Phillips, N. (2009). Twitter: Communication tool or pointless vanity. London, Hansard Society

Williamson, A., Miller, L., & Fallon, F. (2010). Behind the Digital Campaign: An exploration of the use, impact and regulation of digital campaigning. London: Hansard Society

Williamson A. (2010) Digital citizens and democratic participation. London: Hansard Society

Evaluate – building on success, managing faulire

As we have seen evaluation and strategy are intimately linked for reading specifically on evaluation see the further reading list for strategy and evaluation.

For NCVO resources specifically on campaigning see

Coe, J., and R Mayne. (2008) Is your campaign making a difference? NCVO

Ellis, J. (2007) Building on Success: How to cope when you achieve your campaign goal, NCVO

Lamb, B. (2011) Campaigning for Change: learning from the US, NCVO.

And also:

Asibey, E., Parras, T., & van Fleet, J. (2008) Are We There Yet?: a communications evaluation guide, created for the Communications Network by Asibey Consulting.

Gladwell, M. (2008) Outliers – the Story of Success, Little, Brown and Company

Egbert, M., & Hoechstetter, S. (2006) Mission Possible: Evaluating Advocacy Grants. Foundation news and commentary

Lawlor, E. Nicholls, J. and Neitzert, E. (2009) Seven principles for measuring what matters. London: New Economics Foundation

Sennett, R. (2008) The Craftsman. Allen Lane

Whelan, J. (2008) Advocacy Evaluation: Review and Opportunities

For communicating your impact see also http://www.ncvo-vol.org.uk/strategy-impact/learn/impact/communicating-your-impact

Foresight

NCVO's Third Sector Foresight project champions strategic planning with a particular emphasis on providing information about drivers affecting the voluntary and community sector. http://www.3s4.org.uk/

Specific publications include:

NCVO Future Focus: What will campaigning be like in five years time? (2009) Third Sector Foresight

NCVO Future Focus: What will membership be like in 5 years' time? (2010)

Looking out: a practical guide to planning for a changing environment (2009)

Legal issues and governance

Charity Commission www.charity-commission.gov.uk

"CC9: Speaking Out – Guidance on Campaigning & Political Activity by Charities", The Charity Commission http://www.charity-commission.gov.uk/publications/cc9.asp

For legal Issues around advertising it's best to consult the ASA website for latest guidance at http://www.asa.org.uk/Regulation-Explained/The-Codes.aspx

For the codes go to http://www.cap.org.uk/The-Codes/CAP-Code.aspx for the non broadcast code and http://www.cap.org.uk/The-Codes/BCAP-Code.aspx for the broadcast code.

SMK's Campaign Central know how law and campaigning – covering direct action, Protection from Harassment Act, SOCPA and protest and the law http://www.campaigncentral.org.uk/know-how/law-and-campaigning

Data protection http://www.ico.gov.uk/what_we_cover/data_protection/the_basics.aspx

http://www.direct.gov.uk/en/Governmentcitizensandrights/Yourrightsandresponsibilities/DG_10031451

Guidance specifically for trustees see the trustee guide to campaigning and influencing (2010) NCVO http://www.ncvo-vol.org.uk/trusteeguidecampaigning

or the good trustee guide (2008) NCVO

Thanks to Rachael Fisher Lamb for compiling the references.

About us

About Campaigning Effectiveness, NCVO

Campaigning Effectiveness, NCVO supports and empowers people and organisations to change their world through campaigning and influencing policy. We bring together experience and expertise and drive excellence in campaigning and policy work across civil society by providing support, knowledge, tools and resources. For further information about our work go to www.ncvo-vol.org.uk/campaigningeffectiveness

About the author

Brian Lamb, OBE has held Director level posts in campaigning and advocacy in both Scope and RNID. He now runs a consultancy on campaigning, policy and communications for VCO and public sector organisations. He has worked extensively on Government and ministerial working groups. He was chair of a national coalition on and led a national independent Inquiry into special educational needs. He has written widely on campaigning, evaluation and policy issues and is chair of the Campaign Effectiveness, NCVO advisory group. He is a founding board member of Every Disabled Child Matters Campaign and lectures on campaigning and voluntary sector effectiveness.